Praise for Leverage Leadership

"Paul Bambrick-Santoyo has his boots on the ground. This gifted teacher, school leader, and leader of leaders does the work every day in his highly successful North Star Academy schools in Newark, New Jersey. *Leverage Leadership* affirms his rare ability to see what works in school leadership—and to share those best practices with others. This book is as crucial for superintendents as it is for principals, teacher leaders, and policymakers. A must-read!"

> —Kim Marshall, consultant, principal coach, and author of the weekly online newsletter, *The Marshall Memo* and the book, *Rethinking Teacher Supervision and Evaluation*

"*Leverage Leadership* is the educator's definitive road map, plotting the journey from mere teaching to deeply personalized data-driven instruction for all students. Readers will be empowered by learning that the key to replicating remarkable educational success truly lies in their own choices of time, method, and urgency."

> —Tish Howard, principal, Washington Mill Elementary School, Fairfax County Public Schools, Alexandria, Virginia

"Paul Bambrick-Santoyo's career demonstrates a passion for learning both how exceptional school leaders achieve their results, and how to coach leaders to become great—even if they're already good. *Leverage Leadership* effectively communicates how the right leadership actions can build systems and cultures that transform not only individual schools, but also entire school districts."

> —Michael Clough, superintendent, Sheridan School District #2, Denver, Colorado

"In the fight to eradicate the achievement gap, *Leverage Leadership* is the complete arsenal. Culled from thousands of hours of observing extraordinary leaders obtaining exceptional results, this book identifies the seven key levers of school and student success. But it doesn't stop there. The real gems here are the detailed systems and strategies that any leader can apply to transform their schools and replicate the staggering success of Uncommon Schools. Don't just read *Leverage Leadership*, implement it—now! The state of our schools demands it."

> —Elizabeth Topoluk, director, Friends of Education

"Paul Bambrick-Santoyo is one of a small number of game-changing authors who does more than simply capture essential elements of schools: he makes bold choices about which leadership actions matter most for any school committed to closing the achievement gap. In the process, he gives you the tools to make student learning soar."

—Rosemary Perlmeter, co-founder, The Teaching Trust, founder, Uplift Education

LEVERAGE LEADERSHIP

A Practical Guide
to Building Exceptional Schools

Paul Bambrick-Santoyo

With Contributions from Brett Peiser

Foreword By Doug Lemov

JOSSEY-BASS
A Wiley Imprint
www.josseybass.com

Library of Congress Cataloging-in-Publication Data

Bambrick-Santoyo, Paul, 1972-
    Leverage leadership : a practical guide to building exceptional schools / Paul Bambrick-Santoyo ; with contributions from Brett Peiser; foreword by Doug Lemov.
        p. cm.
    Includes bibliographical references and index.
    ISBN 978-1-118-13860-1 (pbk.) ISBN 978-1-118-22538-7 (ebk.)—ISBN 978-1-118-23892-9 (ebk.)—ISBN 978-1-118-26353-2 (ebk.)
    1. School management and organization. 2. School improvement programs. 3. School principals—Professional relationships. I. Peiser, Brett M., 1968- II. Title.
    LB2805.B245 2012
    371.2—dc23
                                                                                    2012010375

Printed in the United States of America
FIRST EDITION
PB Printing   10 9 8 7 6 5 4 3 2

Contents

For children everywhere—

that we can build you schools of excellence that allow you to fly

DVD Contents

HANDOUTS

Rubrics for the Seven Levers

8A—Implementation Rubric for DDI.pdf

8B—Curriculum Plan Rubric.pdf

8C—Lesson Plan Rubric.pdf

8D—Student Culture Rubric.pdf

8E—Staff Culture Rubric.pdf

8F—PD Rubric.pdf

8G—Instructional Leader Rubric.pdf

Action Planning Worksheets

Action Planning Worksheet for Data-Driven Instruction (Chapter 1)

Action Planning Worksheet for Observation and Feedback (Chapter 2)

Action Planning Worksheet for Planning (Chapter 3)

Action Planning Worksheet for Professional Development (Chapter 4)

Action Planning Worksheet for Student Culture (Chapter 5)

Action Planning Worksheet for Staff Culture (Chapter 6)

Action Planning Worksheet for Managing Leadership Teams (Chapter 7)

Action Planning Worksheet for Finding the Time (Chapter 8)

Action Planning Worksheet for Superintendent's Guide (Chapter 9)

Chapter 1: Data-Driven Instruction (DDI)

Action Planning Worksheet for Data-Driven Instruction

9A—Implementation Rubric for DDI.pdf (Implementation Rubric: Data-Driven Instruction & Assessment)

11A—Leading Effective Asst Analysis Mtgs.pdf (Going Deep: Effective Analysis of Assessment Results)

8A—Assessment Analysis Worksheet.doc

4D—Teacher Action Plan.doc (North Star Assessment Teacher Reflection)

8B—Elementary Assessment Calendar.doc (North Star Academy Assessment Schedule)

8C—MS Assessment Calendar.doc (Sample MS Assessment Calendar)

8D—HS Assessment Calendar.doc (Sample HS Interim Assessment Calendar)

11D—Monthly Map—Sample.doc (Principal Monthly Map 2010–11 – On My Radar)

Chapter 2: Observation and Feedback

Action Planning Worksheet for Observation and Feedback

7A—Sample Observation Tracker.xlsx (Observation Tracker 2011–12—OVERALL)

3A—Six Steps for Effective Feedback.pdf (Six Steps for Effective Feedback)

Chapter 3: Planning

Action Planning Worksheet for Planning

4A—Planning Meeting one-pager.pdf (Planning Meetings: Leading Face-to-Face Meetings to Guide Unit/Lesson Planning)

6A—Lesson Plan Rubric.pdf (NSA Lesson Plan Rubric 2009–10)

5A—Curriculum Plan Rubric.pdf (NSA Curriculum Plan Rubric 2010–2011)

Chapter 4: Professional Development

Action Planning Worksheet for Professional Development

2A—Leading Professional Development—One-pager.doc (Living the Learning Model: An Effective Approach for Leading Adult PD)

4A—PD Rubric.pdf

Chapter 5: Student Culture

Action Planning Worksheet for Student Culture

4A—Student Culture Rubric.pdf (Student Culture Rubric)

3B—Student Culture Planning Template.doc (Schoolwide Culture Plan: Template for Mid-Year Correction (In the Moment))

Chapter 6: Staff Culture

Action Planning Worksheet for Staff Culture

8E—Staff Culture Rubric.docx (NSA Staff Culture Rubric)

Staff Culture Tracker

Chapter 7: Managing School Leadership Teams

Action Planning Worksheet for Managing Leadership Teams

7B—Observation Tracker Template.xlsx (Observation Tracker 2011–12—OVERALL)

8G—Instructional Leader Rubric.pdf (North Star Academy Instructional Leader Evaluation Rubric 2010–11)

3A—Six Steps for Effective Feedback.pdf (Six Steps for Effective Feedback)

4A—Planning Meeting one-pager.pdf (Planning Meetings: Leading Face to Face Meetings to Guide Unit/Lesson Planning)

11A—Leading Effective Asst Analysis Mtgs (Going Deep: Effective Analysis of Assessment Results)

Chapter 8: Finding the Time

Action Planning Worksheet for Finding the Time

4C—Model.Schedule.Blank.xls (Daily-Weekly Schedule)

4D—Weekly Schedule ES.xls (ES Principal's Weekly-Monthly Schedule)

4E—Weekly Schedule MS.xls (Principal's Weekly-Monthly Schedule)

3A—Monthly Map Template.doc (On My Radar)

3C—Monthly Map—DDI Sample.doc (Principal Tickler – On My Radar: Data-Driven Instruction)

3D—Monthly Map Sample - Data & Student Culture Sample.doc (Principal Tickler– On My Radar: Student Culture and Data-Driven Instruction)

3E—Monthly Map MS.doc (MS Principal Tickler – On My Radar)

5B—Action Plan Template.doc (Daily Action Plan)

Chapter 9: The Superintendent's Guide

Action Planning Worksheet for Superintendent's Guide

6A—Superintendent Monthly Weekly Planning.xls (Superintendent's Weekly Schedule)

6C—Superintendent Dashboard Template.xlsx (MD Dashboard 2011–12)

6B—Monthly Map—Superintendent 11-12.doc (Superintendent's 2011–12 Monthly Map)

6E—Superintendent Action Plan.doc (Paul's Daily Action Plan)

Chapter 10: Observation and Feedback Workshop

1A—Observation-Feedback reflection template.doc (Observation Feedback and Reflection)

2A—Case Study #1—Choosing Right Levers.pdf (Choosing the Right Levers: Case Study #1)

3A—Six Steps for Effective Feedback.pdf (Six Steps for Effective Feedback)

5B—Action Plan Template.doc (Daily Action Plan)

7B—Observation Tracker Template.xlsx (Observation Tracker 2011–12—OVERALL)

Chapter 11: Leading Planning Workshop

Chapter 12: Leading Professional Development Workshop

POWERPOINT PRESENTATIONS

Chapter 10: 1B—Observation-Feedback PPT.pptx (Observation and Feedback)

Chapter 11: 1—Leading_Planning_PPT.pptx (Leading Planning)

Chapter 12: 1B—Leading_PD_PPT.pptx (Leading Effective Professional Development)

Chapter 13: 1B—Student_Culture_PPT.pptx (Student Culture)

Chapter 14: 1A—Finding the Time PPT.pptx (Finding the Time)

DVD Video Content

Here is an overview of the video clips for your quick reference.

DDI (Chapter 1)—Leading Interim Assessment Analysis Meetings

Clip	Grade Span and Content	Description	Page
1	High School English	Beth Verrilli asks targeted questions to keep teacher Steve Chiger on track toward boosting students' reading comprehension.	22, 42, 47
2	Elementary School Reading	Assessment data lets Juliana Worrell guide Yasmin Vargas toward planning purposefully.	45, 47

Observation and Feedback (Chapter 2)—Six Steps of Feedback

Clip	Which of the Six Steps	Description	Page
3	Overall Model of Feedback	Julie Jackson demonstrates effective feedback in action, debriefing her observations of Carly Bradley's science lesson.	60, 75
4	Step 1: Precise Praise	Specific praise helps Serena Savarirayan set the tone for her observation meeting with Eric Diamon.	80
5	Steps 2-3: Probe & ID Problem—Level 2	Julie Jackson supports experienced teacher Rachel Kashner in finding areas for growth and solutions for improvement.	82
6	Steps 2-3: Probe & ID Action Step—Level 2	Using careful questions, Serena Savarirayan guides Eric Diamon toward strategies that deepen class discussions.	83

Observation and Feedback (Chapter 2)—Six Steps of Feedback (*Continued*)

Clip	Which of the Six Steps	Description	Page
7	Steps 2-3: Probe & ID Problem—Level 3	Evidence-based prompts help Aja Settles correct Kristi Costanzo's misunderstanding and find the right next step for her classroom.	83
8	Steps 2-3: ID Problem/Action Step through Use of Video of Master Teacher	Aja Settles uses video footage of a master instructor to help Kristi Costanzo hone her own practice.	84
9	Steps 2-3: ID Problem/Action Step through Use of Video of Self	Juliana Worrell and Clare Perry use videos of Clare's classroom to find action steps for improvement.	84
10	Step 4: Practice, Level 2-4	Role playing allows Juliana Worrell and Julia Thompson to practice teaching techniques.	86
11	Step 4: Practice, Level 1	Serena Savarirayan and Eric Diamon practice questioning approaches to ensure more rigorous class conversations.	87
12	Steps 5-6: Plan Ahead & Set Timeline	Juliana Worrell and Sarah Sexton plan "Think Alouds" for an upcoming lesson; when Sarah struggles, Juliana supports her through active modeling.	87
13	Step 6: Set Timeline	A set timeline keeps Julie Jackson and Rachel Kashner on the same page.	88
14	Step 6: Set Timeline	Shradha M. Patel closes her feedback meeting with Jamil Sylvester by establishing a timeline for action.	88

Planning

Clip	Technique	Description	Page
15	Opening Sample of Planning Meeting	Kim Nicoll and Jamie Gumpper design specific classroom actions to make an upcoming history unit shine.	110
16	Set Core Content	Serena Savarirayan and Eric Diamon set the core content and objectives for 5th grade English.	122
17	Set Core Content	James Verrilli and Steve Decina decide which science skills to re-teach and how to assess them.	122, 146
18	Diving Deep	Aja Settles and Kristi Costanzo analyze student error to design upcoming lessons.	123

Leading PD

Clip	Technique	Description	Page
19	Master PD Clip	Aja Settles uses the Living the Learning framework to drive her professional development session on improving in-class transitions.	130, 140
20	Airtight Activity—Video	Video footage helps Nikki Bridges lead her workshop on reading comprehension strategies.	142
21	Airtight Activity—Role Play	By role-playing ineffective analysis meetings, Paul Bambrick-Santoyo evokes an emotional response and engages participants in his workshop.	143
22	Large Group Sharing	Julie Jackson asks scaffolded questions to guide a large group toward previously overlooked observations about the airtight activity.	145
23	Application	Participants at Emily Hoefling Crouch's professional development workshop create "book introductions" incorporating what they've learned; Emily offers individual feedback.	148
24	Reflection	Emily Hoefling-Crouch ends her elementary reading workshop by letting participants create lesson plans based on what they've learned.	149

Student Culture

Clip	Technique	Description	Page
25	Morning Routines	Strong morning routines let Stacey Shells set the tone for the day and provide a model for teachers.	164
26	Poke, Pull, Eat	Rochester Prep kindergarteners learn from their teacher Jillian Horvath the "poke, pull and eat" technique to deal with plastic-wrapped breakfasts.	170
27	Dress Rehearsal, Part 1: Master Teacher	The week before classes begin, Andrea Somerville models effective practice during a rehearsal of the entire first day of school, with Julie Jackson.	175, 176
28	Dress Rehearsal, Part 2: New Teacher	The week before classes begin, Alison Komorowski rehearses morning routines under the tutelage of her mentor teacher.	175, 176
29	Monitor & Maintain	Stacey Shells catches small details to maintain a strong student culture.	177

Production work by Silhouette – Art on Video (artonvideo.com) and herbalmedia (herbalmedia.com).

Foreword

In a recent study, the Urban Institute set out to answer a question that had immense ramifications for education and educators. The question had nothing to do with curriculum or governance or instructional methods. It wasn't about the strategic use of data, a topic about which the author of this book, Paul Bambrick-Santoyo, has written the quintessential volume and which, he shows, can cause a sea change in the effectiveness of day-to-day instruction. The study had nothing to do with accountability or human capital management. In short, the study was silent on the issues we most commonly believe—with some justification—drive excellence in schools.

Still, the study yielded critical insight about the things that stand in the way of excellence for a typical school and its leadership team, even if the study's focus seemed a bit pedestrian. The question it set out to answer was how principals spend their time. To do so it followed 65 principals in Miami's public schools as they worked, keeping track of what they did and for how long. The study found that on average principals spent more than 27 percent of their time on administrative tasks—managing schedules, discipline issues, and compliance. They spent 20 percent of their time on organizational tasks such as hiring, responding to teacher concerns, or checking to see if there was money in the budget for projector bulbs or travel to workshops. These two types of tasks, administrative and organizational, were the largest two sources of time allocation.

On the other end of the spectrum, principals, on average, spent less than 6 percent of their time on what it called "day-to-day instruction": observing classrooms, coaching teachers to make them better, leading or planning professional training for teachers, using data to drive instruction, and evaluating teachers. It turned out that day-to-day instruction—what teachers did in the classroom with their students and how—wasn't really the day-to-day focus of the school's leadership. The most important work in the building—the most important work in our society, you could argue—went unmanaged 94 percent of the time in the face of a thousand secondary tasks and petty distractions.

These numbers are dispiriting for a variety of reasons, not least of which is that the tasks described in the "day-to-day instruction" category include, as Paul Bambrick-Santoyo explains in this book, the tasks that essentially determine student achievement levels. The 6 percent of leadership spent on the five tasks amounts to just 36 minutes in a 10-hour day spent on all of them combined, or just over seven minutes per day on each of the tasks. That's about seven minutes a day observing classrooms. Seven minutes a day coaching teachers to make them better. Seven minutes a day developing and leading training for teachers. It's seven minutes a day using data to drive instruction. It's seven minutes a day evaluating teachers.

You almost don't have to read the rest of the study to know what comes of those kind of numbers: lower student achievement and the death spiral of increasing distractions (suspensions, summer school placements, etc.) that increase as achievement declines. The precious minutes spent on key tasks are even fewer and farther between. You can hear the echo of those principals, their shoes striding down the hallway from one low-value task to another (http://www.urban.org/uploadedpdf/1001441-School-Effectiveness.pdf).

In their hearts, the principals probably know the truth—that they are not spending their time doing and getting better at the tasks that would bring about excellence. In many cases, they may even choose not to do them because, in the end, they are not so sure about how to do them well. And this is especially disappointing because the people who run schools are almost all driven, hard-working, committed, and passionate. Given the right tools and protected from distractions, they are capable of running outstanding schools.

An organization or a society ought to be able to remove incentives (or requirements) to spend time on secondary tasks, provide a clear sense for *how* to do the most important tasks well, and provide tools to ensure their ease and efficiency. That's what organizations *should* do for their people, but in fact they are too often looking in the wrong direction—looking for the next new idea rather than studying how to do the core tasks, fighting a philosophical battle when it's the tasks that pop up from below and the systems that manage them that make the champions of school leadership successful.

Turn your sights for a moment to Newark, New Jersey, though. The city not often cited for its educational prowess is a case study in success. There Paul Bambrick-Santoyo and his principals have built the North Star schools, a growing network of elementary, middle, and high schools attended by students almost entirely of poverty and facing every difficulty you might imagine, yet which consistently put students on the path to college—reliable, even predictable excellence in the face of the sort of every day adversity that keeps so many potentially strong leaders from performing their best. The schools have quietly gone about this work for fifteen years now, changing lives and providing the proof that making schools great can be systematically accomplished.

North Star's success, *Leverage Leadership* now reveals, is a result of two things above all. The first is a relentlessness about spending time on the most important things and as little else as humanly possible. The second, far harder, is bringing an engineer's obsession to finding the way to do those things as well as humanly possible. These are simple tools—focus on the right things, intentionally study how to do them well—but their simplicity should not suggest that they are easy. Insights are hard won and implementation is harder. Going from "I get it" to "I can do it" to "I know people in the organization will reliably do it" are gigantic steps. Paul has spent years refining both the answers and the systems that help people use them. Over time he has chosen to focus on making each idea a little bit better every day, turning his insights into a management system that—like the flywheel in Jim Collins' legendary book *Good to Great*—keeps an organization (and a leader) getting better and better as a matter of habit.

Now Paul has made the workings of that system and each of its pieces available to all. It is of course not as sexy as a brand-new pedagogy or shiny technological machine, but in the end it is far more powerful. If you are one of those educators who understands the power of doing the most important things not only well but better over time, of holding fast to what works instead of chasing temporary "revolutions," then this book, I believe, will serve as a touchstone, a guide to which you will return over and over again for guidance, insight, and strategy that can help you and the educators with whom you work to achieve the greatest possible success—to build outstanding educational organizations and to make the greatest possible difference in the lives of your students.

Doug Lemov

Doug Lemov is a managing director of Uncommon Schools and the author of *Teach Like a Champion*, the *Teach Like a Champion Field Guide*, and *Practice Perfect*.

Acknowledgments

Leverage Leadership was born on-site in direct work with school leaders. The ideas stem from observing countless actions—some quite subtle and others more immediately effective—of high-achieving leaders. None of these ideas could have been captured without a tremendous team of support.

First and foremost, Dan Rauch has assisted me once again as a writer extraordinaire—gathering ideas, shaping the drafts, and putting a touch of imagination into each round of edits. He was supported in this project by Alyssa White, who made the professional development section come to life. Without them, this project could never have been completed and the writing would not have been nearly as effective.

I am also indebted to my colleague Brett Peiser, the author of the chapter on staff culture. I have never met anyone who understands organizational culture like Brett does. He has an incredible ability to walk into a school and diagnose exactly what is or is not working with the staff culture. Anything I have learned about staff culture has come from Brett, and so it was an honor that he agreed to author the chapter on the topic. This book is much richer for it, and I eagerly await Brett's book on this area of leadership.

The thought partners in this work were many. Mark Murphy, executive director of Vision Delaware 2015, and Kim Marshall, author of *Rethinking Supervision and Evaluation*, have been two of my closest friends in the work of school leadership. Many an idea was honed over dinner or long emails, and they pushed me every day to make it work for all schools in every context.

The ultimate laboratory for this book was working closely with leaders across the Uncommon Schools network. Doug Lemov, Dana Lehman, and Evan Rudall joined Brett Peiser in bringing so much expertise that sharpened every aspect of this book, from ideas on planning (thank you, Dana!) to how to break down teaching into teachable chunks (where would we be without you, Doug?).

The real heroes of this book, however, are the school leaders who do the work every day. Julie Jackson, Mike Mann, Jesse Rector, Serena Savarirayan, Aja Settles, Juliana Worrell, Kelly Dowling, Juliann Harris, Lauren Whitehead, Yasmin Vargas, and Keith Burnam have inspired me as they have led North Star schools to excellence, and they have been joined by all the school leaders across Uncommon Schools, like Julie Kennedy, Stacey Shells, and Kim Nicolls—and so many more that we couldn't even highlight them all! It was ten years ago when co-founders Norman Atkins and James Verrilli welcomed me to North Star. I wish that everyone gets the chance to work with two people who are as brilliant and humble.

Leaders on the front line are the easiest to see, as they are the face of the school. But as is mentioned in the chapter "Finding the Time," you cannot focus on instructional leadership without someone doing the "dirty work": everything operational. That has been no exception in my own work: Michael Ambriz has silently and effectively managed all key operational issues for our schools, allowing me to focus on growing schools instructionally and culturally. He rarely gets the praise he deserves, but his invisible work made this possible. And I would not have kept my sanity without Angelica Pastoriza managing all my day-to-day tasks: scheduling, organizing meetings, and bringing joy to our office. They were joined by a team of video analysts and project managers who watched countless hours of video, led over the past two years by Melinda Phelps and Jared McCauley. Their work wouldn't have been possible without the support of the entire home office team led by Josh Phillips, Carolyn Hack, and Jessica Ochoa Hendrix.

The other silent partners in this work are even closer to my heart: my wife and children. Ana, Maria, and Nicolas have now watched me write two books, enduring many an afternoon of me watching videos of leaders or pacing as I tried to articulate an idea! My wife, Gaby, continues to be the rock—the steady presence of love and listening.

Thank you to each and every one of you. This book is a tribute to you all.

About the Authors

Paul Bambrick-Santoyo is the managing director of North Star Academies, seven schools that are a part of the Uncommon Schools network. During Bambrick-Santoyo's ten years at North Star, the schools have seen dramatic gains in student achievement, making them the highest-achieving urban schools in New Jersey and winners of multiple recognitions, including the U.S. Department of Education's National Blue Ribbon Award. Bambrick-Santoyo is the author of *Driven by Data: A Practical Guide to Improve Instruction*. He has trained over 5,000 school leaders worldwide in instructional leadership and also serves as the data-driven instruction faculty member for New Leaders, a national urban school leadership training program. Prior to joining North Star, Bambrick-Santoyo worked for six years in a bilingual school in Mexico City, where he founded the International Baccalaureate Program at the middle school level. He earned a B.A. in social justice from Duke University and his M.Ed. in school administration via New Leaders from the City University of New York, Baruch College. Visit Paul at www.PaulBambrick.com.

Contributing author **Brett Peiser** is a managing director of Uncommon Schools, a nonprofit charter management organization that starts and manages outstanding urban charter public schools that close the achievement gap and prepare low-income students to graduate from college. As managing director of Uncommon Schools New York City, Peiser oversees its network of 14 schools in Brooklyn, serving over 3,000 elementary, middle, and high school students, ultimately expanding to 8,000 students in 21 schools. The network's first middle school—Williamsburg

Collegiate—is the highest scoring school in New York City on the NYC Department of Education Progress Reports since the Department of Education began issuing reports in 2006. Peiser is the founder and former principal and executive director of Boston Collegiate Charter School, one of Massachusetts' highest performing public schools. Over Peiser's last four years, Boston Collegiate was the only public school in Boston with 100 percent of tenth graders passing both the math and English MCAS exams, a statewide graduation requirement. Peiser is a graduate of New York City public schools and a former history teacher at Midwood High School in Brooklyn. Peiser received a B.A. from Brown University and a M.P.P. degree from the John F. Kennedy School of Government at Harvard University.

LEVERAGE
LEADERSHIP

Introduction

Julie Jackson knows the obstacles she faces. As principal of North Star Elementary School, Julie works in Vailsburg, one of the many neighborhoods in Newark, New Jersey, that struggle economically and educationally. Most of Julie's students qualify for a free or reduced lunch and are Black or Latino. On the first day of school, only one of Julie's 80 kindergarten students can read; most know only a few letters of the alphabet.

But in a place where most people see challenges, Julie Jackson sees opportunity and promise. After one year at North Star, Julie's students no longer lag behind; they have caught up to—and surpassed—their peers. Incredibly, during their five years at the elementary school, Julie's students collectively score in the median 99th national percentile on the TerraNova in both math and reading/language arts.[1] (See Figure 0.1) Put more plainly, the *average* student in Julie's class scores higher than 99 percent of elementary students in the United States. Their state test scores are similarly striking: with 96 percent proficient in literacy and 100 percent proficient in math on the third-grade state test (and 70 percent advanced), Julie's students match or outperform every other school in the state.[2] Perhaps more important, each day they partake in creative, joyful, and focused instruction, building a genuine and enduring love of learning. Since its 2007 opening, Julie's school has been toured and studied by experts from Chile to China as a model of excellence in urban education. Visitors have praised the school as "wonderful," "inspirational," and "awe inspiring." The reason isn't hard to understand: in the face of vast obstacles, Julie's students have thrived. To all outward appearances, Julie's success seems miraculous.

But Julie Jackson is not a miracle worker. Though she is talented, driven, and hard working, Julie's school has succeeded because of the systems she has put in place and the way she organizes her school. Above all else, *she succeeds because of the choices she makes in using her time:* what she does, and how and when she does it.

How do we know this? Because Julie's success—and the success of leaders like her—has been replicated. In 2010, Julie helped North Star open an additional elementary school: West Side Park Elementary, led by Aja Settles. In temperament, tone, and personality, Aja differs from Julie's. What they share, however, is a set of choices they make in using their time. The results? In the 2010–2011 school year, Aja achieved nearly identical results to Julie, getting her students to the median 99th percentile on the TerraNova in language and math and the 96th percentile in reading.[3] (See Figure 0.2)

At the time of this writing, Julie has led the opening of two more schools, for a total of four elementary schools, and each one is on pace to match the performance of the original. The results speak for themselves. They're not miracles: they're proof that Julie Jackson knew how to spend her time and how to lead others to do the same.

Core Idea

Exceptional school leaders succeed because of how they use their time: what they do, and how and when they do it.

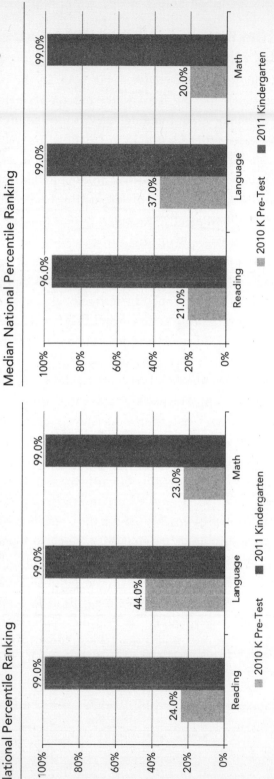

Figure 0.1 Vailsburg Elementary School Kindergarten Median National Percentile Ranking

Figure 0.2 West Side Park Elementary School Kindergarten Median National Percentile Ranking

A PARADIGM SHIFT: LEVERAGING LEADERSHIP MINUTE BY MINUTE

What makes education effective? Great teaching. In the past decade, a host of research has suggested that the decisive determinant of whether students will learn is not school technology, nor building logistics, nor administrative funding, but the presence or absence of high-quality instruction. In recent years, a wide variety of scholars have recognized the quality of teaching as a principal's or school leader's key responsibility. Kim Marshall notes in *Rethinking Teacher Supervision and Evaluation* that "the quality of instruction is the single most important factor in student achievement."[4] Recently, Robert Marzano, Tony Frontier, and David Livingston have built on this work in their book *Effective Supervision: Supporting the Art and Science of Teaching*. They note that "achievement in classes with highly skilled teachers is better than student achievement in classes with less skilled teachers."[5] How much better? Enough, as it turns out, to instigate game-changing improvement. Data suggests that low-socioeconomic status (SES) schools that can offer students three consecutive years of strong teaching *close* the achievement gap, correcting for a host of external factors.[6]

Yet it is much easier to assert that great teaching leads to great learning than to encounter schools where all teachers make this sort of learning happen. Why? Because the typical school leadership model has not been defined precisely enough to work for this purpose. Much of the current research has studied effective school leadership and identified the characteristics of effective schools.[7] Unfortunately, though, these are often the outputs of effective schools, not the actions leaders took to get there. At its best, the current leadership model encourages and develops a handful of great teachers, but it does not succeed in reaching further.

To illustrate this situation, let's consider the performance of a football team. You can watch an effective team like the New England Patriots and describe what that team looks like at game time. You can point out that all players work in unison, that the offensive plays expose the gaps in the opponent's defense, that blitzing is used effectively, and so on. But no one football player can replicate the New England Patriots' success just by watching the team play. That success depends upon what each player knows about what he has to do. The receiver has to read the position of the cornerback to decide to break right or left. The quarterback recognizes the precise moment when he has to throw, based on thousands of drills done in practice. In essence, the team has a detailed step-by-step plan that is capable of adjusting to what happens during the football game. Audibles—changes made to a play at the last minute—can affect the outcome of the game, but only when each member of the team knows what actions to take when the audible is called.

What concrete actions, then, does an excellent school leader take at each moment to make his or her school exceptional? What are the actions that lead not just to somewhat effective learning, but to phenomenal results? What do these leaders prioritize on a day-by-day, minute-by-minute basis? And has anyone done it in a replicable way, moving away from the "Superman" model of outstanding schools?

Answering these questions inspired me to write this book. Over the course of the past ten years, I have had the privilege to work with thousands of school leaders across the country. During that time, I have observed firsthand the challenges facing school leaders. I have also witnessed how many have overcome those obstacles to make a difference in the student learning. My earlier book *Driven by Data* captured a number of those success stories.[8] Yet *Driven by Data* focused only on one critical lever of leadership—data-driven instruction—and didn't try to put all the pieces of great leadership together. How does a leader do it all?

Amid all of the leaders I had the chance to observe, I have been fortunate to work closely with a small group of school leaders who have attained the same extraordinary results as Julie Jackson. These leaders come from the cities in which I have been privileged to work most deeply in my work at Uncommon Schools: Newark, New Jersey; Rochester, New York; Boston; and New York City. They represent school leaders in the broadest sense of the word: they hold roles from department chairperson to principal to superintendent. And they all meet two basic criteria:

1. *Exceptional results that exceed expectations.* By any metrics, the leaders achieved staggering academic successes. Their state test or advanced placement (AP) results marked each leader's school as the top-performing school in its city or state. What makes this even more impressive is the populations that these schools served. In all cases, high percentages of the schools' students qualified for free and reduced lunch, and most students were Black and Latino. But the point bears noting: the schools we found are not "good urban schools"; they are superlative schools outright.[9]

2. *Replication of results.* These leaders didn't succeed in some idiosyncratic way: they used systems and structures that they themselves have effectively replicated at other schools—not just good results, but extraordinary ones. What is most impressive about the leaders we studied is that when they left their original schools, the leaders they left behind achieved *comparable degrees of success.* The successes these leaders built were not the products of unique charisma; they came from strategies and systems that any leader can apply.

Over the course of the next chapters, you will read the stories of Dana Lehman, Beth Verrilli, Mike Mann, Stacey Shells, Julie Kennedy, and many others. Each chapter in this book highlights their success in order to teach us about leveraging leadership. We have also included the experience of additional leaders—like Brian Sims and Jarvis Sanford from Chicago—who have emulated these actions to replicate results or to turn around struggling schools. In examining their leadership up-close, we noticed patterns that separated their practices from those of other school leaders I observed who were doing "well" but not achieving the same results. This comparison allowed me to identify the key levers of leadership that move a school from "mediocre" or "good" to "great." The overwhelming conclusion was this: each of the leaders leveraged more out of each minute of the day. They carefully and intentionally chose the actions that have the biggest impact on student learning—and they avoided those actions that don't.[10] More specifically, they leveraged feedback and time for practice to transform teaching and learning. None of their practices was revolutionary in its own right: success was a result of the combination of and precision with which they implemented them.

So what really makes education effective? The answer: minute-by-minute leadership that ensures great teaching to guarantee great learning.

Core Idea

What really makes education effective is well-leveraged leadership that ensures great teaching to guarantee great learning.

This paradigm has the potential to reshape any school in any context. To harness that potential, however, school leaders must avoid lending credence to these common myths about their work.

MYTHS OF EFFECTIVE SCHOOL LEADERSHIP

Principals Are Administrators and Firefighters, Not Instructional Leaders

One of the largest obstacles standing in the way of school leaders today is the sheer volume of non-instructional work they face. All too often, principals and other school leaders find themselves primarily focused on tasks that do not directly help them improve learning—filling out compliance reports, attending non-instructional meetings, or managing facilities, just to name a few. This has led some to argue that principals should devote themselves to this work and shift instructional leadership to coaches whom they bring into the building. What I saw in exceptional school leaders, however, was an insistence on being instructional leaders. Even when they had coaches to support the development of teachers, they kept their actions and their eyes squarely on instruction. "I am ultimately responsible for the instruction in my building. So regardless of who supports that work, I manage it more closely than anything else," commented elementary principal Stacey Shells (read more about her in Chapter 5).

Comprehensive Observations, Walkthroughs, and Teacher Evaluations Are Sufficient

Also gathering support in the conversation surrounding school leadership is the push for comprehensive teacher evaluation rubrics, classroom observations, and building walkthroughs. All of these elements are important, but they occasionally fall short of their core purpose: to make teachers more effective. Every moment spent filling in a teacher evaluation rubric is a moment not used working directly with a teacher, carefully guiding him or her to improvement. As we'll see in the upcoming chapters, exceptional school leaders are very intentional about how they use observations and walkthroughs, placing the utmost emphasis on the process of giving the right feedback and making sure teachers implement it. (See more in Chapters 1 through 3.)

Change Is Slow: Teacher Development Takes 10 Years

There is a growing sentiment in the educational field that teacher development takes 10 years and that any school change takes multiple years. From this perspective, only slow, gradual change is effective, with change based around the piecemeal introduction of various systems.[11] The leaders in this book disprove that myth on a daily basis. As high school principal Mike Mann says, "Our students cannot wait 10 years for a teacher to become effective—that's their entire educational career." What the leaders in this book do is develop teachers in what matters most: making sure students learn. Whether or not these teachers would be labeled as "master teachers" on a teacher evaluation rubric is beside the point; what's clear is that their students learn as they would in a master teacher's classroom. What were the keys? A detailed structure for teacher development that focused on the highest-leverage teacher actions and that could be adapted to the varying needs of teachers.

There Is a "Principal Personality"

Many people believe that a great school leader has a "principal personality": extroverted, forceful, and charismatic. Many of the "good" schools I observed enjoyed leaders who met this profile, but they struggled to replicate their success. In contrast, the leaders of schools whose successes had been replicated displayed an extraordinary variety of personality types. With the (important) exception of an impressive work ethic, the leaders we studied shared few personal traits. What they did have in common was not so much a character trait as a mind-set: an incredibly self-critical eye and a determination to move from "good" to "great." Each of them was more likely to tell me the five things in his or her school that had to be improved than the twenty things the school was doing extraordinarily well. Their drive to *continuously* improve their schools motivates them far more than the results they achieve. Aside from this, there is no one "principal personality."

Culture Comes Before Instruction . . . or Instruction Before Culture

One of the great debates of school leadership is what should take priority: student instruction or student culture. In the culture camp, some argue that without order, joy, and respect, academic success is impossible. In their eyes, the game plan should be to "delay" improving instruction until culture is "right." On the other side, some argue that instruction creates culture, and that as teachers create engaging and rigorous lessons, student conduct and attitudes will naturally improve. Both views are badly flawed. At schools that decide to wait to improve instruction, the end result is often a "false positive": order without rigor. Yet if instruction is strong but culture is weak, a school's success is crippled. Newer teachers face serious discipline problems, students experience radical inconsistency across classes, and core values cannot be taught. The truth is that both instruction and culture are vital, and both must be led simultaneously. Neither factor will make a school great without the support of the other.

THE SEVEN LEVERS

How did the leaders highlighted in this book dispel these myths and—more important—drive *consistent*, *transformational*, and *replicable* growth in their schools? They structured their work around seven core areas of school leadership—areas to which we refer, throughout this book, as levers. Why? Because, by focusing on those seven areas, the leaders leveraged considerably more student learning from every unit of time they invested in their work. Fundamentally, each of these seven levers answers the central questions of school leadership: *What* should an effective leader do, and *how and when* should he or she do it?

As they look over this framework, many school leaders begin wondering, Can this work for me? That question arises in a variety of ways, such as:

- Can these solutions really work for my school?

- We serve a particularly challenging population; will this turn my school around?

- I lead a big district; is this feasible for us?

The answer to each of these questions is a resounding *yes*. Indeed, this book's goal is to show that the success these leaders enjoy stems, not from some mystic, evasive circumstance, but from practical, specific decisions that *any* leader at *any* school can apply. But don't take my word for it right away. In fact, given the number of impractical solutions and changes you've seen in the past, don't take my word for it at all. This book is committed not simply to "telling" about leadership, but to *demonstrating* that success is possible anywhere.

THE SEVEN LEVERS

Executing Quality Instruction and Culture

Instructional Levers

1. *Data-driven instruction.* Define the roadmap for rigor and adapt teaching to meet students' needs.
2. *Observation and feedback.* Give all teachers professional, one-on-one coaching that increases their effectiveness as instructors.
3. *Instructional planning.* Guarantee every student well-structured lessons that teach the right content.
4. *Professional development.* Strengthen both culture and instruction with hands-on training that sticks.

Cultural Levers

1. *Student culture.* Create a strong culture where learning thrives.
2. *Staff culture.* Build and support the right team for your school.
3. *Managing school leadership teams.* Train instructional leaders to expand your impact across the school.

A "PRACTICAL GUIDE": WHAT YOU'LL FIND IN THE BOOK

In the pages that follow, we offer a concrete, step-by-step method for creating exceptional schools. The first seven chapters are devoted to each of the seven levers, followed by Part 3: Execution, which will explain how to put this all together for school-based leaders (Chapter 8, Finding the Time) and district-based leaders (Chapter 9, The Superintendent's Guide). Part 4 provides all of the materials you need in order to deliver professional development to your fellow leaders in your school or district: handouts, PowerPoint slides, and videos of leaders putting this in action. The sum of all these parts is a practical guide that you can use immediately to develop your own leadership, or that of your school or your district.

Accordingly, this book adheres to a number of commonly held principles of effective professional development, elaborated next.

Seeing Is Believing

For most of us, it is not enough to read about great leadership: we need to see it to believe it. Too many books about school leadership leave readers wondering how the methods in the book look in real life and whether the solutions are truly possible. That's why, in the DVD that accompanies this text, we include a selection of video clips of top-tier leaders in action, working directly with their teachers. These videos are not staged—they are the sessions that took place during these leaders' years of extraordinary results. They are also not videos of interactions with the leaders' strongest teachers. Instead, these videos show teacher–leader interactions with struggling teachers, new teachers, and everyone in between.

In this sense, we bring these schools to you. Every chapter is accompanied by a high-quality video of the lever it presents, broken down to portray both the components of success and how success looks as a whole. We also provide the rubrics and schedules these leaders use behind the scenes in order to make each lever happen, along with a handful of real-life success stories that show every lever's impact on the lives of leaders, teachers, and students alike. Seeing exactly what the leaders in this book do, and how they do it, will make it far easier to replicate their actions.

Here's how to identify and use the materials we've embedded within each chapter of this book.

Videos

 WATCH Clip 8: Aja Settles uses video footage of a master instructor to help Kristi Costanzo hone her teaching practice.

Throughout the book, this symbol indicates that a given video clip on the DVD is crucial to the work and to the reading itself. Although it is possible to use this book without watching the accompanying video, we doubt it will be as effective. Watching exemplars of great leadership in practice will provide insights that words will not. You'll see those same types of demonstrations in our presentation of the training materials in Part 4.

Leader Schedules and Calendars

Each chapter features the weekly schedules or monthly calendars of school leaders to show exactly how the actions outlined in the chapter would fit into a busy schedule. Because determining when to perform those actions is such an instrumental step to accomplishing them, we refer to the calendars as "Making It Work." A sample is presented in Table I.1.

Although we do not explore the details of the scheduling process until Chapter 8, our goal throughout the book is to show how leaders make transformational change feasible. Accordingly, each calendar portrays what a leader's schedule looks like when it includes the actions introduced in the chapters preceding it.

Testimonials

Believing in these school leadership strategies requires not only seeing the actions it takes to wield them, but also seeing the outstanding results they yield. With this in mind, we've asked a wide variety of school community members to write testimonials that describe how high-lever school leadership has improved their own practices and their students' learning. You'll find their stories in boxes with the word *Testimonial* in the title.

A Teacher's Testimonial on Data-Driven Instruction

Stephen Chiger

I came to data-driven instruction as an unashamed skeptic. "This sounds like another round of teaching to the test," I sniffed, as I begrudgingly shuffled in to a professional development workshop that would wind up changing the course of my professional life . . . .

Doing Is Achieving

In addition to showing you how to adopt the practices presented in this book, we give you the materials to do so. Part 4 of this book is devoted to giving you

Table I.1   Making It Work: How It Will Fit in a Leader's Schedule

	Monday	Tuesday	Wednesday	Thursday	Friday
6:00am					
:30					
7:00am					
:30					
8:00am		Meet Wilson	Meet Bradley		
:30		Meet Vargas	Meet Frint		
9:00am	Observe Wilson, Vargas, Jenkins	Meet Jenkins			
:30					
10:00am			Observe Mitzia, Boykin, Devin		Observe Hoyt, Settles, Palma
:30					
11:00am					
:30					
12:00pm	Observe Henry, Bernales, Christian				Meet Bradley
:30		Meet Worrell			Meet Palma
1:00pm		Meet Christian			Meet Settles
:30		Meet Bernales	Meet Boykin		Meet Hoyt
2:00pm		Observe Bradley, Frint, Worrell	Meet Devin		
:30			Meet Mitzia		
3:00pm					
:30					
4:00pm					
:30					
5:00pm					
:30					

■ Work Time   ■ School Culture   ■ Observations   ■ Meetings

everything you need to implement these levers in your school. We've included the key tools and rubrics that leaders can use on the ground to make this work. Is this ambitious? Absolutely. However, the future of our schools depends on the sort of success these tools will bring you. That's why we've also included the actual workshop sessions so that you can turnkey training for school leaders of all sorts—principals, coaches, department chairs, superintendents, and more. These include minute-by-minute annotated agendas, PowerPoint presentations, and all of the accompanying materials to launch these workshops yourself.

In addition to the tools, we give you the space to action plan.

Action Planning Makes Meaningful Change

Each chapter ends with a set of questions designed to help you assess your current school, choose which resources from the book will be most helpful to improving that school, and plan your first action steps. This self-evaluation and strategic work is what makes meaningful change possible.

Pulling the Lever
Action Planning Worksheet

Observation and Feedback

- *Quick Assessment.* What percentage of your teachers are observed every week? How many receive feedback at least twice a month?

Resources Are Provided for Any School, Any Context

Every school is different, and every leader faces different constraints. For some, the challenge will be driving a good school to attain excellent results. For others, the challenge will be taking struggling schools into productive places of learning. Recognizing this incredible variety, we have tried to provide as many resources for differentiation as possible. Each chapter includes numerous tools for adapting the practices presented in it to different subject area, age, and size contexts. Given the daunting challenges faced by many schools, each chapter also includes a section called "Turnaround."

Turnaround

This section focuses on the strategies that turnaround leaders have taken immediately to improve student learning, even when given limited resources and facing great challenges. When tough choices arise, this section will help you make them.

Turnaround: From Crisis to Cohesion

Staff Culture

Get on the same page. The core principle of a staff culture turnaround is that teachers need to know the school's core mission ... and must be unified in putting it into practice. "What most undermines failing schools is that everyone on the staff is doing his or her own thing," Brian Sims explains. "Turning a failing school around demands a culture where everyone is on the same page, supports the school's mission, and accepts what is needed to get back on track." To set this expectation, Brian's turnaround schools each hold a three-week training before school starts to set the new culture's expectations.

WHO SHOULD USE THIS BOOK, AND HOW

This book is for school leaders, but who exactly are school leaders? On the most obvious level, principals engage in school leadership. Yet if instruction and culture are to be the core areas of focus for effective school leaders, then the "circle of leadership" includes not only principals but also instructional coaches, department chairs, lead teachers, teachers, and any other staff whose primary purpose is improving a school's instructional capacity. It also must extend to the level of superintendents and district directors of curriculum, instruction, and assessment (see Chapter 9, The Superintendent's Guide, for a special focus on districtwide leadership). In this book, we highlight the work of leaders at all of those levels, from Beth Verrilli, high school English department chair, to Dana Lehman, superintendent of a growing set of schools. We have taken an intentionally broad view of who can serve as an effective school leader, and of what steps those individuals can take to bring great teaching to the classroom. For the purposes of simplicity of the narrative, we often refer to the principal as the leader in question, but the actions are intentionally designed for all leaders.

Those actions are designed for leaders at all schools, too. We have noted that the methods we offer in this book have worked in some of the most challenging conditions in U.S. education; the fact that our case studies are drawn from underserved urban areas is no accident. The schools and students who most need dramatic change are those that are currently least well served. When used well, though, the systems we propose here can—and have—generated significant impact in *any* school setting.

This being the case, the order in which you will implement this leadership model will depend on you: your needs and your school's level of progress. However, after studying the impact of each of these levers in schools across the country, there has emerged a common order of implementation that is usually most effective. You'll need to adapt this to your school, but here are some global recommendations for principals, coaches, and superintendents, respectively.

For Principals

Step 1: Start with the Super-Levers: Data-Driven Instruction and Student Culture

Of the seven levers, two are the fundamental foundation of any school's success. We have dubbed these the "super-levers." Data-driven instruction (Chapter 1) and student culture (Chapter 5) systems determine your school's *instructional capacity*—the upper bounds of how successfully your school can teach its students. Without instructional capacity, transformational school growth is not possible. Indeed, in cases where once-failing schools experienced turnarounds, these levers were the game changers. In contrast, schools that had not mastered data-driven instruction or student culture found it impossible to significantly boost student achievement despite spending significant time on the other levers. *If you find yourself in doubt, give data and culture priority.* Before you determine whether your school has mastered these levers, read the chapters on those two levers. They will help you determine your next steps even if you have already implemented these to a certain extent.

Step 2: Build the Observation and Feedback Cycle

The observation and feedback cycle changes the feeling of a school—it increases leaders' presence and directly affects the staff culture. It also doesn't infringe in any way on the super-levers—it simply enhances them. As such, this has been the next most important step for most effective schools. It is also the most challenging habit to build for a leader who has not been observing frequently.

Step 3: Implement Remaining Levers as Much as Is Feasible in Year 1

Once leaders have established solid data-driven instruction, strong student culture, and an observation and feedback cycle, the remaining levers can turn good schools into great ones. Whatever you cannot focus on in Year 1 can then become a project for your second year of leadership. It is worth repeating: all of these levers are doable simultaneously. We have given you leaders' schedules throughout the book to prove this. But when it comes to determining the speed of implementation beyond these first levers, you know the needs of your school best.

For Coaches and Other Instructional Leaders

Step 1: Start with Data-Driven Instruction and Observation and Feedback

Combined, the systems outlined in the book for data-driven instruction and observation and feedback systems go a long way in empowering coaches to train teachers more quickly and effectively.

Step 2: Build In Planning

After these two levers have been put in place, coaches may switch their focus to planning (Chapter 3), the next key driver of teacher development.

If Applicable, Add Professional Development

Alternatively, if they have been assigned to lead training for peers, these leaders may benefit from focusing on delivering effective professional development sessions (Chapter 4).

For Superintendents

Studying the implementation for principals is essential to being able to support them effectively. Chapter 9 offers a brief set of guiding points to managing and implementing change at the district or multi-school level. If you have limited time and are not sure where to begin, start with the super-levers of data (Chapter 1) and student culture (Chapter 5) and add observation and feedback (Chapter 2) and finding the time (Chapter 8) before transitioning to the superintendents' guide (Chapter 9).

THE PATH AHEAD

These improvements demand hard work. But one thing we've noticed across the country is that most school leaders already work very hard. This book will not change that. The good news, however, is that this book is about actions, not attitudes. If we've learned anything from these transformational school leaders, it is this: work hard, work smart, and results will follow.

Part 1

Instruction

Chapter 1

Data-Driven Instruction

One-on-One: 90 Seconds That Tell It All

Under Principal Mike Mann's leadership, North Star High School's classrooms usually bustle with rigorous activity. On a typical day, students at this Newark, New Jersey, charter school busily analyze Toni Morrison's writing, complete calculus problems, or perform in community-engaged theater. Today, however, is different. Four times each year, North Star students complete interim assessments (IAs) that track their academic progress. And four times a year, teachers then use their classrooms to meet with instructional supervisors and discuss assessment results.

For Steven Chiger, one of North Star's 11th-grade English instructors, this means conferring with veteran teacher Beth Verrilli. Their conversation begins with a question from Beth: On a standard-by-standard level, what are you noticing about your students' performance?

Steve comments that the students struggle with basic, literal comprehension when they hit dense reading passages like those they'll encounter on the Scholastic Aptitude Test (SAT).

"What I've been teaching them isn't enough to get them over the bar," comments Steve.

Beth quickly responds, "So what happens when they hit something they don't understand? What should we tell them?"

"Let me think for a second . . . ." Steve pauses to consider. "Well . . . we could say something similar to what we tell them in *Macbeth* when they don't understand."

"Exactly," nods Beth.

Steve continues, noting that when the class reads *Macbeth*, "We look for key phrases or words that give us some kind of idea. We know that we may not understand everything, but we can at least highlight those words that give us a foothold of the general gist: Is this something that is positive or negative? What were the sentences around it that we did understand? Does this fit within the context?"

"Right," affirms Beth. "So let's be explicit when we do that with *Macbeth*. This way," she continues, "students will have a clear sense of what strategies to use on complex texts, and how to put them into place."

Steve nods, writing detailed notes in the lesson plans he brought with him for the upcoming week. "We could do that with Act 5 this coming week."

 WATCH Clip 1: Beth asks targeted questions to keep teacher Steve Chiger on track toward boosting students' reading comprehension.

In 90 seconds of discussion, Beth has guided Steve to a strategy that will markedly improve his instruction. By the end of their half-hour meeting, the pair will have found 9 or 10 such solutions: integrating nonfiction articles into novel units, teaching mini-lessons on the difference between tone and topic, and adding activities to build student ownership over classroom data. And in a year's worth of

Figure 1.1 North Star AP Results, Percentage Passing 2007–2011

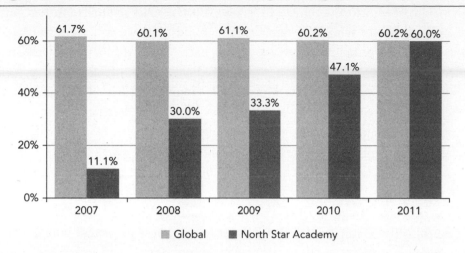

meetings like these, they found 30 or 40. Each week, Steve put one or two of these changes into place, gradually making his classroom more and more effective—so effective, in fact, that over the course of four years, the Advanced Placement (AP) English results in the school rocketed from 11 percent of students passing to 60 percent, even as the percentage of students taking the test quadrupled (see Figure 1.1).

At its essence, data-driven instruction (DDI) begins with and is sustained by meetings like the one we just observed between Beth and Steve, meetings at which principals or other designated instructional leaders create the highest-leverage, most game-changing 30-minute conversations possible—conversations that lead to results. When these meetings succeed, they are the apex of a data cycle that shifts a school's focus to the most fundamental question of education: not "Did we teach it?" but "Did the students learn it? And, if they didn't, how can we teach it so that they do?"

Core Idea

Effective instruction is not about whether we taught it. It's about whether the students learned it.

Putting this simple principle to work fundamentally transforms schools. More important, it transforms *all types* of schools, from district schools to turnaround schools to charter schools, forging success stories that we will see throughout this chapter. Over the past 10 years, leaders nationwide who have implemented effective data-driven instruction at an incredible variety of schools have seen results. Leaders at schools like Morell Park Elementary School in Baltimore,[1] where scores rose 60 points in three years (see Figure 1.2). Leaders at schools like Thurgood Marshall High School in Washington, D.C., and Dodge Elementary School in Chicago, where scores rose 40 points over a five-year span.

As reported in my previous book, *Driven by Data*, there are myriad examples.[2] After spending 10 years observing such systems, I am convinced that data-driven instruction is the single most effective use of a school leader's time. Or, as Beth's principal Mike Mann says, "What is most important is the actual outcome for the student, and data—in its many forms—are the only way to ensure the school is achieving this." Yet knowing that data matter is one thing; truly using them to drive instruction and achieve significant growth is another. What does it take to build a school where 30-minute conversations like Beth's and Steve's can get such dramatic results? For principals like Mike Mann, it takes creating a system of regular data conferences and training teachers in data analysis. For department

Figure 1.2 Maryland State Assessment Percentage of Morrell Park Students At or Above Proficiency

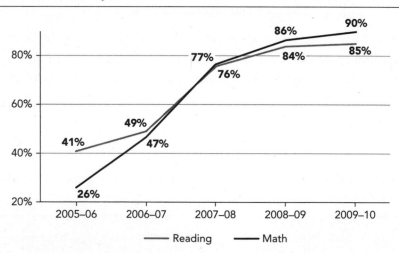

chairs like Beth, it takes asking probing questions and deeply considering the results Steve's assessments produce. To reach this point, though, both Beth and Steve follow a set model.

THE MODEL

Successful data-driven instruction depends on four fundamental keys:

1. *Assessment*. Define the roadmap for rigor.
2. *Analysis*. Determine where students are struggling and why.
3. *Action*. Implement new teaching plans to respond to this analysis.
4. *Systems*. Create systems and procedures to ensure continual data-driven improvement.

In the pages that follow, we look at how North Star leaders Mike Mann (the principal) and Beth Verrilli (the English department chair) put each of these keys into place to make data-driven instruction work.

Keys to Data-Driven Instruction

1. *Assessment*. Define the roadmap for rigor.
2. *Analysis*. Determine where students are struggling and why.
3. *Action*. Implement new teaching plans to respond to this analysis.
4. *Systems*. Create systems and procedures to ensure continual data-driven improvement.

ASSESSMENT: THE ROADMAP TO RIGOR

Most schools strive to offer instructional rigor. But to make rigor a goal raises the question: What is rigor in instruction? Authors from Daggett to DuFour have offered definitions of rigor.[3] In its simplest form, rigor is as the Adams 50 School District in Colorado has defined it: "An expectation that students will demonstrate success with consistent high standards for academic achievement."[4] Yet how can leaders know where the goal for rigor should be set? How can schools determine whether students have learned what they need?

Defining the Roadmap

In pursuit of rigor, leaders often look to state or national standards. Match teaching with these standards, the logic goes, and students will be prepared. The current landscape of the Common Core, whose standards purport to raise instructional rigor across the United States, particularly reflects this thought process. The problem with standards, however, is that they say little about what students must actually master. Consider the following Common Core standard, one that is directly linked to Steve's English class:

> Determine the meaning of words and phrases as they are used in the text, including figurative and connotative meanings (include Shakespeare as well as other authors.)[5]

Seems clear enough. But consider the four possible question prompts in "The Power of Assessment" on page 27, each based around *Macbeth*.

Each question meets the Common Core standard, requiring students to "determine the meaning of words and phrases." Yet the skills required to answer each differ enormously. Question 1 is a relatively straightforward vocabulary-in-context question. The correct response, C, directly connects to both the surrounding sentence and the passage's larger meaning; the incorrect answers have no direct support in the passage. Question 2 presents somewhat more of a challenge, since two of the incorrect responses ("cruel" and "unfamiliar") enjoy some support in the text. To find the correct choice, students will need to figure out which idea *most* relates to the passage; in this case, answer choice B. Question 3, on the other hand, is significantly more difficult, requiring that students interpret the correct meanings of two phrases and select the answer choice that captures both aspects of their connection, B. Two of the "distractor" answers are partially correct, which further complicates this process. Finally, Question 4 requires that students combine vocabulary in context understanding with the larger connotative and figurative meanings of the phrases. Even if students correctly identify the meaning of the phrase "barren sceptre," they may still select answer choice B, unless they can discern that this phrase is not meant as a work of satire, which leaves the best answer as D. Of the four, this is the sort of question that appears on Advanced Placement English examinations.

The Power of Assessment

Assessment Questions for a Passage from *Macbeth*

Directions: In this scene, Macbeth is discussing a prophecy he received from the witches. Read the passage, then answer the questions that follow:

MACBETH:
>   They hailed him [Banquo] father to a line of kings
>   Upon my head they placed a fruitless crown, And put a barren sceptre in my gripe, Thence to be wrench'd with an unlineal hand, No son of mine succeeding. If 't be so, For Banquo's issue have I filed my mind; For them the gracious Duncan have I murder'd.

1. What does it mean that Macbeth has a "fruitless crown"?
   A. Macbeth will soon die.
   B. Macbeth will become a slave.
   C. Macbeth will not be a successful king.
   D. Macbeth will take a long journey.
2. As used in the passage, the word *unlineal* most nearly means:
   A. Cruel to Macbeth
   B. Unrelated to Macbeth
   C. Unfamiliar to Macbeth
   D. United with Macbeth
3. How does the phrase "barren sceptre" connect to the phrase "fruitless crown"?
   A. Both are symbols of kingship.
   B. Both connect authority with infertility.
   C. Both reflect Macbeth's leadership
   D. Both represent negative events.
4. The description of Macbeth's "barren sceptre" contributes to the unity of the passage in which of the following ways?
   A. As a parallel between Macbeth's possible children and Banquo's possible children
   B. As a satirical comment on challenges Macbeth will face with infertility
   C. A comparison between Macbeth's strong formal authority and his lack of popular influence
   D. As an ironic contrast between Macbeth's power and his inability to produce future kings

These examples drive home the essential lesson you need to know about assessment: standards are meaningless until you define how to assess them.

> ## Core Idea
>
> Standards are meaningless until you define how to assess them. Assessments, therefore, are the roadmap to rigor.

Standards alone cannot set the bar for rigor. If teachers know only that students should "determine the meaning of words and phrases," they may only teach to the rigor of questions like number 1, leaving students hopelessly unprepared for questions like number 4. Even sample lesson plans do not suffice. Only in the assessment do we define the rigor.

This distinction can be clearly noted in comparing Steve Chiger's planning process in the opening vignette with that of a traditional teacher, whom we'll call Mr. Smith. Mr. Smith consults the scope and sequence of his curriculum at the beginning of the week and plans his lessons to meet those standards.[6] Without a specific understanding of what sort of assessment item students will need to address, he may build his weekly quiz around questions like number 1 or 2. Doing so may feel easier in the moment, especially if Mr. Smith feels students are not prepared for the challenges of a question like number 4. Simply put, standards alone cannot guarantee that students will learn what they need to—not even when Mr. Smith combines them with good intentions and preparation.

Now consider Steve's planning process. At the beginning of the week he consults the assessment that he will give at the end of the week, which is aligned to the SAT and AP English exams. This assessment has been created by North Star teachers to align with the year-end test and is meant to determine whether students are mastering the core skills they need to. He notes that questions 2 and 4 are on the test. So he asks himself the fundamental question, "What do I need to teach for my students to be able to master questions like number 4?" With the assessment as the roadmap to rigor, Steve's teaching process has been transformed. Write the test first, and the way forward is clear. Wait to write the test until the lessons have been taught, though, and you will end up following the route of Mr. Smith. You will test for what you taught, not for what students need.

> ## Core Idea
>
> Write the assessment first, then ask the question: "What do I need to teach for my students to be able to master the questions on that assessment?"

The assessment-first approach happens in every classroom at North Star's high school. Rather than waste time parsing vague standards, department chairs and teachers like Beth and Steve go straight to the end game: Advanced Placement and other college-ready assessments. By analyzing the specific questions posed on the test, they break down the specific skills—thematic comparison, identification of authorial intent, close textual analysis—that students need in order to succeed on those tests. The point bears stressing: college-ready assessments—not just a list of standards—are Beth and Steve's guide toward rigor.

Advanced Placement and/or International Baccalaureate classes offer a great opportunity for schools to define college-ready rigor, but they are far from the only opportunity. College placement exams (the ones that determine need for remediation) and colleges' expectations for research papers are just two other great sources for well-defined, assessment-driven, college-ready rigor. Indeed, at North Star, and at schools that achieve similar results, well-designed interim assessments aligned to the end game of college rigor are crucial to driving significant student gains. What should these assessments look like? Let's find out.

Building Your Own Assessments

At the heart of every top-tier school we examined lay high-quality assessments that meet the following criteria:

Interim

Great schools schedule interim assessments to identify problems when change is still possible. Year-end tests are autopsies, not assessments: they explain what went wrong after it is too late to change course. The top-tier school leaders in this book gave schoolwide interim assessments four to six times a year, and never more than eight weeks apart. This distribution rate allowed time for teachers to make changes, while not overwhelming students (or faculty!) with "test fatigue."[7]

A Word On . . . Rigor, Multiple-Choice, and Open-Ended Responses

One of the most common criticisms against data-driven analysis is that it reduces learning to "rote-level" or "basic" skills, preventing students from engaging in "real" learning. Underneath that critique is a belief that items like multiple-choice questions are inherently *not* rigorous and are lacking in value. Is that assumption valid? Take another look at the question number 4 about Macbeth:

4. The description of Macbeth's "barren sceptre" contributes to the unity of the passage in which of the following ways?
   A. As a parallel between Macbeth's possible children and Banquo's possible children
   B. As a satirical comment on challenges Macbeth will face with infertility
   C. A comparison between Macbeth's strong formal authority and his lack of popular influence
   D. As an ironic contrast between Macbeth's power and his inability to produce future kings

Consider the skills required to answer this question correctly. Students would need a deep understanding of numerous literary and stylistic devices, the ability to discern meaning using indirect context clues, and the ability to distinguish between competing ideas based on their degrees of evidentiary support. If a rigorous understanding of English is the goal, it's hard to imagine a better way to reach it.

Consider the alternative options: having students write an essay or short answer to one of the following prompts:

- Analyze the following passage of Shakespeare. How does it contribute to one of the central themes of *Macbeth*?
- What does Shakespeare mean by a "barren sceptre"? Cite evidence from the text.

These are quality prompts that could be used to produce a writing sample. The prompt, however, is not what determines the rigor; it is how you score the response. In an open-ended question, the rubric and the text difficulty determine the rigor of the question.

In the end, the multiple-choice question and open-ended question complement each other in very important ways. One requires you to generate your own thesis, and the other asks you to choose between viable theses—with one being the best option. Students need both of those skills: the ability to discern between shades of gray, and the ability to generate their own arguments. To claim that only multiple-choice questions or only essays can capture both is to miss opportunities to develop a student's intellect fully.

Common

If assessments define rigor, then they must be common across all classes and grade levels. Otherwise, we cannot guarantee equal rigor in each classroom. "Common assessments are crucial to keeping all classes at a high level," Beth explained. Teachers occasionally object to this requirement because it creates standards within their classrooms that, to some extent, they cannot control. However, the essential benefit of common assessments—ensuring that all students, in all classes, receive the level of rigor they need—is too valuable to compromise. As Mike Mann, principal of the high school, explains, "Measuring outcomes is only useful if you know what the target should be. If the target is different in each classroom, then we have no way to know how students are doing across the cohort relatively to each other. The students are stuck with varying degrees of rigor depending on which teacher they have. That's not fair to our students."

Aligned

To ensure that they are sufficiently rigorous, interim assessments must be carefully aligned to the end-goal assessments of classes. Establishing that alignment raises the critical question for any teacher or leader: To what end goal for your students will you aspire? It is not enough to say that we want critical thinking or problem solving for our students. Too many schools have fallen into the trap of thinking they're making progress simply by espousing terms like these. Your assessment will define what you mean, and that level of definition will get you results. There are a few levels of alignment:

> *State test–aligned.* I do not know of students who can fail their state tests and be ready for college. That being said, there are many students who pass their state tests and are *still* not ready to attend or succeed in college. State tests, then, are a necessary but insufficient step toward college readiness. Making sure that students can meet this bar is critical. If their ability to do so is in question, then part or most of the interim assessment should be aligned to the preliminary rigor of the state test.
>
> *College ready–aligned.* This is the ultimate goal. For high school, there are many assessments already well defined: Advanced Placement, International Baccalaureate, SAT. These can be complemented by performance assessments

Blazing a Trail: Beth's Approach to "College-Ready Rigor" on Interim Assessments

- Beth's first task is to define, in concrete terms, what it means to design an assessment with "college-ready rigor." Although the specific steps may vary depending on the content area, there are several common features. For example, when designing interim assessments for her English class, Beth notes that the search begins with existing high-rigor materials: "It starts with taking every practice AP and SAT exam out there and looking at the types of passages they have: the lengths, whether fiction or nonfiction; if nonfiction, then what type of nonfiction."
- Once she's identified the right materials, Beth then looks to the type of questions being asked and their level of challenge: literal comprehension, main idea, tone, and perspective.
- Finally, based on the level of challenge identified in order to be college ready, Beth and the English department adapt their curricula accordingly. "The early high school years serve as a bridge between the eighth-grade state test level of challenge and the more rigorous demands of college-ready assessments," Beth explains. "Because we know where our end goal is in Year 4, it makes planning Years 1 and 2 much easier."

---

like a well-designed anchor research paper that all students are required to write. For elementary and middle schools, the task is less well defined, but the leaders cited in this book aspired for above-grade-level proficiency for all their students. That takes the form of integrating algebra earlier into the math curriculum (and assessing accordingly) or setting higher targets for proficiency on leveled reading assessments. In each case, the leaders were not satisfied with state proficiency alone.

Curriculum sequence–aligned. Once you have an assessment that establishes the appropriate level of rigor, then you need to make sure that the assessment is aligned to your curriculum. In the six to eight weeks prior to each assessment, does your curriculum teach the standards that will appear on that assessment? If not, teachers will rightfully protest that you're not testing what they're teaching—which defeats the whole purpose of interim assessments.

Developing interim assessments that meet these high bars can, of course, be challenging. One obvious solution is for schools to create their own. This was the approach that Art Worrell, history teacher and department chair at North Star, took in designing his interim assessments. "Ultimately, going to the source was worth it for me," Art asserts, "especially in figuring out open-ended document-based questions." In this way, teachers like Art ensure that their interim assessments are aligned, relevant, and ready to track student progress.

The drawback, however, is that the whole-cloth creation of new assessments can be incredibly time consuming, especially if a school has not done it before. A second possibility, then, is for leaders to request interim assessments from schools that have already successfully implemented data-driven instruction. This will grow increasingly feasible as the Common Core takes root, influencing more state assessments. For the most part, these schools are happy to share their approach to testing, saving their colleagues an incredible amount of time.

That said, schools must make sure that any "borrowed" assessments they borrow are well aligned. Mike Mann concisely sums up the argument: "Each state has different benchmarks and year-end assessments, and each school and district has a separate sequence of teaching its standards. If you're taking tests from elsewhere, there's a good chance your curriculum won't line up chronologically." This will leave you with one of two options: either change your curriculum sequence to match that of the interim assessment, or change your interim assessment to test standards in the same chronological order as your curriculum.

Finally, for situations in which neither creating nor borrowing assessments is an option, many companies sell interim assessments. Buying from third parties is the least time-intensive approach to building a system of assessment. Yet as tempting as this method may be, "store-bought" assessments are often not aligned enough to your end-goal assessments to ensure that students reach appropriate end goals. AP exams and SAT questions are far more rigorous and challenging than many of the ones drafted by commercial test makers. Steve, whose previous school used such assessments, suggests this policy: "When it comes to third-party tests, buyer beware."

A Word On ... "Teaching to the Test"

One frequent objection to data-driven instruction is that a focus on assessment amounts to empty "teaching to the test." From this point of view, data force teachers to choose between "real" teaching and irrelevant test preparation. If the assessments a school uses are not rigorous enough, or if they are not aligned to what students need to know, then this is a valid critique. However, when interim assessments are well constructed and college ready, they are *an unparalleled resource* in driving student learning. If you want students to be able to write a six- to eight-page paper stating an original argument, why wouldn't you teach so as to get them to do so effectively? In the same way, if students will need to solve a quadratic equation embedded with an area problem in the SAT, shouldn't we teach them how to do that, thus preparing them for success on the SAT?

More pragmatically, in the modern United States, a student's access to admission into the college of his or her choice, and to entry into almost any major career field—from firefighting to medicine—depends significantly upon his or her ability to do well on assessments. One can argue that society ought to work differently, but as educators, we must prepare students to succeed in the real world around them. Here, this means that students who are not prepared for high-quality end-goal assessments have not learned what they need.

In the end, data-driven instruction is not about teaching to the test: it is about testing the teaching. That makes all the difference.

Feasibility Tip: Working Around Imperfect but Mandated Interim Assessments or Pacing Guides

In many large public districts, principals may be required to follow pacing guides that correspond to given schedules or use prefabricated district assessments. If these assessments align with the criteria just outlined, then they will be useful without adaptation. What if they don't, though? Well, fortunately, we've seen public schools use a number of strategies to build effective data systems regardless of what assessments are already in place. Here are a few of the most common approaches they've taken:

- Use the mandated assessment as a base, but on the day of administration, add additional questions you've created that cover the standards that are missing.
- Administer the mandated assessments, but don't spend any time analyzing them—tell teachers and students they're just practice tests. Prioritize, instead, a different interim assessment that meets the criteria established in this book.

ANALYSIS: TEST IN HAND, FACE TO FACE

If assessments set the roadmap for learning, then data analysis lets you know if you're following the path. How a leader uses the time he or she spends analyzing the assessments with teachers is what dictates the results. Beth and Steve demonstrated this in the opening vignette: effective 30-minute analysis meetings between leaders and teachers are the highest-leverage time a leader can spend. Why? Because they can drive 80 percent of all instruction in those few minutes. Here's how.

Consider a principal who is committed to observing class instructions as often as possible. If the principal observed every teacher in his or her school for 15 minutes a week, she would be among the most diligent school leaders in the country. Yet even at this breakneck pace, she would see only 1 percent of the week's learning and teaching time. Don't believe it? Do the math:

- Typical teaching load: 5 classes/day, 50 minutes each
- Total minutes of instruction per week: 5 classes/day × 50 minutes × 5 days/week = 1,250 minutes
- One classroom observation/week: 15 minutes
- 15 minutes/1,200 minutes total instruction = 1.2 percent observation of instruction

Figure 1.3 is a grid of the total percentage of observation of each teacher's lessons given weekly 15-minute observations.

Figure 1.3 Observation Alone

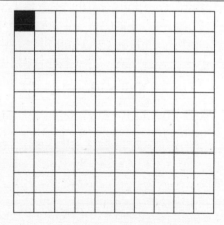

For all her attentiveness, this principal is watching her students through a peephole. Even if leaders are able to identify the most critical 1 percent with these observations, they would still need to make broad, vague conjectures about the standards learned the other 99 percent of the time.

Now consider Beth, who conducts data meetings with Steve after each interim assessment. By using well-aligned interim assessments in leading analysis meetings, Beth can gauge *six to eight full weeks of teaching in 30 minutes*. Indeed, even if the assessment captures only 80 percent of student learning (given that no assessment can capture 100 percent of the learning in a class), leaders have still changed the percentage of instruction they observe from 1 percent ... to a revolutionary 80 percent.

Observation Alone

Interim Assessment Analysis Meeting

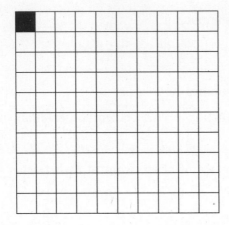

If traditional observations are glimpsed through a peephole, data analysis throws open the doors. "I don't think tests are perfect," Beth says. "But they capture much, much more than I otherwise would be able to see."[8]

Core Idea

A dedicated school leader who does weekly observations of all teachers will see ... 1 percent of instruction. Data analysis meetings see ... 80 percent of the student learning.

If traditional observations are glimpsed through a peephole, data analysis throws open the doors.

Precursors to Effective Analysis Meetings

Frequently, data analysis goes no further than the "scoreboard": Have results gone up, or have they gone down? Such analysis is almost useless. Imagine a soccer coach who skips her team's games and learns the final scores from a newspaper. At best, her advice would be limited to empty platitudes: "Get more goals," "Work harder," "Work on defense." Leaders who look only to a whole class's test scores commit the same error: they see the scoreboard, but never the match. Though they use data, they are not data driven.

By contrast, leaders like Beth Verrilli use interim assessments as a springboard for entering a more probing and detailed discussion of student strengths and weaknesses. Before meeting with Steve, Beth had examined assessments on a question-by-question and student-by-student basis. As Beth succinctly notes, "The more prepared you are, the more fruitful information comes out of the meeting." But before Beth looks at the data, she relies on two key structures: data reports and fast turnarounds.

Data Reports

Great data analysis starts from clear and intuitive data reports: one-page summaries, in table form, of each student's performance on the assessment. At a minimum, these reports must show class performance at four levels:

1. *Question level:* How students performed on each question and what wrong answer choices they made. This is incredibly important; Beth notes, "On a standard like main idea, it's not enough to know the overall percentage. I need to know what makes them struggle: Have they not mastered the skill of main idea in general, or was it the content of this passage that they were unprepared for, the challenge of new vocabulary, a challenging answer choice, or other factors?"

2. *Skill or standard level:* How students performed on each standard or skill.

3. *Student level:* How well each individual student performed.

4. *Global or whole-class level:* How well the class performed.

These templates for data reports are concise and easy to understand, allowing teachers to input and interpret data with as small of a learning curve as possible. "We're always looking to the 'intuition' test," Beth Verrilli explains, "seeing if

Table 1.1 Sample Data Report

First Name	Last Name	Multiple Choice	Overall Proficiency	1	2	3	4	5	6	7	8	9	10	11	12
Question Number				1	2	3	4	5	6	7	8	9	10	11	12
Correct Answer				d	a	c	c	1	1	c	1	1	1	b	b
Standard				Sentence Completion	Sentence Completion	Sentence Completion	Sentence Completion	Sentence Completion	Essay	Extended Reasoning	Literal Comprehension	Perspective	Literal Comprehension	Literal Comprehension	Main Idea
Kate	Smith	75%	75%			b					d		c		
Kendra	Jones	100%	100%												
Sarah	Alba	75%	75%								c		a	c	
Miguel	Menendez	67%	67%					d			d		d	d	
Charles	Wynn	83%	83%									c	c		
Percentage correct		80%	80%	100%	100%	80%	100%	80%	100%	100%	40%	80%	20%	60%	100%

people can pick up the template and use it effectively." If the data report is not intuitive, it will not be informative. Table 1.1 presents a sample data report, and we've also included a few on the DVD.

Fast Turnaround

Each day's delay in scoring assessments and creating data reports is a lost opportunity. That's why the leaders described in this book all make fast turnaround a major priority. As Beth Verrilli notes, "By ensuring that all tests are scored within three days, we're able to quickly shift into problem-solving mode." Ideally, assessment reports should be prepared within 48 hours of the assessment's distribution. This is an ambitious target, but one that can be met with an "all-hands-on-deck" approach. The leaders studied came up with a number of creative ways to make turnaround faster, including:

- Having support staff help with data entry

- Having parent volunteers

- Creating half-day schedules to give teachers extra time to grade assessments

Whatever solution is used, it is vital that assessment turnaround receive high priority. Until they're entered, data are useless.

Analyze in Depth

With data in hand, Beth and Steve can begin their analysis of the results. To do so, they utilize a core set of strategies that ensure that they find the information that matters most. See "Going Deep: Effective Analysis" on page 40.

The Power of Training

Of course, these suggestions are just starting points. Ideally, before any analysis meetings occur, teachers have had the opportunity to learn the fundamentals of assessment analysis hands-on. This means school leaders must, at a minimum, model how to analyze data. At North Star, Mike Mann makes sure that all new teachers participate in a detailed professional development session on data-driven instruction before school begins. "Truly effective data-driven instruction starts from transparency," Mike stresses. "When our teachers understand that the goal is not 'teaching to the test' but rather aligning our practices with what our kids

Going Deep: Effective Analysis

Make a Solid Hypothesis

Look at specific questions:

- Did students all choose the same wrong answer? Why or why not?
- What misunderstandings do the students' errors reveal? What do you think students were doing wrong here?
- What were all the steps students needed to be able to do in order to answer this question correctly? Within those steps, where does it appear that student mastery broke down?

Look *within* standards:

- On questions that measured the same standard, were students better on some questions than on others?
- If so, how do those questions differ in difficulty? Why did students do better on one than on another?

Compare *similar* standards:

- Do the results on one standard influence the other?

Test Your Hypothesis

- Review written student work. Do errors match your hypothesis of why students are struggling?
- Ask students how they solved the problem. Do their errors still match your hypothesis?

Make Explicit Action Steps

- *Explicit instruction.* What would you have to teach to overcome these misunderstandings? How will you teach the information differently this time than you did the last time?
- *Assignments and activities.* What activities or assignments will students need to practice this new skill to the point of mastery?
- *Assessment and checks for understanding.* How will you assess students and check for understanding during the lesson itself?

Repeat the Process for Struggling and Special Education Students

First line of action: Grab the low-hanging fruit first.

- Sort data by students' scores. Are there questions that only the struggling students are getting wrong?
- What are all the steps the students need to take to answer these questions correctly? Which of these steps need to be made more explicit to the students?

- What sort of practice do the students need to master this standard—heavy repetition of computational skills? Following a multi-step protocol?

  Second line of action: Provide in-class support.

- What are the standards that will be reviewed or retaught for the whole class?
- Are the struggling students' misunderstandings different than those of the rest of the students on these standards?
- What additional support or steps will the struggling students need when these standards are being reviewed?

---

need, it lets us build the buy-in we need." To launch your own training session in data-driven instruction, see *Driven by Data*—it includes all the resources and materials you'll need.[9]

Preparing for Analysis Meetings: Using the Back Pocket

Legend has it that when the time came for the Constitutional Convention, James Madison, widely considered the Constitution's "father," was nervous. Prior to the start of the convention, he had drafted his own vision for the founding document, and he feared the others might reject his proposal as pretentious and dismiss it out of hand, regardless of its merits. Madison faced a choice: present and argue for the document he had written, or leave the Constitution in his "back pocket" and guide delegates to independently reach and embrace his solution as their own. Madison chose the latter approach, and the result was an enduring document that included nearly all of his original key proposals.

Whether or not this story is true, it reflects an incredibly important insight: highly effective leaders guide from the back pocket. The strategy works not only for political leaders, but for school leaders, too. A case in point: after analyzing Steve's data report, Beth had many ideas of her own about how Steve needed to adjust his teaching tactics. Yet, rather than simply "dictate" those solutions to Steve, Beth keeps the answers in her back pocket and instead leads by asking questions. Consider just two minutes of their conference:

> "So what happens when they hit something they don't understand? What should we tell them?"

"So let's be explicit when we do that [the new action step] with *Macbeth*."

"Could we follow the *Macbeth* activity with an SAT passage to make explicit what you're doing with Shakespearean language that's giving you trouble? You can use similar strategies when you hit troublesome passages on the SAT." [Waits for teacher to write it down]

"Do you think they're paraphrasing when they get into trouble, or do you think that [strategy] needs to be explicit?"

REWATCH Clip 1: Revisit Beth's meeting with Steve and write down all of the questions that she asks.

Look at Steve's data in Table 1.2. Based on the questions shown in this data report, let's begin by analyzing the data from the standards level.

Table 1.2 Standards-Level Analysis

	Sentence Completion	Main Idea	Extended Reasoning	Supporting Details	Vocabulary in Context
% Correct	73%	55%	**76%**	60%	75%

It's apparent that main idea is a serious challenge for Steve's students. Yet Beth's analysis doesn't stop at noting the most troublesome standards; it also takes into account the specific questions involved. When Beth examines the four questions coded as "main idea," she finds something unexpected:

Question Number	% Correct
10	83%
19	23%
29	45%
32	63%

The students' problem is not with every aspect of main idea, then, but only with certain types of main idea questions. Having determined as much, Beth then returns to the text of the test itself. Question 19, which only 23 percent of students answered correctly, is a logical place for her to start. The question concerns a short passage on the work of Edgar Allan Poe. It reads:

1. The author's purpose in this passage is to (correct answer appears in **boldface**):

    A. Detail the myths and inconsistencies surrounding the personal life of a renowned author

    B. Demonstrate that professional authors can succeed despite scathing criticism

    C. Call attention to the fact that literary critics have erred in their judgment of Poe's writing

    D. Argue that Poe's early negative publicity had continued repercussions throughout his writing career

    E. **Show that contradictions in Poe's life and work do not detract from his popularity**

Once she's identified the key question at issue, Beth takes a final, crucial step: she considers which wrong answer students selected. Looking back to the data, she sees an unmistakable pattern:

Answer A	58%
Answer B	0%
Answer C	0%
Answer D	8%
Answer E	33%

Based on this data, Beth realizes that most students were drawn to answer choice A. Given the amount of time the passage spends discussing inconsistencies in Poe's work, this answer would seem plausible, especially if it were read quickly. Yet the final answer choice, answer E, is the only one to take into account the passage's substantial discussion of Poe's popularity and legacy, a key part of the text that answer choice A misses. In short, students are selecting a "narrow" answer that does not cover the whole passage. Question 29, which saw similarly low levels of student performance, revealed the same error pattern: when students were wrong, their answers did not encompass everything they had read.

Informed by her own analysis, Beth arrives at the analysis meeting with a good sense of how Steve can help his students learn main idea correctly. She knows a few specific strategies that will be effective: prompting students to distinguish ideas that are too limited from those that are sufficiently broad, for instance; and requiring students to link a main idea they've identified back to each paragraph in a text. But just as important as the strategies Beth will suggest are the ones she will not. Why, for example, won't she recommend repeated practice on discarding overly broad main ideas? Because, while developing too-broad main ideas is an error that English students often make, Beth knows it's not one of the mistakes that Steve's English students made. Data get their real clout from the opportunity they give you to analyze student learning at this high of a zoom level—not merely noting which standards students struggled with, but deriving exactly what the questions those students missed were asking.

Even for school leaders who have learned to analyze data closely, guiding teachers to do the same can be quite difficult. Fortunately, outstanding instructional leaders like Beth can provide concrete guidelines to explain how they make "back pocket" leadership a school-changing practice:

- *Analyze teacher's results* before *the meeting*. Premeeting analysis is essential to ensure that leaders enter the meeting with a good idea of where the root causes of problems lie—and of how teachers might fix such problems. Before the analysis meeting, Mike Mann makes sure that both teachers and leaders complete their own analyses of the data report. From Mike's perspective, the reason is simple: "The more intimately teachers are involved in the entire data-driven process, the more likely they are to incorporate the results into their plans and into their teaching."

- *When needed, get help with content expertise*. If school leaders do not have the instructional expertise to analyze certain content areas, they should seek help. This help can come from a coach, department chair, strong teacher, or someone from outside the school. At the high school level, department chairs are essential, because few (if any) high school principals can possibly master all foreign languages, sciences, and other subjects. Mike Mann, for example, asks

Spanish department chair Lina Zapata to lead data conferences with Spanish department faculty. Taking the time to find content help when needed is vital to making analysis meetings as productive as possible.

Leading Analysis Meetings: Diving Deep

For meaningful analysis to occur, leaders must ask carefully prepared questions at the level of specific assessment items. Beth's years of leadership experience, of course, have brought her a keen sense of which questions she should ask, but she and leaders like her do turn to a few common sets of prompts that tend to drive deep analysis. Regardless of how long you've been leading a school, or using data to drive that school's progress, the following examples we've listed are likely to help you lead analysis meetings effectively. (For an expanded list, see "Leading Effective Analysis Meetings" on the DVD.)

- "Let's look at question number _____. What do you think the students are doing wrong here?"
- "What did the students need to be able to do to get that question right? How was this more than what they are able to do with you in class?"
- "What's so interesting is that they did really well on question number _____ but struggled with question number _____ on the same standard. Why do you think that is?"

To see another school leader put this into practice, watch Juliana Worrell, principal of Fairmount Elementary School, push her teachers to identify the error their students were making in decoding.

 WATCH Clip 2: Assessment data lets Juliana Worrell guide Yasmin Vargas toward planning purposefully.

Note that the questions you use will depend on the quality of self reflection and analysis of the teachers. Beth notes, "Reviewing the preliminary action plans of the teachers in advance of the meeting helps you identify where you will most need to support the teacher."

A Word On... Analysis Meeting Size

Analysis meetings can occur either one on one or in teacher teams. The role of the leader changes slightly depending on the size of the meeting, but the keys to effective analysis remain the same. North Star High School employs both models. There, math team meetings often occur in groups led by team leaders, while the English department generally employs one-on-one check-ins. One-on-one meetings are doable even in the largest schools, as we show in the chapter on finding the time (Chapter 8), but that does not preclude schools from choosing group analysis.

ACTION: WALKING THE WALK

During their analysis meeting, Steve and Beth reached a solid understanding of what students did well and generated a host of ideas about how best to strengthen student learning. Even the most cogent analysis, however, is only meaningful if it leads to action. Recognizing this, great leaders make sure that the results of data analysis meetings translate into real classroom changes.

At the Meeting: First Steps Toward Action

As noted earlier, Steve comes to his analysis meeting with an action plan template on which he intends to note specific action steps he wants to take away from the discussion. At the meeting, Beth then supports Steve by giving him time to record on paper the changes they select on the spot. Although action plans like Steve's may be effective in a variety of formats, it is vital that every action plan includes a due date for each key action step. "Assessment is useless until it affects instruction," Mike Mann notes. "Setting clear dates ensures this happens." Attaching due dates to action steps is non-negotiable: it establishes clear expectations, allows for greater accountability, and ensures that the meeting's findings will make a difference in the classroom.

To help teachers respond to the problems they have identified, Beth breaks processes down into smaller steps to facilitate implementation and make accountability easier. For example, rather than instructing Steve to "use *Macbeth* to teach words in context," she works with him to determine specific skills to teach to the students, and they compile a list of those skills right there at the meeting.

A Word On ... Action Plans to Lesson Plans

Converting action plans to lesson plans occurs naturally when you have standing meetings for feedback and planning with each of your teachers. Then, all you need to do is convert that standing meeting to a data meeting once each quarter. You'll learn more about the power of such meetings in Chapters 2 and 3 on feedback and planning.

 REWATCH Clips 1 and 2: Leaders guide teachers from assessment to action.

Action Plans Become Lesson Plans

Rather than stop at pinning down an action plan, Beth and Steve proceed to rewrite upcoming lesson plans based on what they've decided during their meeting. For example, at the close of the meeting, Steve adds lessons on skills for unscrambling confusing passages to his lesson plans for the upcoming week. Rewriting lessons immediately entrenches the new strategies that have been developed at the meeting. Like writing an action plan, this process prevents implementation from being left to chance.

Day 1: TUESDAY	Day 2: WEDNESDAY	Day 3: THURSDAY
Whole class: Do-Now: Review assessment questions 8 and 10 (literal comprehension) Small-group review: *Macbeth* translation think-aloud	Whole class: Do-Now: Practice paraphrasing a difficult sentence or short passage in one's own words—*without* using any of the words in the passage	Whole class: Large group: SAT prep using AP *Macbeth* passage (Predict answers for HW, answer passage in class) Small-group review: Vocabulary-in-context review

After the Meeting: Making Action Happen

Once analysis meetings have been completed in this way, teachers like Steve have a clear guide for what to teach and how to teach it more effectively. To make sure these action steps turn into better student learning, a few more steps follow:

- *Make assessment an ongoing process.* In a data-driven environment, teachers like Steve will use "mini-assessments" to see whether their students are on track. Through quizzes, homework assignments, and even student responses to teacher questions, Steve will know whether he's progressing toward his goal. At the analysis meeting, leaders should encourage this process by brainstorming with teachers: What ongoing assessment will they use to test student mastery of the skills they have targeted? How well these assessments are helping teachers track learning and shape instruction remains part of the leader's discussion with teachers throughout the weeks that follow.

- *Use schoolwide systems to support change.* The heart of change beats in the classroom but needs the support of every second of the school day. Faculty members, such as tutors, who do not participate in assessment or analysis can still get copies of interim assessments and data reports and be included in data-driven instruction. Teacher tutoring, after-school support sessions, or peer instruction should also be linked to action plans. At North Star, for example, teachers Shana Pyatt and Sean Smith lead the "Breakfast Club" to give more individualized attention to students whose interim assessments have revealed difficulty with basic operations in math.

- *Make accountability easy.* Strong action plans make it easy for teachers and leaders to monitor progress. Teachers can make sure their lesson plans are as effective as they can be in promoting learning, and leaders can monitor to see if that is happening. Classroom observations also become more powerful, because observers can better evaluate the teacher's efforts to shape and present a specific lesson that advances agreed-upon goals. We revisit this topic in Chapter 2, Observation and Feedback.

SYSTEMS: LOCK IN SUCCESS

Beth's skills as a questioner and analyst are deeply impressive. However, they would have been squandered without the work that her principal Mike Mann has invested in creating a strong schoolwide structure for data analysis. For data-driven instruction to transform a school, assessment, analysis, and action must be "locked in" through a key set of systems.

The Calendar

Read a principal's calendar, and you'll know his priorities. When he built North Star's yearly calendar, Mike Mann's first step was to lock in the fundamentals of data-driven instruction: interim assessments, analysis meetings, and time to implement action steps. The message is clear: at North Star, student learning is the essential focus.

Consider the calendar outlined in Table 1.3. This calendar outlines the data-related tasks in which a school like Mike Mann's engages during the year. Note that weeks are explicitly marked out in advance for the reteaching of areas where the interim assessment revealed students to be having difficulty. This ensures that North Star has locked in core objectives.

Table 1.3 Building Your Calendar: Sample HS Interim Assessment Calendar

Time Frame	Unit/Assessment	Notes
6 Weeks (8/28–10/20)	**1st Semester, Part 1**	
IA #1 October 16 (7 weeks)	1st semester midterm (Interim assessment #1)	Approximately 1 hour per assessment. All objectives from Unit 1.
1 week (10/17–10/24)	RETEACH objectives from IA #1	Reteach based on test results analysis.
7 Weeks (10/24–12/8)	**1st Semester, Part 2**	
IA #2 December 11 (7 weeks)	1st semester final (Interim assessment #2)	Cumulative: All objectives, units 1–2 (@ 1:30 hours/exam).
1 week (12/13–12/22)	RETEACH objectives from NSA 1 and 2	Reteach based on test results analysis.
8 Weeks (1/2–2/23)	**2nd Semester, Part 1**	
IA #3 Feb 25–Mar 2 (8 weeks)	2nd semester midterm (Interim assessment #3)	Cumulative: All objectives, units 1–3 (@ 1:40 hours/exam).
2 weeks (3/5–3/16)	2nd semester, Part 2 and RETEACH	Reteach based on test results analysis.
SAT March 19–23	SAT	
7 Weeks (3/26–5/18)	**2nd Semester, Part 3**	
IA #4 May 21–25 (8 weeks)	Interim assessment #4 (Juniors and seniors: AP exams)	Cumulative: All objectives, units 1–5 (@ 2 hours/exam).
4 Weeks (5/28–6/22)	**2nd Semester, Part 4 and Final Performance Task Preparation**	
Year End June 25–29	Final exam and final performance tasks	Cumulative: All objectives, units 1–6 (@ 2 hours/exam) and oral presentations/large math projects.

This calendar weaves assessments into the fabric of the school year. Once in place, those assessments provide a valuable tool for scheduling the rest of the year. Imagine the school year calendar as a table, and interim assessments as legs. Each assessment is imperative—without it, the table would topple over. You still have room for mobility, though: if you move the table, all the legs will move with it in unison. For example, if the state moves testing up by one year, your school can simply move everything forward, keeping the assessment cycle in place.

> ## Core Idea
>
> Read a school calendar, and you'll know what matters in a school. Put the assessment cycle in first, and learning will take priority.

Chapter 8 goes into greater detail on creating calendars. For now, the key point is that unless leaders commit to a yearlong program of data-driven growth, they will not realize extraordinary improvements.

TURNAROUND: WHAT TO DO FIRST

As noted in the Introduction, building a strong, data-driven foundation is one of the "super-levers" for schools seeking dramatic transformation. What are the first steps a leader can take to put this into action in a school that is struggling?

In other chapters, you'll find coping mechanisms and shortcuts for working through challenging situations. In this chapter, however, data-driven instruction *is* the turnaround strategy. This is the lever that will jumpstart student learning, right alongside student culture. At the end of this chapter ("How It Fits into a Leader's Schedule"), you'll find the beginning of a monthly action plan, the full version of which is on the DVD. Your task is quite direct: take this monthly action plan and adjust it to meet your school's yearly calendar. Each one of the action steps listed needs to happen, although they can happen at whatever time works for you within the framework we've laid out here.

On the DVD, you have the highest-leverage handouts for use with data-driven instruction. Again, for a full menu of professional development materials, look to my previous book, *Driven by Data*.[10] You do not need to reinvent the wheel here: the work has been done successfully by hundreds of schools across the country. You can attain extraordinary results by simply following their example.

A Teacher's Testimonial on DDI

Stephen Chiger

I came to data-driven instruction as an unashamed skeptic. "This sounds like another round of teaching to the test," I sniffed, as I begrudgingly shuffled in to a professional development (PD) workshop that would wind up changing the course of my professional life.

I'd been teaching in an urban high school for four years, and my idealism, while not extinguished, had begun to seriously sag under the weight of some questions that most teachers in under-resourced communities face. How could I teach well when my students came to me at so many disparate levels? If my students' primary school education had been inadequate, was it too late to change anything by the time they were in high school? And even if I could run my class effectively, were the systemic expectations so low—and the drag of poverty so crushing—that my efforts comprised little more than blowing against the wind?

Suffice it to say, something happened during the course of that PD that altered how I saw education. I read the case studies of schools that had turned around student achievement. I analyzed student data and saw the kinds of insights it provided about learning. I thought of my students—of Zakiyyah, of Dawanna, of Porsalin and Paul and Gwen. Didn't I owe it to them to push myself and my school?

After hearing a segment on using assessments to improve literacy, I called the facilitator over.

"This sounds great," I said. "But this isn't how my department teaches English. We teach poems, we teach stories, we teach the five-paragraph essay."

"Well," the facilitator said, "it's not about which poem or story you teach; it's about how you teach it, assess it, and reteach it. That's what you need to rethink."

I still remember what I was thinking in that moment. First, I thought that this was an incredibly intimidating and outrageous thing to say. Second, I thought that it was exactly right. If we designed tests to measure student literacy, and if we set the rigor of those tests to match what we knew would be true college preparation, we could keep our curriculum focused on the material that really mattered—not just the idiosyncratic whims of the moment. We could, with the backbone of a data-driven program in place, transplant a refreshed academic vision, one to which all of us would be aligned.

A data-driven program wouldn't be teaching to the test; it would be teaching to the kids. More specifically, we'd be teaching to their needs because we'd know—precisely—what those needs were.

I got back to school and immediately began work on developing the system. We hired a consultant who had worked at North Star, a school whose success at that point was legendary in New Jersey. We formed a small cadre of educators who were willing to stick their necks out and develop this system. I split my days between teaching and administrative work.

(continued)

When the opportunity to work at North Star presented itself, I took it. I needed to know—once and for all—whether the student achievement they boasted was really possible for an entire school system. If North Star wasn't doing it, no one was; if they were, I needed to be a part of that.

At North Star I met Beth Verrilli, one of the most astounding leaders and teachers I have ever worked alongside. You'd never know this by talking to Beth: she is humble, soft-spoken, thoughtful, and plenty hard on herself.

Beth doesn't know this, but I'd actually had the chance to meet her at that PD more than a year earlier. Back then, though, the mere thought of someone who'd led students to achieve the results she had intimidated me too much to introduce myself. Beth must be a super-genius or a magician to do the work she did at North Star, I reckoned. Maybe she had a golden binder with the answers to all the teaching questions I privately harbored.

I was wrong. What made Beth a great instructional leader was precisely the opposite. She didn't have all the answers, and—while quite intelligent—she wasn't a mystic with preternatural powers. She was a person, like me, who worked really, really hard. When she didn't have an answer, she set herself to the task of finding one or—more often—creating it herself.

When I got to North Star, another English teacher said to me, "The thing about Beth's leadership is that you'll do everything she asks because you won't be able to imagine letting her down." It was true. At every meeting, it was clear to me that she'd spent as much time poring over my students' data as I had—and, what's more, she'd spent an equal amount of time considering my own analysis. She came prepared to every session as a master teacher does to a lesson: with objectives, ideas, questions, and enough familiarity with the material to think on her feet as the moments demanded. If she was putting this much time into my development as a teacher, I could do no less in return.

I remember in my first year our sophomores tested low on tone questions. I was surprised. I'd predicted they'd do well. They hadn't demonstrated the weakness in my formative assessments—but only because I hadn't been asking the right kinds of questions.

When we analyzed the test, we realized that students weren't differentiating between different types of tone words—for example, disappointed versus sad versus lugubrious. Beth and I co-planned a unit that unlocked the abilities we knew the kids had. We honed it until we were happy with it, until we saw our students master the skill. They did—and now we have these lessons to share with any member of our department who faces the same obstacle.

It would have been easy for Beth to put herself on autopilot. I'd had a good amount of experience with data-driven instruction at my last job, and I was already bought in. I showed up to our meetings having spent hours on developing analysis documents and with as many ideas in tow as I could muster. I was hungry for ideas. But Beth pushed my growth nevertheless. Always keeping one, or two, or ten steps ahead of me, she helped me be my best. Beth understood data-driven culture for what it is: an antidote for curricular complacency.

When I think of Beth I think of my student Kenyatta, who struggled in tenth grade until we deciphered her literacy difficulties ... and who later got into her top college choice. When I think of Beth I think of my student Jessica, who was so surprised at her growth in English—a class she assumed would always be out of her reach—that she set her sights on winning departmental recognition. (She did.)

But, most of all, when I think of Beth I think of someone who took the time and energy to nurture my growth in the same way we try to nurture the growth of our students. I think of someone whose attention to detail and dedication to using data well have earned her own students nationally competitive scores—not just year after year, but each year with stronger results. I think of someone who is my partner, hands dirtied, digging through the messy work of analysis to find the most effective practices for our students. Discovering data-driven instruction changed my career once, but the practice of doing it alongside Beth did so a second time.

Now an instructional leader myself, I try to pay forward Beth's wisdom. I prepare for data meetings with attentiveness and zeal. I analyze my teachers' data with the same alacrity I want them to apply. And I try to meet people wherever they are—whether new or experienced, struggling or masterful—so that together we can find the right answers for our students by analyzing one question at a time.

CONCLUSION: THE RIGHT MAP TO FOLLOW

As the Introduction explained, data-driven instruction functions as a super-lever, sharpening a principal's remaining tools and making learning soar. It gives both leaders and teachers a map of their schools' instructional needs. Stone by stone and change by change, leaders like Mike Mann and Beth Verrilli can then use that map to pave their schools' routes to success. Data-driven instruction asks the most essential question an educator can ask: How can we make sure our students learn? Used correctly, it also spells out the answer.

To help you evaluate the quality of your data-driven "map," we provide a rubric of what makes implementation effective. Intended to be used to assess the present state of data-driven instruction and assessment in a school, the rubric summarizes all the key elements detailed in this chapter. The rubric specifically targets interim assessments and the key levers leading to increased student achievement.

Using this rubric, school leaders can conduct a self-evaluation that will show them where they stand and help them determine what steps they must take to bring data from paper to practice. Follow your map, and results will quickly follow.

Implementation Rubric: Data-Driven Instruction and Assessment

Data-Driven Culture

1. *Highly active leadership team.* Facilitate teacher–leader data analysis meetings after each interim assessment and maintain focus on the process throughout the year. ___/4
2. *Introductory professional development.* Teachers and leaders are effectively introduced to data-driven instruction; they understand how interim assessments define rigor and experience the process of analyzing results and adapting instruction. ___/4
3. *Implementation calendar.* Begin school year with a detailed calendar that includes time for assessment creation and adaptation, implementation, analysis, planning meetings, and reteaching (flexible enough to accommodate district changes and mandates). ___/4
4. *Ongoing professional development.* PD calendar is aligned with data-driven instructional plan: includes modeling assessment analysis and action planning and is flexible to adapt to student learning needs. ___/4
5. *Build by borrowing.* Identify and implement best practices from high-achieving teachers and schools: visit schools and classrooms, share and disseminate resources and strategies. ___/4

Assessments

1. *Common interim assessments* four to six times per year ___/4
2. *Transparent starting point.* Teachers see the assessments at the beginning of each cycle; they define the roadmap for teaching. ___/4
3. *Aligned to state tests and college readiness* ___/4
4. *Aligned to instructional sequence* of clearly defined grade level/content expectations ___/4
5. *Reassess* previously taught standards ___/4

Analysis

1. *Immediate turnaround* of assessment results (ideally 48 hrs) ___/4
2. *User-friendly, succinct data reports* include item-level analysis, standards-level analysis, and bottom line results ___/4
3. *Teacher-owned analysis* facilitated by effective leadership preparation ___/4
4. *Test-in-hand analysis* between teachers and instructional leader ___/4
5. *Deep:* Moves beyond what students got wrong and answers why they got it wrong ___/4

Action

1. *Plan new lessons* collaboratively to develop new strategies based on data analysis ___/4
2. *Implement explicit teacher action plans* in whole-class instruction, small groups, tutorials, and before- and after-school supports. ___/4
3. *Ongoing assessment.* Utilize in-the-moment checks for understanding and in-class assessment to ensure student progress between interim assessments. ___/4
4. *Accountability.* Instructional leaders review lesson and unit plans and give observation feedback driven by the action plan and student learning needs. ___/4
5. *Engaged students* know the end goal, how they did, and what actions they are taking to improve. ___/4

TOTAL: ___/100

Note: 4 = Exemplary Implementation, 3 = Proficient Implementation, 2 = Beginning Implementation, 1 = No Implementation

Table 1.4 August–October Monthly Plan: Data-Driven Instruction

August	☐ Present first DDI PD session to staff (use *Driven by Data* for PD agenda, materials).
September	☐ Week 2: Have the first round of interim assessments (or the closest proxy) finalized. ☐ Week 2: First interim assessments (or the closest proxy) have already been seen by the teachers (transparency) so that they can plan for mastery. ☐ Week 4: Develop plan to determine how test scoring and analysis will be completed.
October	☐ Week 1: Have teachers predict performance on interim assessment #1. ☐ Mark each question: "Confident" (sure that the students will get it right), "Not sure," and "No way" (students will definitely get it wrong). ☐ Week 2: Interim assessment #1. ☐ Week 2: Deliver PD to school's instructional leaders in DDI analysis and leading analysis meetings (use *Driven by Data* for PD agenda, materials, and resources). ☐ Week 3: Teacher analysis and action plan templates are in place; teachers complete assessment analysis instructional plans. ☐ Week 3: Instructional leaders run test-in-hand analysis meetings with teachers. ☐ Compare performance to what the teacher predicted: highlight areas of discrepancy (for example, teacher over- or underpredicted how well the students were going to do on certain test questions). ☐ Follow one-pager: "Leading Effective Analysis Meetings." ☐ Week 3: Principal observes analysis meetings, giving feedback to instructional leaders about their facilitation. ☐ Week 4: Staff PD. ☐ Run results meeting to plan to reteach challenging standards. ☐ Have teachers add rigor to their lessons using "Data-Driven Best Practices for Increasing Rigor."

Making It Work: How It Fits into a Leader's Schedule

None of the systems mentioned here require blocking out time in a leader's schedule every week. Rather, they are tasks that occur on a quarterly basis around each interim assessment. Thus, rather than a weekly schedule, they are best driven by a monthly plan. A sample is shown in Table 1.4.

On the week of assessment analysis, a leader's calendar would include conferences with all the teachers involved in the assessment. This would look something like Table 1.5.

Stop Here

Take a moment and evaluate your school on the data-driven instruction implementation rubric. Then follow the steps below:

Table 1.5 Sample Schedule

	Monday	Tuesday	Wednesday	Thursday	Friday
6:00am					
:30					
7:00am					
:30					
8:00am		Meet Wilson	Meet Bradley		
:30		Meet Vargas	Meet Frint		
9:00am		Meet Jenkins			
:30					
10:00am					
:30					
11:00am					
:30					
12:00pm					Meet Bradley
:30		Meet Worrell			Meet Palma
1:00pm		Meet Christian			Meet Settles
:30		Meet Bernales	Meet Boykin		Meet Hoyt
2:00pm			Meet Devin		
:30			Meet Mitzia		
3:00pm					
:30					
4:00pm					
:30					
5:00pm					
:30					

◻ Work Time   ◻ School Culture   ◼ Observations   ◼ Meetings

If your school is below a 70 on the DDI rubric:

The point bears reiterating: data-driven instruction is the super-lever *without which none of the other instructional levers work effectively*. If you don't think your school is proficient on this DDI rubric (that is, it doesn't earn a score above 70), then this chapter should remain your primary focus for building your school's success (combined with student culture—Chapter 5). While you may successfully implement other instructional levers now, too, don't launch anything yet that will inhibit your ability to implement DDI thoroughly. Consider using *Driven by Data* as an additional resource—it includes all the professional development materials and tools you need to launch this effectively in your school.

If your school is above a 70 on the DDI rubric:

Move on to the next chapter to see how observation and feedback, planning, and professional development can support your school's journey from good to great.[11] These chapters are listed in the order of the extent to which the levers they describe will impact your school.

Pulling the Lever
Action Planning Worksheet for Data-Driven Instruction

Self-Assessment
- Assess your school on the Implementation Rubric for Data-Driven Instruction and Assessment. What is your score? /100
- What items on the Implementation Rubric need the most improvement?

_____

_____

_____

_____

_____

Planning for Action

- What tools from this book will you use to develop data-driven instruction at your school? Check all that you will use (you can find all on the DVD):
  - ☐ Implementation Rubric for DDI
  - ☐ Leading Effective Analysis Meetings One-Pager
  - ☐ Assessment Analysis Spreadsheet
  - ☐ Teacher Action Plan
  - ☐ Assessment Calendars: Elementary, Middle, or High School
  - ☐ Monthly Map: Data-Driven Instruction Sample
  - ☐ Videos of Observation and Feedback Meetings

- What are your next steps for launching data-driven instruction?

Action	Date

Chapter 2

Observation and Feedback

If data-driven instruction (DDI; Chapter 1) and student culture (Chapter 5) are the "super-levers" of successful schools, observation and feedback is arguably the next most effective. Let's look at the following feedback conversation.

One-on-One: 10 Minutes That Make the Difference

An enormous wooden table dominates the conference room at North Star Elementary School. In a building that pulses with the energy of two hundred students, the room is strikingly quiet: a space for contemplation. On this Wednesday morning, Principal Julie Jackson and third-grade teacher Carly Bradley sit at one corner of the table, ready for their weekly feedback meeting. Yesterday Julie observed Carly delivering a science lesson on the classification of animals. She noticed that every time a student struggled, Carly lowered her expectations of that student instead of pushing him or her to continue working out the right answer. Today, Julie sits down to give Carly feedback about that lesson.

After praising the progress Carly has made, Julie shifts the focus to Carly's questions. "Carly," she begins, "what happened with Simon when you called on him to answer a question about mammals?"

Carly thinks for a moment before responding, "He couldn't think of an example of a mammal."

"Right. And then what was your next prompt after that?"

"I asked someone else to give me an example."

Julie continues, "What does that do to Simon's ability to master the problem?"

Carly hesitates, then slowly answers, "It makes it … too easy."

Julie nods. "Yes! So you reduce the rigor too quickly. That's what I want to get at today. When you're prompting, you want to maintain the rigor and not go immediately to the easiest level of questioning."

As the meeting goes on, Julie and Carly discuss ways that questions could keep the level of question rigor higher during the lesson.

"So let's break this down a little more. Let's say Simon gives you an example that's not a mammal—for example, 'fish.' What might you say next?" Carly first comes up with an overly simplified question, catches herself, and starts generating less scaffolded questions that maintain the rigor. Julie comments, "What do you notice about the level of questioning you just modeled?"

"The rigor is raised and the questioning will definitely be more effective," Carly says, smiling at her own improved questioning. Julie pulls out Carly's lesson plan for tomorrow and they both review it. Then, after Carly makes a note in her lesson plan, she and Julie begin to practice, rehearsing exactly what Carly will say tomorrow morning.

 WATCH Clip 3: Julie Jackson demonstrates effective feedback in action, debriefing her observations of Carly Bradley's science lesson.

In just 10 minutes, Julie leads Carly through an incredibly powerful process: a targeted focus on, and practice of, exactly what Carly needs to improve. For Julie, teacher feedback is not about the volume of observations or the length of written feedback; it's about bite-sized action steps that allow a teacher to grow systematically from novice to proficient to master teacher.

Becoming a master teacher is often considered a slow process. Recently, some have argued that it takes as long as 10 years, since the "10-year rule" has been successfully applied to fields other than education.[1] Yet for teachers who take part in the sort of observation-feedback loop Julie sets in motion, highly effective teaching comes after just one or two years. The proof? Julie gets outstanding results not only from experienced teachers but from rookies as well. One of the most striking statistics from North Star Elementary School is that the median national score on the TerraNova for kindergarten, first-, second-, *and* third-grade students, in reading, language, *and* math, is in the 99th percentile. You don't get these results by placing your best teachers strategically—you get them by coaching each and every teacher to do excellent work.

How is this possible? It takes two steps: spending much more time coaching, and using much more effective coaching tactics. A recent study found that in major metropolitan areas, the median new teacher receives only around two observations a year; the median veteran teacher is only observed once every two years, and, incredibly, nearly one in three veteran teachers were observed only once every three years.[2] Julie Jackson's school is radically different: there, every teacher is observed and receives face-to-face feedback every week. That means that each teacher is getting feedback at *least* 30 times per year—as much as most teachers get in more than 20 years. And Julie's teachers develop accordingly. They might not earn scores of "master teacher" on every teacher evaluation rubric, but they do get master teacher–like results.

Core Idea

By receiving weekly observations and feedback, a teacher develops as much in one year as most teachers do in twenty.

When we observe teachers, much of our focus tends to be (rightly) on making every individual observation as meaningful as possible. In the process, though, we often lose sight of any systematic way to track how teachers grow, or to grasp schoolwide trends in teaching practice. For everything we know about teaching from individual visits, there's a lot we can't know, like:

- How frequently is each teacher being visited?

- Who are the teachers you are not seeing often? Why aren't you seeing them?

- What feedback was this teacher given a week ago? A month ago? Last year? How have they put it into practice?

- What are the schoolwide strengths in instruction? What are the areas for growth?

- What feedback has led to meaningful changes for teachers? What feedback has not?

For the leaders we present in this book, the uncertainty surrounding these questions was agonizing. At Julie's school, there now exists a process that answers each of these questions and a system that ensures that the hard work of teacher observation bears results far greater than the sum of its parts. In short, Julie and her colleagues have recognized that observation and feedback are only fully effective when leaders systematically track which teachers have been observed, what feedback they have received, and whether that feedback has improved their practice.

Core Idea

Observation and feedback are only fully effective when leaders systematically track which teachers have been observed, what feedback they have received, and whether that feedback has improved their practice.

THE TRADITIONAL MODEL: OBSERVATION ADRIFT

Sadly, all too many schools still observe less diligently than North Star does—and less frequently. At these schools, observations are stress-packed rituals that occur no more than once a year. Months in advance, each teacher learns when his or her "day of destiny" falls and plans accordingly: shining classrooms to sparkling, honing lessons to perfection, and badgering students to behave well. When the annual 45-minute encounter finally unfolds, the principal observes the year's most dynamic lesson. Unused to the leader's presence, students display stellar conduct. The lesson is successful, and one month later, each teacher receives a carbon-paper checklist with each box marked "Satisfactory." With a sigh of relief, the whole ceremony ends. Teachers are "safe" for another 11 months. Yet despite all the anticipation, school leaders haven't learned much—nor have they done much to nurture meaningful improvement.

Over the past 20 years, some school leaders have tried to improve this model by using more detailed feedback, more engaged observations, or detailed teacher rubrics that judge instruction. The most prominent such teacher rubric, proposed by Charlotte Danielson in 1996, calls for assessing teaching through a comprehensive framework of elements. Danielson lists 76 elements of teaching that leaders must evaluate, elements that are said to "honor the complexity of teaching … [and] constitute a language for professional conversation [and] provide a structure for self-assessment and reflection on professional practice."[3] Yet while the notion of a comprehensive rubric for teacher assessment is certainly an improvement over the traditional one-observation-per-year model, it still does not address the most fundamental issue. Both normed rubrics and more traditional observations share a fatal flaw: at their essence, they are judgments of teacher quality. Whatever the merits (or accuracy) of these judgments, they neglect a much more relevant question: How can teachers be coached to improve student learning?

Core Idea

The primary purpose of observation should *not* be to judge the quality of teachers, but to find the most effective ways to coach them to improve student learning.

This gets at the heart of what most teacher observations miss. Effective observation and feedback isn't about evaluation—it's about coaching.

Recognizing this, school leaders like Julie Jackson have re-envisioned the observation-feedback model, emulating the best practices of other high-achieving principals and of successful leaders from other fields. To meet her primary goal—coaching teachers in ways that drive student learning—Julie has embraced a core commitment:

- Weekly 15-minute observations of each teacher, combined with . . .
- Weekly 15-minute feedback meetings for every teacher in the building

Take a moment to remember how great a difference this commitment makes: it increases the speed of teacher development exponentially!

At each feedback meeting, Julie offers direct, readily applicable feedback. The next week, she checks that her feedback has been put in place and looks for further areas for improvement, building a veritable cycle of improvement. The result is a set of observations meant not to evaluate but to coach—a change that makes all the difference.

The sum total of these changes is a complete shift in the staff culture of the school. Yet the shift is not to a nerve-wracking, "gotcha" environment. Instead, provided that the main goal of the observations is for teachers to improve practice, the result is greater staff investment, with teachers realizing that their development matters. As Carly herself notes, "The conversations may seem intimidating at first, but in fact it shows just how careful Julie Jackson is as a leader, and how important my own development is to our school." Paradoxically, the fact that the observations occur at varying times and on a weekly basis makes them *less*, not more, stress intensive. "Because Julie comes by so often, I never worry that one bad lesson will give a false impression of what class is really like," Carly explains. Carly is not alone: as Marzano, Frontier, and Livingston note in *Effective Supervision*, frequent observation leads to *less*, not more, apprehension, taking a lot of the stress out of the observation process.[4]

Like the other leaders we studied, Julie Jackson uses a powerful model of observation and feedback:

Scheduled observations. Lock in frequent and regular observations.

Key action steps. Identify the one or two most important areas for growth.

Effective feedback. Give direct face-to-face feedback that practices specific action steps for improvement.

Direct accountability. Create systems to ensure feedback translates to practice.

In the pages that follow, we will see how she creates each of these core components—and the pitfalls she avoids along the way.

Core Idea
Keys to Observation and Feedback

Scheduled observations. Lock in frequent and regular observations.
Key action steps. Identify the one or two most important areas for growth.
Effective feedback. Give direct face-to-face feedback that practices specific action steps for improvement.
Direct accountability. Create systems to ensure feedback translates to practice.

SCHEDULE OBSERVATION AND FEEDBACK

If the goal of leaders is to coach teachers, it is foolish to observe only once or two times a year. Imagine if a tennis coach said that he would only watch players once every six months, but that he would fill out a detailed report after each visit. If this seems ridiculous, remember that *teaching is no different*. Teachers, like tennis players, need consistent, regular feedback and practice to improve their craft. At North Star Elementary School, teacher improvement is the name of the game. As one teacher noted, "Julie is all about driving us to the next level, and every week she makes us a bit better."

Core Idea

Teachers are like tennis players: they develop most quickly when they receive frequent feedback and opportunities to practice.

Although frequent observation has many benefits, it comes at a cost: time. On first reading, Julie Jackson's extraordinary commitment to observation may seem unsustainable. Where, in the midst of a busy schedule, is the time for weekly visits? In part, Julie is able to observe her teachers weekly because of the systems she has put in place:

• *Shorter visits.* In contrast to the traditional, hour-long block, Julie observes only for roughly 15 minutes per teacher. As long as leaders are strategic about what they are looking for, this shorter length of time is sufficient for thorough and direct feedback. Indeed, significantly longer observations are often inefficient, especially when they come at the expense of observing far fewer teachers.

• *Observation blocks.* Grouping observations in hour-long blocks reduces inefficiencies in traveling between rooms and transitioning between tasks. Scheduling three or four brief observations back to back is a good way to gain extra time. On Wednesdays, for example, Julie saves a great deal of time by watching six teachers back to back in a two-hour block.

• *Locked-in feedback meetings.* Each of Julie's observations is accompanied by a face-to-face feedback meeting. To keep herself on track, she makes a point of scheduling these meetings from the beginning of the school year. Teachers know when they'll meet, which brings stability, and there is no wasted time in email exchanges or tracking down teachers to deliver the feedback. "Even during my busiest weeks," Julie remarks, "having the meeting on my calendar means I keep making observation a priority." Locking in feedback meetings also helps leaders stay accountable and committed to the observations they need. Julie affirms, "If I know I have to give that teacher feedback on Thursday morning, I have an extra incentive to get that observation done—I don't want to walk into the meeting empty-handed!"

• *Feedback meeting combined with other meetings.* Rather than only meet to discuss feedback, Julie combines observation feedback with her other agenda items for her teachers. Almost every week, that includes a discussion on the next week's plans (discussed at length in Chapter 3); four times a year, the whole meeting converts to a data analysis meeting (discussed in Chapter 1). Even if your school does not engage in weekly planning, because feedback and planning are so directly connected, scheduling both in one block is a powerful synergy, making both much more effective. Here is the breakdown:

• 10 minutes: Observation feedback (this chapter)

• 20 minutes: Planning (Chapter 3)

- *Distributed observation load among all leaders.* Of course, most schools—like Julie's—have considerably more than 20 teachers, and it is impossible for one leader to observe all of them every week. Recognizing this, as North Star Elementary grew, Julie empowered other instructional leaders to conduct observations and give feedback. This is consistent with a poll I made of principal coaches in eight urban districts: Chicago, New York City, Charlotte, Memphis, Baltimore, Oakland, Washington, D.C., and Newark, New Jersey. In these districts, the ratio of total teachers to total school leaders (including vice principals, nonteaching personnel, coaches, lead teachers, special education coordinators, and so on) was never greater than 12:1. We are often reluctant to count every leader ("but they're a floating coach" or "but they don't currently do instructional leadership"), but the reality is that we have the capability to create a 15:1 ratio of teacher to leader in almost every public school.[5] (Chapter 7, on school leadership teams, discusses this process in much greater detail; for now, it is important to note here that almost every school has enough potential observers to make this approach work.)

Making It Happen

Your first reaction might be to think this is not all possible in a school leader's day. Let's show how by doing the math:

- Typical teacher-to-leader load (when all leaders are counted): 15 teachers per leader

- One classroom observation per week: 15 minutes

- Total minutes of observation per week: 15 teachers × 15 minutes = 225 minutes = less than 4 hours

- One feedback and planning meeting: 30 minutes

- Total minutes of feedback and planning meetings: 15 teachers × 30 minutes = 7.5 hours

- Total hours devoted to teacher observation and feedback: 4 hours of observation + 7.5 hours of feedback and planning meetings = 11.5 hours

Percentage of a leader's time (assuming a 7:00 a.m.–4:00 p.m. school day): 25 percent. Table 2.1 shows how that looks in Julie's schedule.

Table 2.1 Sample Calendar with Observations and Meetings

	Monday	Tuesday	Wednesday	Thursday	Friday
6:00am					
:30					
7:00am					
:30					
8:00am		Meet Wilson	Meet Bradley		
:30		Meet Vargas	Meet Frint		
9:00am	Observe Wilson, Vargas, Jenkins	Meet Jenkins			
:30					
10:00am			Observe Mitzia, Boykin, Devin		Observe Hoyt, Settles, Palma
:30					
11:00am					
:30					
12:00pm	Observe Henry, Bernales, Christian				Meet Bradley
:30		Meet Worrell			Meet Palma
1:00pm		Meet Christian			Meet Settles
:30		Meet Bernales	Meet Boykin		Meet Hoyt
2:00pm		Observe Bradley, Frint, Worrell	Meet Devin		
:30			Meet Mitzia		
3:00pm					
:30					
4:00pm					
:30					
5:00pm					
:30					

☐ Work Time   ☐ School Culture   ☐ Observations   ☐ Meetings

As you can see, committing to observation and feedback does require a significant time investment—but not an unreasonable one. You can schedule observation blocks and feedback and planning meetings and still have plenty of time for everything else. (See Chapter 8, Finding the Time, for more strategies to keep non-instructional items from interfering with your ability to observe teachers.)

Once you have developed a schedule like this one, you are one step closer to making dramatic improvements to teacher development. The next step is the knowhow to observe effectively.

IDENTIFY KEY ACTION STEPS
Criteria for the Right Action Step

After 15 years of teaching and school leadership, Julie Jackson doesn't miss much. When she enters Carly's classroom, she immediately sees dozens of areas for comment, from student engagement to the quality of questioning to lesson materials. Recognizing this, some researchers have suggested that ideal observations attempt to capture every significant aspect of teaching at once. In *Effective Supervision*, for example, it is suggested that observers complete a 41-point rubric for each observation.[6] Yet Julie is not looking to find a "laundry list" of faults or make a radical overhaul of Carly's pedagogy. Instead, she limits herself to a narrow, specific action step to increase student learning: "When a student answers incorrectly, ask that same student a scaffolded question to give her a chance to get it right." She limits herself to just this one key change. Why? Because that method conforms to the way adults actually learn.

Think about the times when you have received a long list of feedback in one meeting. There is no way for you to implement all of that feedback at once. So you are stuck with the task of trying to prioritize what to do first, and many of the other pieces of feedback you've received are left unattended. So why does this happen so often? Because principals using a traditional observation and feedback model feel—rightly—that they have limited opportunities to share all of the feedback they come up with. With a weekly observation model, however, that framework completely changes. Julie Jackson uses weekly observation to take the guesswork away from her teachers. Instead of leaving each teacher to wonder what to prioritize, she answers that question during feedback meetings by limiting her feedback to what is most important.

Core Idea

We learn best when we can focus on one piece of feedback at a time. Giving less feedback, more often, maximizes teacher development.

Focusing on one key piece of feedback also makes more sense given the length of Julie's observations. There is simply no way to assess 40+ points of a teacher rubric in 15 minutes. You would spend more time reading the rubric than observing the class! As Kim Marshall, author of *Rethinking Teacher Supervision and Evaluation*, notes, "Shorter visits are fine . . . if they are effective." So how does Julie Jackson make sure she's focused on the right thing?

There are a number of core criteria Julie uses to separate the high-impact changes from the low-impact and to ensure that the key action steps she chooses are the right ones:

Is the action step directly connected to student learning?

As noted at the start of the chapter, observation works best when it draws on the resources of data-driven instruction. For example, Carly's interim assessment data revealed that her students struggled with "high-rigor" questions, that is, those questions in which students are engaged in more of the cognitive work. From this insight, Julie narrowed her focus to creating higher-level prompting. Of course, many key changes, such as how well disciplined a class is, may not be directly revealed by the data. As a direct record of student learning, however, strong data analysis is a great starting point for coaching teachers forward. Even though she may not be hitting every area for improvement, Julie knows from data and experience that this step will make a concrete difference and will make class better.

> ## Core Idea
>
> Weekly observations, coupled with the interim assessment cycle, means you can coach teachers not only based on their needs but on the specific learning needs of students. You see the right things because you know where to look.

Does the action step address a root cause affecting student learning?

Julie's next concern in picking an action step is whether it addresses a root cause of problems in the class or merely a symptom of them. For example, in observing a noisy classroom, it may be tempting to focus feedback on stopping students from acting out of place. But as Julie notes, "Often, classroom management or discipline problems aren't really about how teachers deal with misbehavior; they're about the design of classroom procedures. If the teacher simply worked on building the expectation that all hands stay on student laps, it's easier to prevent students from pushing each other." Distinguishing a root cause from a superficial symptom takes practice, but there are a few areas where confusion is particularly likely. Consider these examples:

- *Common surface problem:* Students off-task during group work.
    Often the root problems: Lack of explicit roles and instructions for the group work; lack of guidelines for what to do when students get stuck.

- *Common surface problem:* Students appear bored by content that is not engaging.
    Often the root problem: Teacher hasn't created the illusion of speed with effective in-class transitions, all-class responses, and other pacing techniques identified by Doug Lemov in *Teach Like a Champion*.[7]

Is the action step high-leverage?

The final criterion is whether the action step notably improves many facets of instruction or is a necessary step for other improvements. Given leaders' limited time and the difficulty teachers face when they try to make many changes simultaneously, it's important to identify the action steps that have the most leverage—that drive improvement for the greatest number of aspects of the lesson at once.

Julie Jackson's Highest-Leverage Action Steps

On some level, identifying the most effective feedback possible is a matter of experience; with practice, it becomes far easier. Yet some shortcuts exist. A good way to start is by studying the best literature around classroom instruction. *Teach Like a Champion* and *The Skillful Teacher* were the most-mentioned resources by the leaders in this book.[8]

Even more valuable is learning from these top-tier leaders themselves. Although there are many facets of classroom instruction that can affect multiple areas, leaders like Julie Jackson think about two critical areas for feedback: management and engagement, and intellectual engagement. While every teacher has different experiences of what works to drive improvements, Julie has identified the areas outlined in "Julie's Top 10 Areas for Action Steps" as the highest-leverage based on her experience. If you want to make effective, immediate impact in teacher instruction, these areas are a good place to start.[9]

This list isn't complete, and it isn't intended to be. Every teacher needs the action steps that will most affect their instruction. However, by looking for these areas and practicing giving feedback in them, you can greatly develop your eye for teacher development.

Making It Bite-Sized

In *The Talent Code*, author Daniel Coyle tells a remarkable story about Coach John Wooden, who led the UCLA basketball team to an unprecedented 10 national championships in the 1960s and 1970s. When he studied Wooden's practices, he noticed few pep talks, and *no* conversation that wasn't accompanied with immediate practice of the skill. Moreover, Wooden wouldn't focus on mastering every aspect of basketball: he would work with each athlete to practice one small part at a time. As Coyle notes, quoting Wooden: "Don't look for the big, quick improvement. See the small improvement one day at a time. That's the only way it happens. And when it happens, it lasts."[10]

Julie's Top 10 Areas for Action Steps

Most Frequently Used Action Steps by Top-Tier Instructional Leaders

Engagement and Management

1. *Develop routines and procedures.* Write up and rehearse minute by minute.
   - Write out every routine and procedure down to the smallest detail of what is said and done.
   - Rehearse these routines with a colleague in the classroom before the students are there.
   - Introduce each procedure with short sequential steps.
   - Practice routine to perfection: have students do it again if it is not done correctly.
2. *Narrate the positive.* Describe what students are doing well, not what they're doing wrong.
   - "I like how Javon has gotten straight to work on his writing assignment."
   - "The second row is ready to go: their pencils are in the well and their eyes are on me."
   - Narrate the positive while looking at the student(s) who are not complying.
3. *Challenge and build momentum.* Give the students a simple challenge to complete a task.
   - "The last class was able to transition to small groups in 45 seconds. I bet you can do even better."
   - "Now I know you're only fourth graders, but I have a *fifth*-grade problem that I bet you could master. Get ready to prove how smart you are!"
4. *Increase teacher radar* (awareness of when students are off task) and *implement least-invasive immediate intervention* (when the first student is off task).
   - Deliberately scan the room for compliance: choose three or four "hot spots" (places where students often get off task) to continually scan.
   - Circulate with purpose by moving to different locations on the perimeter of the room.
   - Give an instruction, narrate the positive, then redirect student who is not complying.
   - Redirect from least to most invasive:
     - Use proximity.
     - Use a nonverbal.
     - Maintain eye contact.
     - Say student's name quickly.
     - Give a small consequence.

(continued)

- Anticipate student off-task behavior and pre-rehearse the next two things you will do when that behavior occurs.

5. *Use a strong voice.* Use these five techniques to establish a teacher's authority in the classroom:
   - *Square up and stand still.* When giving instructions, stop moving and strike a formal pose.
   - *Use economy of language.* Give crisp instructions with as few words as possible.
   - *Do not engage.* Keep repeating your core instruction and ignore student complaints.
   - *Employ quiet power.* Lower your voice and change your tone to communicate urgency.
   - *Do not talk over.* Use a reset (for example, all-school clap) to get students' full attention before continuing to speak.

6. *Develop pacing.* Create the illusion of speed so that students feel continually engaged.
   - Use a timer for each aspect of your lesson and let students see how much time they have left during each activity.
   - Use brief 15–30-second turn-and-talks.
   - Cold-call students.
   - Elicit choral responses to certain questions.

Rigor (Intellectual Engagement)

1. *Establish the right objective.* Write precise learning objectives that are
   - Data driven
   - Curriculum plan driven
   - Able to be accomplished in one lesson

2. *Check for understanding.* See whether students have learned the material frequently using a variety of techniques.
   - Actively monitor student work, making note of students who have wrong answers.
   - Poll the room to see how many students answered a certain question correctly.
   - Track right and wrong answers to class questions.
   - Implement an exit ticket (brief final mini-assessment) and collect at end of class to see how many students have mastered the concept.

3. *Increase the think ratio.* Get students to do more of the thinking.
   - Script out what you will ask and do when students do not answer correctly.
   - Script out the questions and activities that will facilitate students getting to the right answer.
   - Push students to use habits of discussion to critique or build off each other's answers.
   - Provide wait time after posing challenging questions.

4. *Encourage effective independent practice.* Make sure student independent practice meets the assessment objective.

- Build into each class at least 10 minutes of independent practice.
- Support struggling students during independent practice (identify the first two or three students you will support) while continuing to scan the room for compliance (position yourself so that you can still scan the entire room).
- Align independent practice to the rigor of the upcoming interim assessment.

Observing the leaders highlighted in this book, one finds an eerily similar practice. Picking the right area of focus only gets you part of the way there. The next challenge is making sure it is bite-sized: teachers can accomplish it in one week. Julie limits herself to one or two pieces of feedback like this in each meeting, noting that "I try to make sure that every change is a '10-second' change: that you can walk into a classroom at the right time and know, in 10 seconds, whether it has been put into place." No single small step will dramatically change a classroom in and of itself. Multiple small changes, though, implemented week after week, add up to extraordinary change. The key insight of leaders like Julie Jackson is that feedback and observation make big shifts by focusing on small changes in quick succession. Let's turn back to Clip 3 to see what shape this may take:

 REWATCH Clip 3: Julie's feedback and observation meeting with Carly. This time, focus on the specific action steps Julie gives Carly.

To illustrate, page 76 shows the actual bite-sized action steps Julie used week after week with a new teacher who was struggling to increase student engagement and on-task behavior. While such feedback may seem simple or low level, it is precisely these sorts of changes that allow real change to be possible.

Can you imagine how quickly this teacher can develop with this sort of feedback? Incredibly, despite a challenging start, she went on to have all of her students perform in the 99th percentile on the TerraNova. Without this sort of feedback, classroom engagement would have interfered with learning.

> ### Core Idea
>
> Action steps need to be bite-sized: changes teachers can make in one week. Effective feedback makes big shifts in teacher practice by focusing on small changes in quick succession.

One Teacher's Action Steps

A Sample of Julie Jackson's Feedback

Week 1
- Reduce teacher talk in the introduction by using cold calling and turn-and-talk.
- Get closer to the students in order to keep them on task.

Week 2
- When you are engaging with one student, deliberately scan the room to make sure all other students are on task.

Week 3
- During the turn-and-talk, listen in briefly on two or three pairs of students so you can select a pair who had a good discussion and an answer that you want to be heard by the whole group.

Week 4
- Do not engage. Just give the consequence with your "teacher look" and refrain from getting into the details of why (because it interrupts the flow of your lesson). You can go into the why once the rest of the group is working.

Week 5
- When you or a student is talking, reinforce other students listening by signaling nonverbally for students to put their hands down.

Week 6
- Vary the students you are calling on during homework review.
- Pose a critical thinking turn-and-talk and then quickly check in with any students who are confused.

Week 7
- Check for understanding prior to students doing the "You-Do" portion of the lesson by calling on a student to explain the task.
- Set a timer during independent practice so you have time to close the lesson and check for mastery of the objectives of the lesson.

Week 8
- After giving directions, allow a quick pause to wait for compliance. Avoid using more language.
- When doing it again, use nonverbals.

Your Turn

Converting Poor Action Steps into Effective Ones

Instructions: As you read each problem, read the poor action step while covering the better action step with your hand or a piece of paper. Try to generate your own bite-sized action step and then compare to the one given here.

1. *Scenario 1 problem:* Students are talking while the teacher is talking.
   - *Poor action step:* Reduce student talking when you're speaking.
   - *Better action step:* Don't talk over the students. Stop and make eye contact with the student who is talking. Throughout the lesson walk with purpose toward students who may have a hard time staying on task.
2. *Scenario 2 problem:* Students never get enough time to practice the skill independently.
   - *Poor action step:* Be careful about your pacing so as not to sacrifice independent practice.
   - *Better action step:* Set a timer to go off with 20 minutes left in the lesson to remind you when you need to begin independent practice.
3. *Scenario 3 problem:* You have a student in your guided reading group who always jumps in, eager to respond to every question and dominate the conversation.
   - *Poor action step:* Don't let students jump into the conversation.
   - *Better action step:* Give think time and use cold calls to call on students who haven't yet raised their hands. For the eager student, have her write her response on a whiteboard.
4. *Scenario 4 problem:* Students are rowdy as they come into class.
   - *Poor action step:* Keep students calm when entering the classroom.
   - *Better action step:* Have students reenter the room and set the mood for learning and reinforce good behaviors.

Note: Not all of these should be used simultaneously. As noted, only one or two major changes should be pursued at a given time.

Ultimately, finding the right action step takes time. Here we include a practice exercise to consider what the strongest action step should be. Use this exercise as a guide to determine your readiness and sharpen your skills as you move toward finding and articulating key action steps in your own school.

Naming the key action step is a critical step to improving teacher practice. When action steps are fuzzy, teachers must figure them out on their own. That doesn't allow you to be 100 percent successful with 100 percent of your teachers.

Core Idea

Effective action steps are

- *Measurable, observable.* You can see whether this has been accomplished when observing and reviewing lesson plans.
- *Bite-sized.* Teacher can accomplish in the next week.
- *Data and goal driven.* They are connected to larger professional development (PD) goal and/or DDI goals for the teacher.

EFFECTIVE FEEDBACK

Naming the key action step is critical to improving teacher practice. However, for Julie's insight to be effective, it must be delivered effectively. To do so, first she avoids some common myths of feedback. You'll find these myths, or "errors," outlined in "The Five Errors to Avoid."

Six Steps to Effective Feedback

Julie successfully avoided all of those errors by following six key steps. Together, these six steps form the backbone of an effective school leader's feedback process. Of course, seeing is believing. In going through the feedback steps, this book breaks down each one with video clips and accompanying descriptions.

Six Steps to Effective Feedback

1. *Provide precise praise.* Start off the meeting with one or two pieces of precise praise from your observation.
2. *Probe.* Ask a targeted open-ended question about the core issue.
3. *Identify problem* and *concrete action step.* Identify the problem and state a clear, measurable, observable action step that will address this issue.
4. *Practice.* Role-play or simulate how the teacher could have improved the class.
5. *Plan ahead.* Design or revise upcoming lesson plan to implement this action.
6. *Set timeline.* Determine time by which the action will be accomplished.

The Five Errors to Avoid

Error 1: More is better.

Top-tier Truth: Less is more. Many leaders fall prey to the temptation to deliver feedback on every aspect of the lesson. While that is a useful tool to demonstrate your instructional expertise, it won't change practice nearly as effectively. As we can learn from coaches in every field, bite-sized feedback on just one or two areas delivers the most effective improvement.[11]

Error 2: Lengthy written evaluations drive change as effectively as any other form of feedback.

Top-tier Truth: Face-to-face makes the difference. The reason why this error persists nationwide among school leaders is that there is a subset of teachers for whom lengthy written evaluations are effective (just like there is a small group of learners for whom lengthy lectures are most effective). This leads to the dangerous conclusion that all teachers develop well by reading lengthy evaluations. In what other field do we subscribe to this idea?

Error 3: Just tell them; they'll get it.

Top-tier Truth: If they don't do the thinking, they won't internalize what they learn. In classroom instruction, highly effective teachers push the students to do the thinking. If teachers eclipse this thinking by providing conclusions or answers too quickly, students will disengage. Feedback is not any different: if teachers don't participate in the process of thinking about their teaching, they are less likely to internalize the feedback. This is metacognition applied to teacher development: having teachers think about their teaching improves their performance.

Error 4: State the concrete action step. Then the teacher will act.

Top-tier Truth: Guided practice makes perfect. If a surgeon simply tells a resident how to perform an operation, the resident will be less effective than if she practices with the surgeon's guidance. Teaching is the same: practicing implementation of the feedback *with the leader* is at the heart of speeding up the improvement cycle. It also allows teachers to make mistakes before they're in front of the students again.

Error 5: Teachers can implement feedback at any time.

Top-tier Truth: Nail down the timing. Having a concrete timeline in which feedback will be implemented serves two purposes: it makes sure everyone has clear expectations as to when this will be accomplished, and it will expose action steps that are not really able to be accomplished in a week.

Step 1: Precise Praise

In the opening video clip, Julie Jackson began her meeting by complimenting Carly on her energy level and enthusiasm. This was not accidental. This was the precise area of feedback from the last meeting, and Julie intentionally observed for this in the previous classroom visit. By linking praise to the previous core action step, Julie triples its impact. Not only is the praise genuine and affirming, but it also gives the teacher the fundamental satisfaction that comes from achieving in a goal that she has worked hard on. Even more, it lets the teacher know that Julie is observing her to see if she implements feedback—it is built-in accountability in the form of praise! Of course, when teachers are not making progress in these core areas, leaders may focus their praise elsewhere. Yet the best praise focuses on the key areas of progress teachers have identified.

> ## Core Idea
>
> The most effective praise is directly linked to the teacher's previous action step: you validate the teacher's effort at implementing feedback.

Julie Jackson's fellow principal Serena Savarirayan gives another example of effective praise in Clip 4.

 WATCH Clip 4: Specific praise helps principal Serena Savarirayan set the tone for her observation meeting with Eric Diamon.

Step 2: Probe

As Beth and Steve's example in Chapter 1 showed, people are much more likely to embrace conclusions they've reached than directives they've received. Recognizing this, Julie leads her feedback discussion with a targeted open-ended question, guiding Carly to come to the solution on her own. While there is no one way to craft a generalized set of probing questions—each question will depend on the action step you are focusing on—Julie follows a few core guidelines in the questions she asks:

- *Narrow the focus.* The first step is to focus in on one aspect of the lesson. Avoid general questions like "How did your lesson go today?" and prioritize the area where you will generate the action step: questions, transitions, pacing, and so on.

- *Begin with the purpose.* Ask teachers to articulate the essential reason why they are employing a given practice that is your area of focus. For example:
  - "Why do we use student prompting?"
  - "What is the purpose of independent practice?"

> ## Core Idea
> When giving feedback, start with a probing question that narrows the focus of the teacher to a particular part of the lesson.

Step 3: Identify the Problem and the Concrete Action Step

Once the probing question has been asked, the goal is to get the teacher to articulate the problem and concrete action step on her own. What makes Julie Jackson's leadership so skillful here—and it mirrors the techniques of Beth Verrilli in data analysis meetings from Chapter 1—is her ability to guide any sort of teacher toward the action step. The teacher's ability to be reflective and metacognitive will determine what level of scaffolding she needs to provide. Here are the four levels of support that Julie provides based on the responsiveness of the teacher:

Level 1: 100 percent teacher driven. Teacher identifies the problem.

Level 2: 50 percent teacher driven. Teacher can identify the problem when leader prompts with appropriate scaffolded questions.

Level 3: Leader guided. Leader needs to present the classroom data for the teacher to be able to understand the problem.

Level 4: Leader driven (when all else fails). When teacher has been unable to identify the problem despite the attempts outlined, the leader identifies the problem for the teacher.

Let's look at how each of these levels plays out with real teachers.

Level 1: Teacher Identifies the Problem

Some teachers are capable of identifying the core issues in their lessons. In that case, Julie's role is simply to guide them to articulating a specific action step. For example, in Clip 5, she can be seen working with Rachel Kashner around a science lesson on understanding the parts of the backbone. Rachel immediately identifies that the weak spot in her lesson was a lack of an assessment of all students' learning. "I didn't have an assessment to check the understanding of all the students." With that opening, Julie simply asks Rachel questions about why this was an issue and how she could address it in the future. At the last prompt, Rachel notes, "Next time, I will add a written component before the class discussion so I can monitor how all students understood the concept." See what it looked like in Clip 5.

WATCH Clip 5: Julie Jackson supports experienced teacher Rachel Kashner in finding areas for growth and solutions for improvement.

Even in the case of such a reflective teacher, Julie's role is still actively present in asking questions that narrow the focus on a specific action step and ensure that a teacher understands the rationale for that action step. Julie simply asks the right questions, and the teacher can do the rest of the thinking on her own.

Level 2: Leader Asks Scaffolded Questions

When a teacher cannot identify the problem from the first probing question, Julie Jackson asks additional scaffolded questions that help the teacher get there. These prompts usually involve recalling what happened in class. Examples include:

- "What did you say when you went to prompt Simon?"

- "How much time did you leave for independent practice?"

- "Do you remember what happened with Jessica during opening procedures today?"

What makes these questions so effective is that if the teacher is able to remember what happened during the lesson at this point, he or she often realizes the issue on the spot. These questions allow a teacher to see his instruction with fresh eyes, guiding his focus to something he didn't realize was so important in the midst of teaching. For many teachers, this process feels like switching the lights on to their instruction.

In other cases, the teacher needs more than just questions. Let's revisit the opening vignette of this chapter. In this case, Julie followed up her opening question with a piece of evidence from the classroom observation: "What happened with Simon when you called on him to answer a question about mammals?" After Carly answers the question, Julie asks her, "What does that do to the level of questioning?" Then Carly is able to figure out what happened.

Watch as Serena Savarirayan and Aja Settles use this same technique.

 WATCH Clip 6: Serena Savarirayan guides Eric Diamon toward strategies that deepen class discussions.
WATCH Clip 7: Evidence-based prompts help Aja Settles correct Kristi Costanzo's misunderstanding and find the right next step for her classroom.

Core Idea

Guiding a teacher to remember a specific moment in his or her lesson when the highest-leverage problem occurred is like turning on the lights: the teacher can analyze his or her instruction with new eyes.

Level 3: Leader Presents Classroom Data

Sometimes scaffolded questions targeting a moment in the lesson are not enough. A teacher might not be able to recall what happened or have a blind spot. For these reasons, it is vital for the leader to be prepared with specific, fact-based observations about what happened at what time. Consider the following exchange:

- *Ask scaffolded question.* "Do you know how long it took students to enter the classroom?"

  [Teacher does not have an accurate answer.]

- *Present the data.* "I timed students, and it took them four minutes from the time they entered the room to the point where every student was working."

  [Teacher is surprised by the answer.]

- *Ask why this is important.* "What does that do to the student learning?"

  [Teacher notes the lost time for learning; leader can add detail if teacher answer is insufficient.]

- *State the action step.* "This is what we're going to focus on today: reducing classroom entry to two minutes to save instructional time and also start in a more productive fashion."

By following this sort of exchange, leaders help teachers to realize the discrepancy between their self-awareness and the reality of the lesson, thus increasing their metacognition and building their capacity to self-correct. By doing so, the leader helps the path toward finding a solution for any problem become clearer.

Another effective tool for getting teachers to identify the problem is to watch a video of best practices from a master teacher and compare it to their own teaching. Watch as Aja Settles uses this approach.

 WATCH Clip 8: Aja Settles uses video footage of a master instructor to help Kristi Costanzo hone her teaching practice.

Of course, if feasible, leaders can also have teachers record their own practice and use the video as a jumping off point. As Mike Mann, principal of North Star High School, has noted, "Teachers, especially early career teachers, can get so caught up in delivering their lessons that they miss the big picture. Videotaping their classes is a great way to bring in perspective and guide teachers toward improvement." Watch Clip 9 to see how Juliana Worrell, school leader at North Star's Fairmount Elementary School, uses this footage to help a teacher reach the right action steps.

 WATCH Clip 9: Juliana Worrell and Clare Perry use videos of Clare's classroom to find action steps for improvement.

Level 4: Leader States the Problem Directly

In a few cases, despite all the scaffolding and presentation of the classroom observation data, a teacher still won't be willing or able to recognize the challenge. In these rare moments, the principal simply needs to state the problem and the clear, precise action step. This strategy should only be used if a teacher fails at the other levels or has consistently struggled to improve his or her practice.

In general, leaders err too much in reverting to this level simply because of its convenience. Remember: Even if you are observing weekly, you are still only observing 1 percent of instruction. As such, it is critical for teachers to develop the craft of self-analysis and self-correction.

Summary of the Four Levels

What Julie is doing here is following a strategy: she provides only the scaffolding that the teacher needs to get to the answer. The order of strategies is as follows:

1. Probe.

2. Ask additional scaffolded questions.

3. Present evidence (classroom data).

4. (When all else fails) Tell.

Why is this model so effective? By leading this way, Julie pushes the onus of the thinking onto the teacher. This practice develops reflective teachers who are capable of critiquing themselves when they're not being observed. As Julie notes, "As teachers get in the habit of looking for the root cause, my job gets much easier." Little by little, a novice teacher starts to identify more of his or her own errors and make on-the-fly adjustments. What Julie has done is turn on the light bulb for more effective self-analysis of one's teaching.

Step 4: Practice

John Wooden famously said, "The importance of repetition until automaticity cannot be overstated. Repetition is the key to learning."[12] Too many interactions between leaders and teachers end in a description of what will happen but no actual practice. That puts the burden of implementation on the teacher alone. But for Julie Jackson, in-the-moment practice represents an essential commitment to good coaching. "Basketball coaches don't lead by conversations; they have players practice their dribbling," Julie explains. "It's in the repeated and careful practice that teachers learn the skills they need and really get it down." That sounds very much like Mr. Wooden!

This reflects a crucial insight: for feedback to truly be effective, leaders must allow teachers to practice "on the spot," whether through role plays or by scripting changes into their lessons (depending on the action step). Great teaching is not learned through discussion; it's learned by doing.

Core Idea

Great teaching is not learned through discussion. It's learned by doing—or, more specifically, by practicing doing things well. Supervised practice, then, is the fastest way to make sure all teachers are doing the right things.

While it flies in the face of conventional school customs, in-the-moment practice separates the top-tier leaders from the rest. Consider what happens in Julie's meeting with Carly when Julie begins with the question, "If we want to think about next steps, what might you do in order to make sure that your prompts split complex questions into smaller parts to guide students?" At that point, Julie has Carly practice asking the questions to her as if she were a student. Juliana Worrell takes the same approach in her work with Julia, as shown in Clip 10.

 WATCH Clip 10 to see Juliana Worrell coach Julia Thompson in the immediate role-play practice of her decoding lesson. Role playing allows Juliana and Julia to practice teaching techniques.

Practice is not just for novice teachers; it can also allow you to be a thought partner with your strongest teachers as together you plan out implementation. Watch Serena Savarirayan take the role of the teacher as she works with Eric to develop effective questions for the classroom conversation in Clip 11.

WATCH Clip 11: Serena Savarirayan and Eric Diamon practice questioning approaches.

The speed of teacher development rises dramatically. This high rate of development is one of the distinguishing characteristics of top-tier leaders, and these clips show you why.

Step 5: Plan Ahead

Now that Julie and her teachers have identified an action step and practiced it, they can write it into future lesson plans to lock it in place. In some cases, the nature of an action step will make designing lesson plan components or activities unnecessary. If, for example, the action step is related to addressing student noncompliance when it arises, it won't fit neatly into a lesson plan. Even then, though, the precise words a teacher will use can be written down, possibly on a note card he or she will attach to a clipboard. You can see how Juliana Worrell leads her teacher through that very exercise in Clip 12.

 WATCH Clip 12: Juliana Worrell and Sarah Sexton plan think-alouds for an upcoming lesson; when Sarah struggles, Juliana supports her through active modeling.

In the next chapter (Planning), we go into more depth on how leaders shape effective lesson plans to prevent problems from happening.

> ## Core Idea
>
> Practicing and planning ahead go hand in hand: practice the skill and then adjust upcoming lessons.

Step 6: Set a Timeline

Julie leaves nothing to chance: in every feedback session, she has a concrete timeline for implementation. Because action steps are already designed to be accomplished in a week, Julie finds it easy to monitor these timelines. She still records each implementation component when needed: when a teacher will turn in lesson plans, when she will change the classroom setup, and other phenomena.

Writing a timeline might seem like an obvious step, but I cannot emphasize enough how many leaders I observe who skip it. They assume that teachers will implement action steps without a timeline to use as a guide. This will be true for the large majority of your teachers, but if you're striving for excellence for 100 percent of your teachers—and that is the only way to get exceptional results—you need to set a timeline. Timelines are basic, but they help all of us stay on target to what we're trying to accomplish! See how Julie ends her meeting with Rachel Kashner with a timeline in Clip 13.

WATCH Clip 13: A set timeline keeps Julie Jackson and Rachel Kashner on the same page.

Shradha M. Patel sets an even more basic timeline that is just as effective in Clip 14.

WATCH Clip 14: Shradha M. Patel closes her feedback meeting with Jamil Sylvester by establishing a timeline for action.

For the vast majority of teachers, the observation-feedback system outlined in this chapter will have a tremendous impact. By putting action steps into place, teachers will witness phenomenal improvement in their own practice and, most important, in student learning. Moreover, greater accountability will also reveal the exceptions to this rule: the teachers who are struggling to improve and who are not putting actions into practice effectively. What happens when you discover teachers like these?

WHEN FEEDBACK ISN'T WORKING: STRATEGIES FOR STRUGGLING TEACHERS

Julie Jackson knows this well. Although most teachers at her school improve tremendously in their first months, there are occasionally teachers who struggle. Three years ago, Erin Renz began teaching at Julie's school. Erin was hard working, determined, and enthusiastic, but she was struggling tremendously and student learning was suffering. As she wrote in her reflection from that time period:

> I felt like there were hundreds of things I needed to change, and I pulled randomly from the bank of examples I had been sponging up and tried to balance this unsuccessfully with a growing task list.

Erin seemed to be on the road to failure. Even Julie noted, "By the end of October, I didn't know if she would make it through to the end of the year."

Yet despite this concern, Julie—and her team—rallied to help Erin. Let's look at Erin's own reflection on that process:

> I was convinced I lacked some sort of fundamental connector allowing me to effectively implement something I saw modeled. It was then that Julie said, "You are already working hard. We need to teach you to work smart." This became my new mantra. I found that the key was not in implementing what I saw—it was in understanding what was important, or most important about what I saw. Julie would point out the important things to notice—the really strong elements of taxonomy, or the nuances of classroom management I was missing. Afterward, in our frequent meetings, we would compare notes. I wasn't just learning how to teach, I was developing an eye for good teaching. We set up a system of identifying the goals I was to implement that day, the next day, and the next week.

Over the course of eight months, Erin slowly began to see her teaching transformed. She made bite-sized change after bite-sized change: speaking more economically when giving directions, rearranging desks to more easily transition to and from group work, creating clearer posters to reinforce instruction, providing more time for students to think about questions, and a host of others. With each change, she got a bit better. The results, by year's end, were dramatic: Erin's students matched the performance of her colleagues in scoring well above the 90th percentile. She had made it through the year, and her students had learned. Her final reflection of the year:

> From where I stand now, it is almost impossible to believe that only eight months ago I felt completely unsuccessful. I am writing this as I sit at my desk during curriculum planning week, working with the team to develop curriculum. I feel like I am making a meaningful contribution. This year will still be an uphill race, but I feel strong and confident and ready.

Erin's story is inspirational, and it continues to bear fruit. Erin currently is a manager of teacher leadership development for Teach For America, sharing her experience and coaching a cohort of teachers to follow in her footsteps.

Erin's success—and that of many teachers like her—is a product of far more than Julie's unwavering commitment to her staff. Desire and dedication alone do not make a leader effective. This level of success with a struggling teacher also reflects a number of crucial systems and approaches that can be put in place for any teacher who needs them.

> ## Core Idea
>
> Desire alone will not help you improve a struggling teacher. You need effective systems and approaches that can be put into place immediately for teachers who need them.

Early Warnings: Yellow Flag Strategies

If several feedback cycles have elapsed and teachers have failed to improve, leaders should consider the following strategies. We've labeled these techniques "yellow flag" strategies. A yellow flag at a beach is raised when danger is mounting. Similarly, the strategies listed here should be employed when teachers are continuing to struggle, and the standard observation and feedback cycle needs additional structure.

- *Provide simpler instructions and techniques.* Sometimes, the bite-sized action steps need to get even smaller. One of my personal favorites from watching Julie Jackson in action was with a teacher who lacked enthusiasm. What became apparent was that the teacher was not a morning person and generally got better later in the day. So Julie's feedback addressed that directly: "Drink some coffee before work, stand up straight, and talk louder!"

- *Give face-to-face feedback more often.* If the usual observation and feedback cycle is not making change, leaders can extend it through more informal face-to-face contact.

- *Plan immediate post-feedback observation.* Rather than waiting a week to see if feedback is being implemented correctly, drop by the struggling teacher's classroom the next day. Shortening the feedback-observation loop ensures that if action steps are not working out, leaders know this as soon as possible.

- *Arrange for peer observation.* Strong leaders recognize that struggling teachers often benefit from sitting in on a star teacher's class. A word of caution: Jon Saphier, author of *The Skillful Teacher*, notes the perils of this action, because the observer can look at the wrong things.[13] To mitigate this, leaders like Julie Jackson observe alongside the struggling teacher, pointing out key moments.

- *Choose interruptions with care.* Occasionally, if teachers are continuing to struggle, strong leaders interrupt their class to model the technique. For example, a principal might interrupt an elementary school teacher during "guided reading" to demonstrate how students should be questioned. This technique sounds far more disruptive than it is in practice. For example, an instructional leader observing a class might say, "Mrs. Smith, an idea occurred to me. Could I ask the class a question?" Students are unlikely to see this as a break in instruction, and the teacher has an opportunity to observe new techniques put to use in her own classroom. Note, however, that leaders should only try this if they have instructional expertise in that classroom area. Otherwise, they risk putting the students further behind than they were before. As important, teachers may feel that their trust has been violated or feel disrespected, and feelings like these may damage relationships. Pick only the interruptions that will produce the biggest gains in learning. If the expected gains from the interruption aren't large, find another way to model the techniques you'd like to try.

Continued Struggles: Red Flag Strategies

If the strategies outlined fail to produce reasonable results, then more intense interventions may be needed. These strategies can be thought of as "red flag" strategies, just as the red flag on a beach signals serious danger. These solutions should be used only when other means have failed and when more drastic options, such as termination or radically reducing the teacher's course load, are being considered.

- *Model entire lessons.* For a struggling teacher, it can be extraordinarily helpful to see an entire lesson taught by a master teacher and then repeat it himself later that same day. Before the lesson, the model teacher should talk to the struggling teacher and explain exactly what he or she plans to do and what to look for during the class. Of course, this sort of change is time intensive, and as a result, it should only be used when warranted.

- *Take over.* Takeover is the most extreme form of intervention, but in rare instances it's the best strategy available to you. During a takeover, a master teacher takes over a struggling teacher's class twice a week for six weeks. The struggling teacher observes these classes and works closely with instructional leaders to improve his or her teaching.

Of course, takeover takes a tremendous amount of dedication and resources, and in many cases, you will not have that flexibility. The fundamental reality of Erin's situation—and the situation of teachers like her—is that it takes a tremendous investment of time to bring them back on track.

ACCOUNTABILITY: TOOLS FOR KEEPING TRACK OF IT ALL

The final piece of the puzzle is accountability: ensuring that feedback becomes practice. The number one challenge is keeping track of it all! Julie and the other leaders highlighted in this book have found a simple, novel solution: an observation tracker. This is a simple tool with which they can record their weekly observations. In the Excel version of the tracker, each tab represents a different teacher. (I'm certain that a specific software application for teachers will not be far behind!) Let's take a look at the tracker for a middle school principal and her observations of a math teacher.

The Observation Tracker

Up to this point, we've considered how Julie makes each individual observation as effective and meaningful as possible. Yet while each of her observations is influential, Julie's impact on instruction is far greater than the sum of her visits. Even the most astute classroom observer faces significant limitations on the information he or she has about teacher development. What are these?

- *Patterns across time: What has the teacher been working on for months? What goals have been met already?* Without this information, leaders may have no way to evaluate how teachers have developed over time, to assess where they are now against where they once were.

- *Patterns across teachers: What challenges are problems for the whole school? Which are limited to just the new teachers? Just the math department?* Leaders may have no way to systematically track trends in teaching practice across their school or to quickly recognize areas for improvement that cross different classrooms.

- *Patterns of visits: Who are the teachers you are avoiding observing? Whom do you always see?* Leaders often do not know which teachers have been visited and how often these visits have happened.

- *Patterns of effectiveness: What feedback is solving the problem? What's falling flat?* Most important, leaders often have no way to quickly check whether the feedback they give is effective in changing practice.

Gathering this information can be game changing; if leaders had a way to quickly and intuitively record it, they would be able to drive instructional feedback well beyond any one visit. Through her observation tracker Julie Jackson has found a way. The observation tracker is a tool for keeping track of:

- How often you observe
- Patterns of your feedback
- Teachers you're avoiding
- Precision of your feedback

The tracker is a spreadsheet document containing two sets of information: a tracker for each individual teacher, and a schoolwide tracker for all teachers in the building. Table 2.2 presents a sample observation tracker.

Table 2.2 A Sample Observation Tracker: Individual Tab

Date	Time/Class	Key Lever (small, measurable, targeted)	Evidence of Change from Previous Observation	Summary of Observation (OR Cut and Paste "Things I'm Impressed by" and "Things I've Noticed")
9/7	RM	1. When choral response isn't 100% call the name of the student who made the error to give him a second chance. 2. Use a timer during oral review to keep up the pace.		1. Great teacher energy. 2. Good use of narrating the positive.
9/10	RM	1. Do not allow students to opt out. Use the call-ahead strategy so students are ready to answer. 2. Give all directions for the take-home prior to students doing the take home.	Much better choral response.	1. Great teacher energy. 2. You immediately hooked the students at the start of the lesson.
9/14	RM	1. Lower your voice when you are working one on one with a student. 2. No opt out: First, repeat the question. Then, if the student cannot get it, give a prompt.	Pacing has improved during opening procedures.	1. All directions were explained prior to the start of the activity and you checked for comprehension. 2. All materials were prepped and ready to go.

Date	Code		
9/24	RM	1. Put your clipboard on your lap (or in an area) so when you have to give a check it does not interrupt the flow of your lesson. 2. Give a clear and crisp nonverbal prompt when you want the entire group to answer. 3. When you are saying the sounds, exaggerate your mouth so students are doing the same.	1. Your teacher Student Chart is a great way for students to see who is "winning." 2. Pacing is quick and engaging. 3. You held students accountable throughout by using the point system—well done.
10/12	SS/SC	1. During the do-now, circulate with purpose. Walk by the students who need proximity or whom you need to check in with for understanding of the task. 2. Give think time after you ask a critical thinking question. 3. Feign ignorance when an incorrect response is given so you do not tip the student to what you are thinking.	
11/1	RM-M	1. Lower your voice when you are working one on one with a student so you do not distract rest of your group who is working independently. 2. Have students read three or four sentences before you ask a comprehension question. They read one sentence and then you asked a comprehension question. This assesses their ability to retell, not to comprehend the story.	1. During instruction you consistently narrated expectations. 2. Pacing is engaging. 3. You are carefully listening in to make sure students are saying the sounds correctly. 4. During the independent practice portion of the lesson you circulate with purpose.

As you can see, the individual tracker provides the basic details of each observation: when, what action step, whether that action step was implemented, and a space for general notes. Julie and the rest of the leaders in this book carry their laptops to every observation and record the action step on the spot. That way there is no additional work to maintain the tracker. Then she simply pulls it up during the feedback meeting to remind herself of what she observed.

By contrast, the schoolwide summary sheet of the observation tracker gives you the quick facts about each teacher: how many times you've observed, the date of your last observation, and the PD goals and latest action steps for every teacher. Table 2.3 presents a sample from Julie's schoolwide tracker.

In one brief glance, Julie can make a quick review of the professional development goals of staff and the latest action steps, making it easy for her to know what she is looking for on her next set of observations. This summary can drive decisions on what PD she should deliver given patterns that might emerge across her teachers. Just as significantly, the tracker tells the real truth on how often Julie is observing, and it is easy for anyone to see that, including her supervisor. (We talk more about this in Chapter 9, The Superintendent's Guide.)

Julie Jackson does not personally coach every teacher in the building—there are too many to do weekly. Instead, just as Beth served as instructional leader for Steve in Chapter 1, Julie has chosen several veteran teachers to serve as instructional leaders at North Star. Each of these leaders also owns an observation tracker, even if he or she is a mentor teacher working with only one teacher. This tracker becomes the essential tool for Julie to support leader effectiveness and make sure every leader is working effectively. (See more about the power of this tool for school leadership teams in Chapter 7.)

Core Idea

An observation tracker holds you accountable to your quantity and quality of observations, and it also allows you to supervise others who are doing the same.

Table 2.3 Julie's Observation Tracker

Name	Total Observations	Major PD/Instructional Goals	Latest Key Lever
Lear	13 (Nov 22)	1. Frequently check for understanding of students meeting the objective. 2. When students are confused regain focus by pausing and then restating the expectations in a calm tone.	1. After giving directions give a quick pause to wait for compliance. 2. When doing it again use nonverbals. 3. Avoid choral responses when the response has multiple answers.
Jones	14 (Nov 22)	1. Implement "break it down" when students give an incorrect response. 2. Increase thought ratio without tipping during whole-group and small-group instruction.	1. Select three different ability levels when you are calling on students to retell the story. 2. Avoid summarizing a student's thinking before asking him or her to tell you more. Use clear and concise language to explain the task for independent practice and check for understanding. 3.
Smith	8 (Sep 10)	1. Implement "control the game": keep the length of the reading unpredictable and mark it. 2. Ask high-order questions by using prompts from Bloom's Taxonomy guide.	1. Prior to turn-and-talk, restate the question so they know what they are discussing. 2. During comprehension conversation, ask students to tell you why they think that or how do they know.
Roth	10 (Nov 22)	1. Increase thought ratio without tipping. 2. Use a question prompt from the reading guide to respond to student error.	1. Share the pen. During the review of the do-now have a student do the editing. 2. With your reading class students, use prompt "Is there something that you know about this character that can help you understand them now?"
Phelps	14 (Nov 22)	1. Wait until you get 100% compliance before continuing instruction. 2. Allow one or two students to comment on a given response from another student to increase student thinking.	1. Lower your voice when you are calling on different readers in order to keep the focus on the text and not on your voice. 2. Use the economy of language—just state what you need them to do. For example, "Re-read with expression."

Table 2.3 (Continued)

Name	Total Observations	Major PD/Instructional Goals	Latest Key Lever
Bernard	18 (Nov 23)	1. Use cold call throughout the lesson to check for understanding. 2. Use turn-and-talk during guided practice during writing to increase pacing.	1. Implement the turn-and-talks as they are scripted in the plan: during turn-and-talk listen in carefully so you know what students you are going to call on. 2. Cold-call on students at a faster pace—four students every minute.
Downing	13 (Nov 22)	1. Employ controlled urgency (hushed excitement, circulating purposefully, slow pacing of talking) during the beginning of class. 2. Narrate the positive and use nonverbals for student noncompliance.	1. When you give a redirect, scan and then pause for compliance. 2. Use nonverbal prompts to redirect student behavior without breaking up the flow of the lesson. 3. Employ more frequent individual checks for understanding of the material so you can assess whether students are really mastering the objectives of the lesson.
Donald	10 (Nov 16)	1. Diagnose student misunderstanding in guided reading, and then selecting a strategic prompt to lead to misunderstanding. 2. Have students break down the process of how they are making an inference (text evidence + schema) to strengthen understanding. 3. Use the break-it-down techniques beyond the initial prompt to continually scaffold student understanding.	1. In guided reading, stop the student with a quick nonverbal and use one of your prompts from the K–4 reading taxonomy.
Total Observations	100		
Average per Teacher	12.5		

A Teacher's Testimonial on Observation and Feedback

Sarah Sexton

I began teaching at North Star after spending one year working in another public school. On my first day of orientation, I remember thinking that this transition was going to be a piece of cake. Between my education classes in college and my year of teaching experience, I told myself, I was ready for anything!

I have never been more wrong in my entire life. Before my new students had even entered my classroom, I had become overwhelmed and anxious about the weeks to come. My year of "teaching experience" began to look more like an overzealous babysitting session as I learned what it would take to be a master teacher. Feeling as if I were starting my first year of teaching, I doubted my ability to keep twenty-five scholars actively engaged for 50 minutes—or, even more important, to bring joy into my classroom. Much to my dismay, a number of these doubts became realities when the school year kicked off.

At this point, I don't know what I believed would make me a better teacher, but I definitely didn't foresee it being North Star's observation and feedback system. It wasn't that I didn't appreciate the support of my instructional leader, Juliana Worrell, and my school leader, Julie Jackson. The consistency with which they came to my classroom to observe my teaching and provide feedback was a powerful testament to their commitment and care. It was just that it didn't seem to be helping me. I would try to think constructively about my feedback, telling myself, "Okay, these are my strengths, these are my areas of growth, and these are my quick hits." But remaining positive grew increasingly challenging as I struggled to be successful. Suddenly, goals that I had expected to achieve easily felt unobtainable and frustrating.

A turning point came during one of my check-ins with Juliana. I told her my teaching performance was still falling short of the level it needed to reach if I was to guide my scholars to success. She, in turn, suggested that I begin videotaping myself as often as I possibly could. That way, I would see what she and Julie saw when I delivered my lessons.

Without the footage I collected after that conversation with Juliana, I would never have gathered the insights I can now share about my old teaching habits. It turned out that I rarely showed outward excitement for the material I was teaching—my body language and posture made me appear disengaged from my students and the lesson. I looked like the kind of teacher that I had always wanted *not* to be. With renewed dedication, I dove into the task of improving. I listened to feedback, watched videos, and tried to fix my mistakes. Whenever I made gains in one area of growth, I would start working on another, still trying to figure out exactly where my failures were coming from.

My breakthrough finally came on the day that Julie intervened in one of my vocabulary lessons. She took over the lesson just long enough to model how to get students to figure out the meaning of an unknown word. I then took her cue and followed

(continued)

her example for the remaining unknown words in the lesson. And something clicked. If I observed a successful teacher in action and then immediately implemented that teacher's technique in my own lesson, I became a successful teacher, too. From that point on, whenever Julie or Juliana observed my lessons, they would jump in to help guide me. They always knew just when to intervene, and I quickly learned the right time to take my class back and effectively execute the remainder of the lesson.

What made me a better teacher wasn't just observation and feedback: it was instantaneous feedback, modeled directly in front of me. Not every teacher—or even every first-year teacher—needs that level of guidance. But following a regular observation and feedback schedule is what enables Juliana and Julie to identify the teachers who do. It tells them what each of their teachers does well and what each of their teachers need. And when they fulfill their teachers' needs, they fulfill their students' needs, too.

Without Juliana's and Julie's diligent attention to my work, I would not be the teacher I am today. Remembering the lessons from my first year at North Star, I still observe other skilled teachers as often as I can. Meanwhile, I also continue to receive continual observation and feedback from my leaders. I no longer worry that their support is merely a gesture of care, because I know for certain that it strengthens me as a teacher.

TURNAROUND: WHAT TO DO FIRST

A legitimate question to ask is how to implement a new observation and feedback cycle like this one with teachers who have never experienced anything like this before. Won't they resist such a change? I look no further than Kim Marshall, who was a pioneer for shorter observations as principal of the Mather School, an elementary school in Dorchester, Massachusetts. Many years later, he recounted his personal experience about how he started to move to briefer observations in his book *Rethinking Supervision and Evaluation*. Marshall notes:

> At first, teachers had their doubts about the mini-observation idea. I had introduced it at the beginning of the year, but teachers were still uncertain about what to expect. Several were visibly relieved when I gave them positive feedback after their first mini-observation. One primary teacher practically hugged me when I said how impressed I was with her children's Thanksgiving turkey masks. But others were thrown off stride when I came into their rooms, and I had to signal them to continue what they were doing. I hoped that as my visits became more routine, these teachers would relax and be able to ignore my presence. And that's what happened in almost all cases.[14]

A Word On . . . The Power of Frequent Feedback

Steve's Story

The transition toward an environment where observation occurs continually may seem scary. Steve Decina agrees. "When I started at North Star in 1999, observation meant a twice-a-year meeting and some vague directions: Teach more on the Civil War or get more engagement." When North Star first adopted a system of weekly observation, teachers like Steve were skeptical. Today, his opinion has changed significantly. "Observation and feedback have driven my practice in ways I'd never imagined," Steve explains. "I feel like without that regular coaching, it would have been impossible for me to develop as quickly as I did." Steve's story didn't just help him; it's helped his students. When Steve started at North Star, his students achieved an average of 80 percent on the New Jersey Assessment of Skills and Knowledge test. Today, they achieve higher than 95 percent every year, a notable improvement that Steve attributes to the school's culture of data-driven instruction and regular observation-based feedback.

Based on his experience and that of other leaders, there are two key points to highlight with your staff when launching this model:

- Make it clear that the purpose is coaching and improvement, not evaluation.
- Frame progress positively.

The greatest source of buy-in? The answer is as simple as it was for data-driven instruction: results, results, results. When teachers see their practice gradually improving and that they are getting consistent feedback, it really pushes them forward and gets them much more excited. Of course, a small handful of teachers may still remain recalcitrant. At this point, however, the challenge shifts from apathy to intentional defiance, a question we take up in Chapter 6 on staff culture.

When launched effectively, the real turnaround will not be teacher resistance, but your own resistance: resistance to stepping foot in people's classrooms far more often, getting out of your office, and so on. That's the heart of turnaround, and that is something you can control.

Core Idea

The real turnaround challenge will not be teacher resistance, but your own. Lock in your schedule for observation and feedback meetings, and you will make the turnaround a success.

CONCLUSION: COACHING TEACHERS TOWARD GREATNESS

The more time people spend in education, the more cynical about the observation and feedback process they seem to become. This doesn't have to be the case. Our exposure to the traditional model of observation and feedback can blind us to the possibility of doing the job well, but we must cast our cynicism aside. Leaders like Julie Jackson highlight the axiom that great teachers aren't born—they're made. And there is no better way to drive student learning than to develop the talents of the teachers who spend hours educating them every day.

Keys to Observation and Feedback

1. *Scheduled observations.* Lock in frequent and regular observations once a week.
2. *Key action step.* Identify the two or three most important areas for growth.
3. *Effective feedback.* Give direct face-to-face feedback and offer specific action steps for improvement.
4. *Direct accountability.* Create systems to ensure feedback translates to practice.

Six Steps to Effective Feedback: Leading Post-Observation Face-to-Face Meetings

Leader should bring:	Teacher should bring:
Observation Tracker One-Pager: Six Steps for Effective Feedback Preplanned script (questions, observation evidence, and so on)	Laptop and school calendar Curriculum plan, lesson plans, materials, data or student work

<table>
<tr><td rowspan="2">1
Praise</td><td colspan="2">Praise: Narrate the positive</td></tr>
<tr><td colspan="2">What to say:

"We set a goal last week of _____ and I noticed this week how you [met goal] by [state concrete positive actions teacher took]."

"What made you successful? How did it feel?"</td></tr>
<tr><td rowspan="2">2
Probe</td><td colspan="2">Probe: Start with a targeted question</td></tr>
<tr><td colspan="2">What to say:

"What is the purpose of _____ [certain area of instruction]?"

"What was your objective or goal for _____ [the activity, the lesson]?"</td></tr>
<tr><td rowspan="2">3
Identify
Problem
and
Action
Step</td><td colspan="2">Identify Problem and Action Step: Bite-sized action step (do in a week) and highest lever; add scaffolding as needed</td></tr>
<tr><td colspan="2">What to say

Level 1 (Teacher-driven): Teacher identifies the problem:

"Yes. What, then, would be the best action step to address that problem?"

Level 2 (More support): Ask scaffolded questions:

"How did your lesson try to meet this goal/objective?"

Level 3 (More leader guidance): Present classroom data:

"Do you remember what happened in class when _____?" [Teacher then identifies what happened.] "What did that do to the class or to learning?"

[Show a video of the moment in class that is the issue.] "What happened in this moment?" [or the appropriate question to accompany the video]

Level 4 (Leader-driven; only when other levels fail): State the problem directly:

[State what you observed and what action step will be needed to solve the problem.]

[If you modeled in class] "When I intervened, what did I do?"

[Show video of effective practice] "What do you notice? How is this different than what you do in class?"</td></tr>
</table>

(continued)

Six Steps to Effective Feedback: Leading Post-Observation Face-to-Face Meetings

Leader should bring:	Teacher should bring:
Observation Tracker One-Pager: Six Steps for Effective Feedback Preplanned script (questions, observation evidence, and so on)	Laptop and school calendar Curriculum plan, lesson plans, materials, data or student work

4 **Practice**	**Practice: Role-play or simulate how to improve current or future lessons**
	What to say: *Level 1:* "Let's practice together. Do you want me to be the teacher or the student?" *Levels 2–4:* "Let's try that." [Jump into role play.] "Let's replay your lesson and try to apply this." "I'm your student. I say/do _____. How do you respond?" *Level 4:* [Model for the teacher, and then have them practice it.]
5 **Plan Ahead**	**Plan Ahead: Design or revise upcoming lesson plans to implement this action**
	What to say: "Where would be a good place to implement this in your upcoming lessons?" "Let's write out the steps into your [lesson plan, worksheet/activity, signage, and so on.]"
6 **Set Timeline for Follow-Up**	**Set Timeline for Follow-Up**
	What to say: "When would be best to observe your implementation of this?" *Levels 3–4:* "I'll come in tomorrow and look for this technique." **What to do:** Set timeline for: *Completed materials:* When teacher will complete revised lesson plan/materials *Leader observation:* When you'll observe the teacher (When valuable) *Teacher observes master teacher:* When they'll observe master teacher implementing the action step (When valuable) *Video:* When you'll videotape teacher to debrief in upcoming meeting

Table 2.4 Making it Work: Where It Fits in a Leader's Schedule

	Monday	Tuesday	Wednesday	Thursday	Friday
6:00am					
:30					
7:00am					
:30					
8:00am		Meet Wilson	Meet Bradley		
:30		Meet Vargas	Meet Frint		
9:00am	Observe Wilson, Vargas, Jenkins	Meet Jenkins			
:30					
10:00am			Observe Mitzia, Boykin, Devin		Observe Hoyt, Settles, Palma
:30					
11:00am					
:30					
12:00pm	Observe Henry, Bernales, Christian				Meet Bradley
:30		Meet Worrell			Meet Palma
1:00pm		Meet Christian			Meet Settles
:30		Meet Bernales	Meet Boykin		Meet Hoyt
2:00pm		Observe Bradley, Frint, Worrell	Meet Devin		
:30			Meet Mitzia		
3:00pm					
:30					
4:00pm					
:30					
5:00pm					
:30					

■ Work Time ■ School Culture ■ Observations ■ Meetings

Note that the meetings labeled in this schedule (Table 2.4) are for both feedback *and* planning. If you choose a planning system that completes planning work at the start of the year, these meetings can be half of the length they are shown above. (See Chapter 3 for more on different approaches to planning conferences.)

Pulling the Lever
Action Planning Worksheet for Observation and Feedback

Self-Assessment

- How frequently are your teachers being observed? _____/year or _____/month
- Which of the six steps of effective feedback are being used to give your teachers feedback?

  _____

  _____

  _____

- Which of the six steps would most enhance the quality of your schools or your own feedback?

  _____

  _____

  _____

Planning for Action

- What tools from this book will you use to improve observation and feedback at your school? Check all that you will use (you can find all on the DVD):

  ☐   Sample Observation Tracker

  ☐   Six Steps of Effective Feedback One-Pager

  ☐   Videos of Observation and Feedback Meetings

  ☐   PD Materials for Observation and Feedback

- What are your next steps for improving observation and feedback?

Action	Date

Chapter 3

Planning

One-on-One: Planning with a Purpose

Though the first day of school is still weeks away, Roxbury Prep is already abuzz with activity. In these last weeks of August, Principal Kim Nicoll is meeting with each teacher to review his or her yearlong curriculum plan.

Andrew, a veteran eighth-grade history teacher, arrives first. Kim begins by asking Andrew what changes he has been making to his plans. They narrow their focus to his unit on U.S. history in the 1830s, and Andrew starts commenting on his opening activity.

"For this activity I focused in on asking kids 'Why?' as the key question. But, if I explicitly asked 'What's your evidence?,' this would definitely make the activity more demanding and challenging." For the remainder of the 45-minute meeting, Kim and Andrew discuss the rest of Andrew's plans, spending extra time on his new 1830s unit.

Five hours later, Kim meets with another history teacher, Jamie. Jamie is less experienced than Andrew, and it's his first time teaching sixth grade. Kim asks Jamie what he notices about his plans. "Well," said Jamie, "I guess we need to do more work on research."

"Okay," Kim presses, "how could we get kids into the habit of using their research resources?"

After a moment, Jamie slowly answers, "I guess we could start questions with . . . 'What is your evidence?'"

"Great idea," Kim responds.

 WATCH Clip 15: Kim Nicoll and Jamie Gumpper design specific classroom actions to make an upcoming history unit shine.

At most schools, lesson planning is a solitary process. Each teacher, whether veteran or novice, is left to his or her own devices. Under the guidance of then-principal Dana Lehman and her successor Kim Nicoll, Roxbury Prep, a middle school outside Boston, has taken a different approach. Before the first day of school, each teacher plots out the year and reviews a comprehensive curriculum plan with an instructional leader. Though these meetings are usually calm and collegial, they are also intensely focused on two questions: What do students need to be able to do, and how will we get them to do it? All teachers, from novice to superstar, leave this process with a clear idea of what they will teach and, more important, why they will teach it.

The impact of this planning is nothing short of phenomenal. In 2009, 98 percent of Roxbury Prep's eighth-grade students were proficient or advanced proficient in English on the Massachusetts Comprehensive Assessment System (MCAS) state test, a score that marked the school as one of the top ten in the state. Even more impressive, the school's 96 percent proficient and advanced proficient in math left it tied for being the number one middle school in the state. And as Figure 3.1 shows, this success was not a one-off occurrence.

Figure 3.1   Eighth-Grade MCAS Math Performance 2005–2009

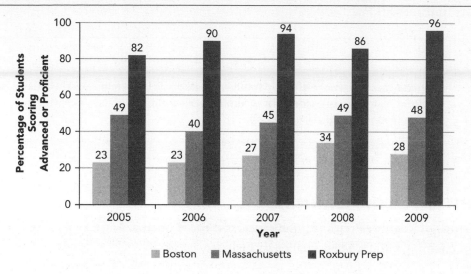

In explaining this remarkable and consistent high achievement, Dana recognizes the impact of all seven levers of exceptional schools, and she particularly highlights systematic, effective teacher planning:

> I think we underestimate the tremendous power we have by deciding what kids learn and how they learn it. As teachers we're constantly making choices about how our classes will look. Good instructional leadership is about making these choices explicit. When teachers are making truly systematic decisions about their practice, it has a real impact on the educational trajectory that students have.

On the surface, an emphasis on teacher planning does not seem novel or unique. McTighe and Wiggins have championed this cause with *Understanding by Design*, and many others have followed.[1] What distinguishes Dana's and Kim's process is the systematic approach they have built to continually drive teachers to make tough choices and catch problems early, leading to profoundly improved instruction.

Roxbury Prep is not alone. At schools that work at this level, leaders set the foundation for great lessons through great planning: they take the time to ensure that every teacher asks—and answers—the right questions. The results are transformational.

> ### Core Idea
>
> Every day teachers make choices about what students learn and how they learn it. Good instructional leadership is about making these choices explicit, and *making teachers choose intentionally.*

PITFALLS OF PLANNING

Much of Roxbury Prep's planning success is based on avoiding a well-known set of planning pitfalls. These challenges include:

- *Not becoming "end goal driven."* Today, the things that many consider good instructional strategies may be little more than highly engaging activities. An explicitly end goal–driven plan, by contrast, focuses squarely on the learning objective students need—as you have defined by your interim assessments. Schools whose planning does not align with these end-goal assessments risk creating plans that focus less on what students need and more on what a teacher's or district's pacing guide chooses to emphasize.

- *Treating all content equally.* Whether planning a week or a year, planning is all about making tough choices. As Dana notes, "One of the most common mistakes I see rookie teachers make is trying to cover all content with equal time; the result is a mile wide and an inch deep." A yearly pacing guide does not entirely resolve the problem; teachers still need to determine what aspects of each unit require greater importance and depth.

- *Providing insufficient guidance.* The most common error is that leaders implicitly or explicitly act in a way that suggests that all teachers, including rookie teachers, need maximal freedom and autonomy in planning to develop as educators. Though autonomy is valuable, planning is a challenging and often counterintuitive skill that requires leader guidance, especially early on. Imagine if, in the name of autonomy, a piano teacher did not teach students how to read music, time notes, or switch keys. The only "freedom" that piano teacher offers is the freedom to fail. Likewise, leaders who give teachers the "autonomy" to plan without guidance are doing their teachers a significant disservice.

Core Idea

Autonomy in lesson planning for all teachers only guarantees one thing: that some teachers will have the "freedom" to fail to plan effectively.

- *Believing leaders lack content expertise.* Often, principals or coaches assume that until they have "curriculum expertise," they cannot effectively lead planning meetings with teachers. In fact, the process works in reverse: conducting planning meetings builds curricular understanding, not the other way around. "My background isn't in mathematics, but years of observing teachers and following the data have allowed me to effectively lead math teachers," comments Dana. True expertise is achieved by devoting hours to working with teachers and to building lessons that drive student achievement.

- *Letting plans gather dust.* Across the country, many districts and school leaders have spent countless hours assembling detailed plans, binders of worksheets, and carefully calibrated curricula. Thousands of hours and millions of dollars have been spent on incredibly intricate curricula, pacing guides, and "curriculum coaching" experts. Too often, however, all of this investment comes to nothing because the teachers don't see these resources' relevance in planning each day's lesson. Even if detailed, careful, and rigorous plans exist, schools may still fail to execute them.

The primary reason why Dana's planning succeeds is not the level of detail the plans reflect (though Roxbury Prep's plans are quite intricate) or the volume of plans produced. Indeed, it does not rest in any specific format but rather in an unswerving commitment to planning out the year with the right content—and making sure those plans get implemented. When leaders know the questions to ask—and ensure that they are answered with actions—the plans that result pave the way for outstanding student achievement. Let's take a look at both components: yearly planning and then weekly lesson planning.

YEARLY CURRICULUM PLANNING: TEACHING THE RIGHT CONTENT

How a school approaches yearly curriculum planning depends entirely on curriculum context. For many schools, a district central office has already developed mandated curriculum plans and pacing guides. If you are a leader in this situation, you can skip forward to the next section of the chapter: supporting teachers in their weekly planning. If you are a district-level leader who can influence the development of curriculum plans and pacing guides, or if you are a school leader who has the autonomy to develop your own, then read on.

Two core questions guide Dana's and Kim's selection of the right content:

1. What, specifically, must students be able to do at the end of each unit?

2. Given limited time, how will teachers get them there?

On their own, these questions are not unique. What separates elite leaders from countless others, however, is the criteria by which they answer them.

Question 1: What Do Students Need?

The first key set of questions that leaders must ask relates to what students must be able to do in order for teaching to have succeeded. At the yearlong level, as we saw in Chapter 1, the end-goal assessment determines this destination. Remember, *standards are meaningless unless you define how to assess them.* Even the most specific academic standard is open to ambiguity, interpretation, and confusion until you know how it will be assessed. Curriculum design is no different: until a yearlong plan defines the end-goal assessment and then maps all objectives to that end, it will not be a meaningful guide.

Core Idea

Planning works when it starts from assessment, not from standards. That is the roadmap to rigor.

At Roxbury Prep, leaders and teachers begin from their end-goal assessment: both paper-and-pencil tests and work products that students will produce. Far from rote teaching, alignment with these tests creates curricula that teach an array of extremely rigorous skills, from complex research writing to analyzing nonfiction texts. In each case, principals take the final assessment and work product students must create—such as a one-act play for theater class—and work backward. For Roxbury Prep's advanced science curriculum, for example, Kim, Dana, and the science team chose a high school engineering assessment as the end-goal benchmark because "this was what truly college-level rigor demanded." The planning process then works because it starts from that assessment, not from standards alone.

Once an end goal has been chosen, the process of alignment can take several forms. More experienced teachers may simply be given exemplars of the end-goal assessment and be left to design their curricula accordingly. For newer educators, this process should be completed with the assistance and support of instructional leaders. Providing that support ensures that the challenge of determining what skills and competencies should be taught is met as well by a novice teacher as by a veteran.

Question 2: How Can We Get Them There?

With proper end-goal assessments in place, teachers and leaders can break down the units into the activities and objectives they'll need to implement to master those assessments. Table 3.1 presents a sample curriculum plan from Roxbury Prep. You'll note the larger standard, a specific objective, the assessment question that defines the standard, the activity, and the necessary vocabulary.

When looking at all of the exceptional school leaders presented in this book, I did not see one consistent format for curriculum plans. What I did see, however, was how clearly these leaders followed the steps mentioned earlier.

So how do leaders ensure this quality for yearlong plans? To truly drive instructional planning, school leaders like Kim and Dana review each teacher's yearlong plans for at least an hour. As Kim explains, "Before I can ask the right questions, I need to really sit down and review the plans on my own. Sometimes, I'll even call in other instructional leaders to make sure that my input is on point and that I'm seeing the right things." Accordingly, at each school studied, teachers are expected to submit their plans in advance of meeting, allowing leaders time to review them.

After briefly reading or skimming the entire plan, Kim and Dana will spend the bulk of their preparation time considering the assessments and activities. Rather

Table 3.1 Eighth Grade-Science Curriculum Plan Sample: Roxbury Prep

Standard	Objective: Students Will Be Able to …	Assessment Question	Learning Activity	Vocabulary
Relate the position of an element on the periodic table to its electron configuration and compare its reactivity to the reactivity of other elements in the table.	… use the periodic table to identify the number of valence electrons for a given element.	How many valence electrons do Li, Mg, and Sn each have?	Inquiry: Identifying Patterns	Valence Electron
	… draw a Lewis Dot Structure for a given element.	Draw a Lewis Dot Structure for Li, Mg, and Sn.	Lewis Dot Structure Periodic Table Human/manipulative Lewis Dot Structures Partner drawing and peer check	Lewis Dot Structure
Differentiate between physical changes and chemical changes.	… identify and differentiate between physical and chemical changes	An iron nail left outside will rust. Is this a physical change or a chemical change? How do you know?	Demonstrations Inquiry activity with stations of changes and classification of these changes into groups Mystery Powders Lab	Chemical change Physical change
Explain how atoms combine through ionic and covalent bonding. Predict chemical formulas based on the number of valence electrons.	… explain how atoms combine through ionic and covalent bonds	Compare and contrast what happens to the electrons in an ionic bond and a covalent bond. Include an example of each to support your explanation.	Acting-out scenarios Analogies to sharing and stealing materials Venn Diagram or, Compare and contrast ionic and covalent bond using an example of each	Ionic bond Covalent bond
	… draw ionic and covalent bonds for given elements	Draw a bond between hydrogen and oxygen. Draw a bond between sodium and phosphorus.	Drawing bonds with different colored pencils Marshmallow manipulatives	
	… predict the chemical formula of the compound that two elements will form based on their number of valence electrons	Calcium and oxygen react to form a new compound. What is the chemical formula of the compound that they will make?	Inquiry: Find the chemical formula for different compounds	Chemical formula

than serve as "proofreaders"—assessing each and every objective—strong leaders use their preparation time to search for broad patterns or for lessons that seem particularly disconnected from the goals they are trying to achieve. At that point, Dana and Kim ask teachers to make tough choices.

At its core, the concept of making tough choices rests on the principle that as teachers become more intentional about their instructional decisions, the quality of their instruction will improve.

Core Idea

As teachers become more intentional about the decisions they make about what to teach, the quality of their instruction will improve.

Such choices are necessary, because, as any school leader can attest, time is incredibly limited. To illustrate why this is so important, consider this example from Dana's practice.

At the start of the year, a sixth-grade teacher had created a plan aligned to the state test objective that "students will be able to write an essay around ancient Egypt." Accordingly, the teacher's end-of-day assessment was a short essay response to the prompt "What do you know about Egypt's political system?" But as Dana explained, "This objective—in and of itself—could be asking any number of things: Is it an acceptable response to say 'Egypt had Pharaohs'? Or did they want a detailed description of the Ancient Egyptian theocracy?" Probing can be important in determining what the objective is in the first place.

Kim Nicolls shares another example. A set of Massachusetts sixth-grade state standards calls for students to "use a map key to locate countries and major cities" on every continent in the world, including 14 nations in Latin America, 17 in Southeast Asia, and 56 in Africa.[2] Initially, the teacher was tempted to present each country rapid fire—not very rigorous, as it would be a mile wide and an inch deep. During her meeting with the teacher, however, Kim prompted the teacher to go continent by continent and split the nations into categories based on desired end-goal assessment: those countries that students would simply need to be able to identify on a matching test, those countries that students would need to identify on a blank map, and those countries that students would need to be able to describe in detail. The result of this exercise was a more targeted focus of the standard.

While there is no exact science for identifying these areas, there are several key areas that leaders like Kim and Dana always consider in reviewing a teacher's plans:

- *What students will need to do.* Carefully consider alignment between the activities teachers propose and the objectives they have selected. Often, the skills taught in class will not match up with the rigor that the end-goal assessment demands. Recognizing this at the planning stage will ensure that instructional problems are addressed before they even begin.

- *Order and prioritization.* Are students learning the skills they need in a pedagogically appropriate order? Be conscious of how skills build off each other and how they should be structured.

- *What's left out and what's kept in.* It is an unfortunate reality that there is simply not enough time in the school year to teach everything about every objective. In reviewing yearlong plans, it is vital that instructional leaders take the time to consider the choices teachers have made in deciding what to teach and what to leave out.

- *Activities over objectives.* Do activities seem to have been chosen simply because they are fun or exciting for the teacher to teach? Dana offers an instructive example: "During the ancient civilizations unit, our veteran history teacher had set aside time for students to build elaborate replica pyramids. While the project was very involved and detailed, the teacher offered no way to determine whether students had actually learned anything from their creations."

- *High-cost activities.* Some class activities require far more intense planning and coordination than others, and they tend to be especially challenging to do well. Among others, these include group projects, computer-based assignments, and long-term, multipart work. Although these projects can be vital educational experiences, it is particularly important that they have been carefully planned. Identifying these activities early allows school leaders to support teachers as they design these lessons and ensure that the lessons are given the care they need to be effective. At the same time, leaders may also identify moments where such high-cost activities will not offer benefits to match the effort they require. That way, leaders can suggest changes at the planning meeting.

Core Idea

When planning, nail down what to leave out as much as what to keep in. You'll have far more time to teach deeply and comprehensively.

Note that the purpose of considering these areas is not limited to finding areas of improvement (though this is a very important benefit). Instead, even if teachers have done nothing "wrong" in their planning, these areas mark important points of discussion during the yearlong planning, allowing leaders to generate the sorts of questions that will push teachers to very carefully consider why they take the approaches they do. This is particularly important for more experienced teachers who can use these conversations as "sounding boards" to hone their own practice.

Committing to Action

The final step of the planning meeting process is to ensure that teachers capture the insights gained during their planning meetings. During the meeting, teachers should record the changes they will make on the spot, either electronically or on paper. Leaders should require teachers to update their plans to reflect these changes and to resubmit them by a reasonable deadline. Setting a concrete expectation that changes will be directly put into plans and implemented will ensure that the hard work and insights of the meeting are translated to action and, in the process, improve instruction. With this final step, Dana, Kim, and leaders like them ensure that each lesson presented by each teacher is one that advances the goal of student learning.

At Roxbury Prep, the end result of this process is a detailed plan that outlines the year's specific objectives. Who produces plans like these is different in each exceptional school mentioned here. In the case of Roxbury Prep, every teacher does. In the case of North Star Elementary, only veteran teachers create the plans, while less experienced teachers focus primarily on implementing them. Yet regardless of the model embraced, effective planning demands that teachers have narrowly focused in on what students will be able to do on each day.

At many schools, the creation of the sort of document outlined here would mark the end of the planning process. Indeed, many schools would view the creation of such comprehensive plans as a triumph in its own right. Yet on their own, even the most specific objectives and assessments cannot ensure effective learning. The quality of planning gets solidified when you drill down to the level of daily lesson planning.

WEEKLY AND DAILY LESSON PLANNING: ENSURING ACCOUNTABILITY

In most cases, a master teacher will be capable of taking a high-quality curriculum plan and building effective daily lessons. For most teachers, however, this is still a highly complex task. At a number of the schools mentioned in this book, leaders have committed to supporting their teachers in the daily lesson plan process, and they find that it flows naturally from the observation and feedback process. Quite simply, they utilize the 30-minute check-in with each teacher (you locked that into your schedule in Chapter 2 on observation and feedback) to give feedback and then dive into next week's lesson plans:

- 30-minute weekly teacher–leader meeting
  - 10 minutes: Observation feedback (Chapter 2)
  - 20 minutes: Dive into lesson planning (this chapter)

Almost every school can build a 15:1 teacher-to-leader ratio, which means locking in fifteen 30-minute check-ins alongside the observations. For a reminder of what that looks like, see the table at the end of this chapter. As you can see, no additional time for planning meetings is needed beyond what we already locked in!

How do leaders use that time productively? There are three key steps that they follow to ensure high-quality lesson plans.

Three Steps for Effective Daily Lesson Planning

There are three basic steps to effective daily lesson planning:

1. *Map out the week.* Determine how school events, classroom routines, and carryover work from last week will influence the week.
2. *Set the core content.* Establish the key objective for each day.
3. *Dive into key lessons.* Develop tight activities for key lessons.

Let's look at each one a little more closely.

1. *Map out the week.* Proficient lesson planners do not need much help mapping out their week, but it may be a daunting task for less proficient planners. Leaders can work with those teachers to lay out the week, taking into consideration the following:

   - *Carryover standards from previous week:* Standards that the teacher didn't finish from the previous week

   - *School events:* Changes to the weekly routine that will reduce the amount of class time

   - *"Always" tasks:* Establishing where to place the common routines each week—fluency work in an English language arts (ELA) class, computational practice in a math class, labs in a science class, and so on

   These are rather basic tasks, but you'd be amazed by how many problems you can prevent by doing them effectively.

2. *Set the core content.* Deciding on core content sounds so simple: Don't you simply follow the curriculum plan? Not so fast. If a teacher is striving for results—student learning—then the degree to which students are mastering the learning will speed up or slow down the pace of the original curriculum plan. In essence, setting the core content is combining the data-driven instruction (DDI) six-week action plan (see Chapter 1 for a reminder of what this looks like) with the original curriculum plan. Leaders can use the

following questions to align a data-driven six-week plan to a curriculum plan:

- What objectives require more time, given student misunderstanding on the last assessment?

- What units can be reduced to build in that time? Where will we cut those units?

Watch as Serena Savarirayan helps teacher Eric Diamon work through the core content for his English class.

 WATCH Clip 16: Serena Savarirayan and Eric Diamon set the core content and objectives for fifth-grade English.

Taking the time to set objectives carefully can ensure that teaching is directly aligned to what students need to learn, and that reteaching is used as strategically as possible. Consider how school leader James Verrilli and science teacher Steve Decina use their planning meeting to determine which skills to teach and how to check for progress when setting the core content.

 WATCH Clip 17: James Verrilli and Steve Decina decide which science skills to reteach and how to assess them.

3. *Dive into key lessons.* Once steps 1 and 2 have been completed, leaders and teachers can dive into a key lesson for the week. What constitutes the "key lesson" will vary based on the teacher's development. It most likely will be a lesson that is essential to student understanding (for example, day 1 of a new unit, a new skill). For a newer teacher, however, it could be the lesson that has the most potential for classroom management problems (for example, new activity, small-group work, lab). It also could be the lesson that is most directly connected to the teacher's action step from the observation and feedback cycle. In any case, the "deep dive" process is the same:

- Develop the objective for the lesson.

- Start with the interim assessment or the unit's end product: What do students need to be able to do to master that assessment?

- Set the lesson's objective: What do you want students to be able to do at the end of this lesson that will prepare them for the end goal?

- Design the assessment for the day (for example, exit ticket, check for understanding, or quiz).

- Link activities to the objective.

  - Design and evaluate activities based on their alignment to the objective.

- Go even deeper (for teachers who need it): Practice:

  - Design the actual work products (worksheets, end products, rubrics).

  - Role-play or practice implementing the plan.

 WATCH Clip 18: Aja Settles and Kristi Costanzo analyze student error to design upcoming lessons.

Core Idea

There are three basic steps to effective daily lesson planning:

1. *Map out the week*. Determine how school events, classroom routines, and carryover work from last week will influence the week.
2. *Set the core content*. Establish the key objective for each day.
3. *Dive into key lessons*. Develop tight activities for key lessons.

These steps are not revolutionary: all they do is take what has already been established as best practice in planning and place it in a concrete set of steps that any leader can follow.

TURNAROUND: WHAT TO DO FIRST

In a school in which teachers are not engaged in this depth of curriculum and lesson planning, leaders need to decide where to begin. Your school's circumstances will dictate your choice.

A Teacher's Testimonial on Planning

Jamie Gumpper

In the months leading up to my first year as a teacher, a trusted mentor told me and some other newbies, "Plan as much as possible in August. If you don't, you're going to regret it for the rest of the year." As somebody who had always survived by adhering to the maxim, "Never do today what you can put off until tomorrow," I carefully listened, nodded in acknowledgment, then promptly frittered away the weeks leading up to the school year. Unfortunately (but unsurprisingly), my first years of teaching were filled with lessons finished just hours before the school day, nights of 4 or 5 hours of sleep, and far too many cups of coffee.

It wasn't until I reached Roxbury Prep that I felt I could act on my mentor's original advice. I was teaching a new course, ancient history, in a new city, Boston, and I didn't want to repeat the mistakes I had made in previous summers. On my first day, Kim Nicoll, our principal, warmly greeted the new teachers in the room, and we introduced ourselves. Then we opened our orientation binders to the section on curriculum. Kim explained that teachers at Roxbury Prep used something called a CAT—a Curriculum Alignment Template—to plan their year. Initially, I assumed this would be similar to the planning documents I'd used—and misused—in years before. The spreadsheet in front of me seemed to confirm my thoughts: I would be taking the state standards and breaking them down into daily objectives, a task I was familiar with from my previous school. Based on that experience, I figured I would spend a day on the CAT and then go all-out on planning my first unit so I was ready for September.

Kim, however, breezed right through the part about standards and objectives and instead focused her time on other categories: assessment questions, learning activities, and methods. At Roxbury Prep, it wasn't enough to define our objectives; Kim expected us to know exactly what questions we were going to ask to assess whether or not our students had met the objective. It also became clear that we should know what answers we were looking for to those questions. Kim also expected us to have a reasonable idea about what the learning activities for each day would be, so that I would know what the third class in my fourth unit would be by the middle of August. Last, Kim asked us to indicate the method for delivering content in each day of class. Would I be lecturing while students took notes? Presenting readings for small-group work? Facilitating student writing about some aspect of ancient history? Kim left the choice up to us, but she reminded us that there should be a variety of methods within any given unit.

I was floored by how high the bar was set. I had expected to be solidly set for my first unit and have a passing familiarity with the yearly curriculum by the end of August. Now, I was being asked to come away with a deep knowledge of what, when, and how I planned to teach ancient history . . . for the entire year. It would be a lie to say that I developed perfect CATs in August. Still, I think I spent at least 60 hours last summer doing meaningful planning for the upcoming year with a fresh brain (and getting plenty of sleep while doing it).

For Schools Without Curriculum Planning Autonomy

The most common context for public schools is that you have a district curricular pacing guide that you must follow, but it doesn't address the depth of each lesson plan or the quality of each learning objective. If this is your context, making sure the data-driven instruction model (Chapter 1) is in place is *always* the most effective step to accompany a pacing guide. Then your core focus is to find ways to give teachers feedback on how to set data-driven objectives and to align activities to those objectives. This is most easily accomplished during those same weekly check-ins that we've already locked into leaders' schedules. Follow the guide to leading these meetings (embedded in this chapter), and you'll start to see results. Leaders who carefully plan with teachers will more consistently identify potential pitfalls and increase the quantity of effective teaching.

For Schools with Curriculum Planning Autonomy

Having curriculum planning autonomy gives leaders more options but also makes it more challenging to determine where to start. For one, it is often challenging to secure uninterrupted planning time before the school year begins. Unless a substantial amount of time (at least two to three weeks) can be committed to such planning, it cannot go into the week-by-week depth needed to drive truly effective instruction. In this case, it is best to see if you can acquire quality curriculum plans from another school and devote your efforts to supporting teachers in their daily lesson planning. When this is not possible, some schools have decided to simply map out the assessments and work products for each unit at the beginning of the year—creating a skeletal curriculum plan—and then dive into the weekly planning. The subsequent year, they fill in their curriculum plans with the experiences gained in that past year.

CONCLUSION: PLANNING MAKES PERFECT

As Dana notes, "Time invested in planning is paid back many-fold." By ensuring that she has seen all lessons and deeply examined all key lessons, she allows all teachers to plan to succeed and succeed through planning.

The work of instructional leadership has come full circle, all in the course of one standing check-in with each teacher. We have seen how this can drive learning via data analysis meetings, feedback from observations, and lesson planning. Data is the super-lever, and once that is in place, the levers of feedback and planning increase in size and impact. Up next: how to leverage professional development in support of the other levers.

Planning Meetings: Leading Face-to-Face Meetings to Guide Unit and Lesson Planning

Leader should bring:	Teacher should bring:
Laptop One-Pager: Leading Planning Meetings Copies of teacher's lesson plans and curriculum plan	Laptop and school calendar Curriculum and unit plan, lesson plans, class materials, data and student work

1 **Map Out the Week**	**Weekly Grid: Map out calendar** *Proficient Planners* • Teachers map this out ahead of time. *More Support* Leader and teacher map out the week jointly: • Carryover standards from previous week • School events (changes to the weekly routine) • Always tasks (where to place the common routines each week: fluency work in an ELA class, labs in a science class, and so on)
2 **Set Core Content**	**Core Content: Decide the core content for each day of the week** *Set the content for each day of the week that is:* • Data Driven: Aligned to six-week assessment analysis action plan • Curriculum Driven: Aligned to curriculum and unit plan *Use these questions to align DDI six-week plan to curriculum plan:* • What objectives require more, time given student misunderstanding on the last assessment? • What units can be reduced to build in that time?
3 **Dive into Key Lessons**	**Key Lessons: Develop objectives and activities** *Choose a key lesson based on whether the lesson:* • Is essential to student understanding (e.g., day 1 of a new unit, a new skill). • Has potential for management problems (e.g., new activity, small groups). • Directly connects to teacher's action step from the observation feedback. *Develop the objective for the lesson:* • Start with the interim assessment/unit's end product: What do students need to be able to do to master that assessment? • Set the lesson's objective: What do you want students to be able to do at the end of this lesson that will prepare them for the end goal? • Design the assessment for the day (foe example, exit ticket, check for understanding, quiz, and so on). *Link activities to the objective:* • Design and evaluate activities based on their alignment to the objective. • Going even deeper (for teachers who need it)—Practice. • Design the work products (worksheets, end products, rubrics). *Role-play or practice implementing the plan.*

Pulling the Lever
Action Planning Worksheet for Planning

Self-Assessment

- How frequently are your teachers getting feedback about their lesson and curriculum plans? _____/year or _____/month
- What percentage of your teachers' lesson and curriculum plans are well aligned with interim assessment data? _____ percent
- What percentage of the activities students do in class would you say are well aligned with lesson objectives and classroom assessments? _____ percent

Planning for Action

- What tools from this book will you use to improve planning at your school? Check all that you will use (you can find all on the DVD):
  - ☐ Planning Meeting One-Pager
  - ☐ Lesson Planning One-Pager
  - ☐ Lesson Plan Rubric
  - ☐ Curriculum Plan Rubric
  - ☐ Videos of Planning Meetings
  - ☐ PD Materials for Leading Planning

- What are your next steps for improving lesson and curriculum planning?

Action	Date

Chapter 4

Professional Development

The Impact of One: Leading a Professional Development Session on Reading Transitions

"All right team, get ready!"

As the video continues, an audience of 30 teachers watches Laura Palma's first-grade class transition from a reading fluency game to a comprehension activity. Led by then-vice principal Aja Settles, the teachers of North Star's elementary schools had been discussing a case study about an otherwise strong classroom that lost hours of learning time because of slow switches between activities.

As the clip ends, Aja offers the next step: "Take a minute to write your answer to the core question: What actions did Laura take to make her transition so effective?"

Across the large classroom, all the teachers begin to write, knowing they'll soon have a chance to share what they saw. Under Aja's guidance, this sharing will form the basis of concrete and applicable strategies that will tighten every class in the building.

 WATCH Clip 19: Aja Settles uses the Living the Learning framework to drive her professional development session on improving school-day transitions.

At some point, nearly everyone in education attends a great professional development (PD) session. The speaker is charismatic, the material is relevant, and the participants are excited. Years later, attendees may even remember catchy anecdotes, corny jokes, or key phrases. But once the session ended, how many of the changes were put into place? Too often, even the "best" professional development ends where it begins—in the conference room.

For the leaders like Dana Lehman, Julie Kennedy, and Mike Mann, this is an unacceptable outcome. "Increasing student achievement is the ultimate goal," Mike Mann explains. "If PD isn't changing how our students learn, it's useless."

Core Idea

Professional development only matters if it translates from paper to practice, driving real improvements to student learning.

One particularly strong example comes from the work of Aja Settles. From 2007 to 2010, Aja served as a lead teacher under Julie Jackson's tutelage at North Star Elementary. Later, she became the principal of North Star's second elementary school, West Side Park (see her results in the Introduction of this book) and played a critical role in improving reading instruction for a host of elementary schools across the United States. Her primary lever for doing so was creating a number of professional development lessons around every aspect of K–4 literacy. Her success in PD contributed significantly to the outstanding results of Julie

Jackson's school, Aja's own school, and a host of other elementary schools. This chapter explores just how Aja—and leaders like her—have been able to develop PD that translates to results.

Great professional development workshops can be divided into three parts. In the pages that follow we look at each in more detail.

1. *What to teach: Follow the data.* Focus PD on the areas that will meaningfully drive student results.

2. *How to teach: Lead the training effectively.* Actively engage teachers in the skills they need.

3. *How to make it stick: Hold teachers accountable.* Build systems that guarantee that PD jumps from paper to practice, genuinely changing classrooms.

WHAT TO TEACH: FOLLOW THE DATA

Determining What Your Staff Needs

Leading Up to the PD on Reading Transitions

It is June, and Aja Settles is sitting down with her fellow leaders to determine the summer PD needs for the staff. They review the notes from their observation trackers and notice how much time newer teachers lose on mid-lesson transitions during reading instruction. After the meeting, Aja begins to work on professional development training for literacy teachers, focused around tightening those transitions.

At the start of this chapter, we saw a moment from Aja's professional development session. There is no doubt that Aja's training was engaging: she's a confident leader, and her content knowledge is staggering. Yet what makes her training relevant isn't her delivery; it's how she selected the material she taught. Aja's session on reading began with data—in this case, observation data. As a result, Aja knows that this session will directly affect what matters: student success.

Great professional development starts with knowledge about what teachers need. No one knows that better than a leader using all of the tools presented in the previous chapters. When leaders employ regular data analysis meetings

(Chapter 1), weekly feedback and planning meetings (Chapters 2 and 3), and school culture evaluations (upcoming in Chapter 5), they have locked in tools that guarantee they will know what teachers need. They are no longer dependent on external consultants or other opinions: they can generate the right focus themselves. This is what separates the content of PD of highly effective schools from the rest: they continually focus on the right things.

Core Idea

Great professional development starts with knowledge about what teachers need. Interim assessment results, observation trackers, and culture walkthroughs are the easiest places to find that information.

In the following sections we review how each instructional and cultural lever sets up leaders to identify the right content for their PD.

How to Choose Your Content

Responding to Data

Interim assessments are the most logical place to find schoolwide areas for curricular or instructional improvement. During data analysis weeks, leaders should be on the lookout for larger patterns that cut across classes and grade levels. Mike Mann notes, "On the schoolwide level, data can confirm suspicions about problem areas or point out concerns you might overlook if you only saw one classroom." Consider again the data in Table 4.1 that we presented in Chapter 1 for Mike's English teacher Steve Chiger 1.

When Steve and his instructional leader, Beth Verrilli, analyzed this data, they concluded that the sticking point for Steve's students was comprehending the main idea of a passage—especially when the passage included unfamiliar words or phrases. When Beth saw a similar problem among her other teachers, the next PD topic for the English department was easy to choose.

Learning from Observations and Planning

As noted in Chapter 2, leaders use observation trackers to monitor teachers' development goals and key action steps for each week. A quick review of the summary page allows a leader like Julie Jackson to find common or persistent

Table 4.1 Data Report

	Sentence Completion	Main Idea	Extended Reasoning	Supporting Details	Vocabulary in Context
% Correct	73%	55%	76%	60%	75%

Sentence Completion	Main Idea	Extended Reasoning	Literal Comprehension	Perspective
92%	100%	100%	40%	80%

action areas across many classrooms. Consider a sample of Julie's tracker in Table 4.2.

When reviewing the latest key action steps, a number of teachers are struggling with the technique for questioning and checking for understanding. Not only can Julie Jackson plan to lead a session on checking for understanding, but she can also differentiate her leadership and exempt a teacher whose observation data suggests he or she doesn't need that session. Teachers are happier, because they know that if a leader asks them to attend a workshop, it will address something they personally need.

Culling from Culture Walkthroughs

Finally, as you will see in the upcoming chapter on student culture (Chapter 5), leaders can use school culture rubrics to take a subjective area like student culture and quantify it—and then to focus on particular aspects of student culture that they'd like to improve. Consider the excerpt (Table 4.3) taken from a walkthrough of the teachers that Aja Settles was leading; note that the observations are aggregated to show the overall level of proficiency of teachers at the school.

Using this rubric, Aja has hard evidence that transitions between activities are the area that needs focus to improve student culture; thus she planned the PD that was presented in the opening session of the chapter.

By using interim assessments, classroom observations and culture walk-throughs to find areas for professional development, leaders know that they will have picked a relevant area of practice. Once this is done, the next key step is to land on a specific objective for the session.

Table 4.2 Julie's Observation Tracker

Name	Total Observations	Major PD/Instructional Goals	Latest Key Lever
Lear	13 (Nov 22)	1. Frequently check for understanding of students meeting the objective. 2. When students are confused regain focus by pausing and then restating the expectations in a calm tone.	1. After giving directions give a quick pause to wait for compliance. 2. When doing it again use nonverbals. 3. Avoid choral responses when the response has multiple answers.
Jones	14 (Nov 22)	1. Implement "break it down" when students give an incorrect response. 2. Increase thought ratio without tipping during whole-group and small-group instruction.	1. Select three different ability levels when you are calling on students to retell the story. 2. Avoid summarizing a student's thinking before asking him or her to tell you more. 3. Use clear and concise language to explain the task for independent practice and check for understanding.
Smith	8 (Sep 10)	1. Implement "control the game": keep the length of the reading unpredictable and mark it. 2. Ask high-order questions by using prompts from Bloom's Taxonomy guide.	1. Prior to turn-and-talk, restate the question so they know what they are discussing. 2. During comprehension conversation, ask students to tell you why they think that or how do they know.
Roth	10 (Nov 02)	1. Increase thought ratio without tipping. 2. Use a question prompt from the reading guide to respond to student error.	1. Share the pen. During the review of the do-now have a student do the editing. 2. With your reading class students, use prompt "Is there something that you know about this character that can help you understand them now?"

Phelps	14 (Nov 22)	1. Wait until you get 100% compliance before continuing instruction. 2. Allow one or two students to comment on a given response from another student to increase student thinking.	1. Lower your voice when you are calling on different readers in order to keep the focus on the text and not on your voice. 2. Use the economy of language—just state what you need them to do. For example, "Re-read with expression."
Bernard	18 (Nov 23)	1. Use cold call throughout the lesson to check for understanding 2. Use turn-and-talk during guided practice during writing to increase pacing.	1. Implement the turn-and-talks as they are scripted in the plan: during turn-and-talk listen in carefully so you know what students you are going to call on. 2. Cold-call on students at a faster pace—four students every minute.
Downing	13 (Nov 22)	1. Employ controlled urgency (hushed excitement, circulating purposefully, slow pacing of talking) during the beginning of class. 2. Narrate the positive and use nonverbals for student noncompliance.	1. When you give a redirect, scan and then pause for compliance. 2. Use nonverbal prompts to redirect student behavior without breaking up the flow of the lesson. 3. Employ more frequent individual checks for understanding of the material so you can assess whether students are really mastering the objectives of the lesson.
Donald	10 (Nov 16)	1. Diagnose student misunderstanding in guided reading, and then selecting a strategic prompt to lead to misunderstanding. 2. Have students break down the process of how they are making an inference (text evidence + schema) to strengthen understanding. 3. Use the break-it-down techniques beyond the initial prompt to continually scaffold student understanding.	1. In guiced reading, stop the student with a quick nonverbal and use one of your prompts from the K–4 reading taxonomy.
Total Observations	100		
Average per Teacher	12.5		

Table 4.3 Walkthrough Observations

Classroom Systems	Advanced	Proficient	Working Toward	Needs Improvement
Transition Between Activities	Efficient, time-saving (30-second) routine Teacher initiated using economy of language (Teacher says "Transition" and students move) Immediately after the transition students begin task Students know how to adjust the physical setting (MS/HS teacher initiated) Evidence of a routine	Efficient, time-saving (up to 1 minute) routine Teacher facilitated After the transition students are waiting for directions Students know how to adjust the physical setting (MS/HS Teacher facilitated) Evidence of a routine	Inefficient, more than 1 minute Off-task talking, too noisy Teacher has to repeat directions After the transition students are off task Physical setting is not adjusted Not a clearly established routine; teacher has to redo the transition	Inefficient, more than 1 minute Off-task talking, too noisy Teacher has to repeat directions After the transition students are off task Physical setting is not adjusted Not a clearly established routine; teacher has to redo the transition
Student Joy and Engagement	Students seem to be joyful and excited to be in school 90–100% of students are engaged in classroom activities	Most students seem to be joyful and excited to be in school 80–90% of students are engaged in classroom activities	While many students seem joyful, there are notable instances of student arguments and/or lack of joy 70–80% of students are engaged in classroom activities	Students generally seem disinterested in school Fewer than 70% of students are engaged in classroom activities
Exit	Class ends on time with sufficient time to line up students Teacher uses a consistent system to have students line up that is organized, quick, and efficient Teacher leads students to the next class	Class ends on time Teacher uses a consistent system to have students line up that is organized, quick, and efficient Teacher leads students to the next class	Class ends in a rushed or hurried way or goes over time Teacher lines up students in a disorganized way or does not check to see that all students are ready to be lined up Teacher does not lead students all the way to the next class	Class ends late or in a rushed or hurried way No evidence of a systematic dismissal process is evident Teacher does not lead students to the next class Students are loud and disorganized during the transition

A Word On ... Who Should Lead the PD

One of the most intuitive questions to ask about PD is who, exactly, should lead it. This session on deciding what teachers need makes one point clear: it should be someone who is intimately familiar with the school's data, observations, and culture. While a natural choice would be a principal, in all of the exceptional schools I observed, PD presentations were distributed among the principal, other instructional leaders, and master teachers.

Allowing other staff to lead PD can be especially fruitful in developing greater leadership capacity and in content areas where your own expertise may be more limited.

Only in rare occasions, however, did these great school leaders rely on external PD consultants. "It is just so difficult for an external presenter to understand the full context of the school and exactly where our teachers are," comments Julie Jackson. "The only cases where it has been effective are when the presenter spends notable time in the school observing teachers with a school leader *before* delivering the workshop and then implements the Living the Learning framework for their PD. There are few presenters who can effectively do both of those."

Building Better Objectives

A key first step for an effective PD session is to clearly articulate the objective. As Julie Kennedy (highlighted in Chapter 6) notes, "It's not enough to say 'This session will focus on management'; you need a clear goal in mind of what you want to happen." Like the one-on-one training of feedback meetings, professional development will succeed only if it is a clear, measurable, and bite-sized objective. The same skill leaders developed in Chapter 2—observation and feedback—can be used here. Effective PD must simply answer the question: What will teachers be able to *do* at the end of this session? It is not enough for teachers to "know" something or to "be aware of" something. The bottom line is, What will they be able to do when they walk into their classrooms the next day?

> ### Core Idea
>
> Effective PD must start by answering a basic question: What will teachers be able to *do* at the end of this session?

Building Better PD Objectives

Examples of Weak and Strong Objectives for a 60-Minute Session

Imagine you have 60 minutes to lead a professional development session. While that's a good amount of time, if you hold yourself to the expectation that teachers will be able to *do* something by the end of the session, you quickly realize you cannot accomplish as much as you would like. Narrowing the objective, then, becomes a critical tool. Of everything you could discuss on the topic, what is most important?

See the examples on page 139. We have started with a weak objective that is way too broad. Take a look, then, how these objectives were made narrower until they reached a size that could be accomplished in 60 minutes. Try it out for yourself. Read only the broad objective and cover the rest with your hand or a piece of paper. Try to come up with more specific objectives that could be accomplished in 60 minutes, and compare your answers to the ones written here. They likely will not be identical, because in narrowing the focus you could choose many options within one broad category. But still, compare your specificity to the examples provided.

While a seemingly reasonable question, most errors in PD come from not answering this question effectively. This question can be divided into three parts:

1. *Is it actionable?* Does it articulate what teachers will be able *to do* when they walk out of the workshop?

2. *Is it evaluable?* Will you be able to easily evaluate whether they accomplished the objective? What evidence will you have that teachers now know how to do this?

3. *Is it feasible?* Can you accomplish this objective in the time that you have allotted?

Thinking this way about the objective of your PD session might feel unnatural at first. Many a leader who has attended a workshop on this process has initially felt that their topic didn't apply. But unless you are simply giving an information session (for example, how the state's benefits program works), these questions really do apply. Following are a few examples to show how this works.

Reading

Weak: Too Broad

- Teach reading effectively.

Weak: Still Too Broad

- Teach guided reading effectively.

Strong: Specific and Bite-Sized

- Teach students two strategies for decoding.
- Respond to student errors at Fountas-Pinnell levels D–F with the appropriate prompt.

History

Weak: Too Broad

- Understand the importance of primary source documents in the teaching of history.

Weak: Still Too Broad

- Use primary source documents in history class.

Strong: Specific and Bite-Sized

- Teach students the S.P.R.I.T.E. (Social, Political, Religious, Intellectual, Technological, Economic) technique for interpreting a primary source document.

Student Culture

Weak: Too Broad

- Understand the characteristics of students who struggle to follow directions.

Weak: Still Too Broad

- Identify methods to help struggling students follow directions.

Strong: Specific and Bite-Sized

- Implement one of three techniques for redirecting a student who is struggling to follow directions.

Diversity

Weak: Too Broad

- Be aware of the diversity of our students and the experiences that they have had.

Weak: Still Too Broad

- Understand the current political and social challenges of our urban environment and how they affect our students.

Strong: Specific and Bite-Sized

- Redirect a noncompliant student with one of the three nonbiased strategies presented in the workshop.

The more often you do this exercise of narrowing your objective, the more proficient at it you will become. And with a specific objective, effective training becomes possible. The next question is, What is the most effective way for you to teach that objective?

HOW TO TEACH: LIVING THE LEARNING

The Impact of the "How"

Breaking Down Aja's Reading PD

As Aja's session gets started, participants move from resolving a failed case study to watching a video, writing down ideas, discussing, and sharing. What's striking is not what Aja is saying; it's what she's not saying. In fact, over the course of a 30-minute segment, she's spoken for less than five minutes. In this room, it's participants who are doing the talking—and the thinking.

 REWATCH Clip 17: Note how rarely Aja herself speaks when leading this session.

Objective in hand, Aja must design a lesson. As this moment in the video shows, Aja is deeply committed to having participants do the talking, thinking, and practicing. This reflects a simple but often overlooked truth: if you want to get good at a skill, you have to perform it yourself.

Core Idea

If you want to get good at a skill, you have to implement it yourself. Participants—<u>not</u> the presenter—need to do the heavy lifting in a workshop.

Tennis players don't practice by listening to speeches about ground strokes; they improve by hitting thousands of practice shots. Pilots don't watch PowerPoint presentations about flying; they spend hours in simulators. Teaching is no different: unless participants can truly "live the learning," their skills will not improve. Recognizing this, Aja breaks her training down into five key components that form what we call the Living the Learning cycle:

1. *Airtight activities.* Activities ensure participants will independently reach the key ideas.

2. *Sharing.* Participants discuss and formulate the conclusions reached in airtight activities.

3. *Framing.* The leader assigns formal language to the audience's conclusions.

4. *Application.* Time is allowed for participants to begin directly putting activities into practice.

5. *Reflection.* Time is set aside for participants to take notes and gather their thoughts.

To see each of these components in action, let's break down Aja's session on literacy instruction.

Airtight Activities

Airtight activities are the training wheels of PD sessions. If a new rider sits on a bike with training wheels and pushes the pedals, the bike will go straight. If PD participants put the cognitive work into an airtight activity, they will come to the right conclusions. Just as training wheels ensure a new biker cannot fall, good airtight activities are built so that participants cannot fall into flawed ways of thinking about the PD topic. The responsibility to learn—physical in the case of the bike and cognitive in the case of professional development—remains with the learner.

Airtight activities have one central premise: guide participants to the right conclusions with minimal facilitation from the presenter. Let's look at two examples: a teacher video and a role play. In the first example, Principal Nikki Bridges is delivering a session on how to teach a reading comprehension skill using guided practice (I-Do, We-Do, You-Do). She begins the session with a video of a teacher implementing an effective I-Do. There are some subtle but important actions she takes to set up this video correctly. Take a look.

WATCH Clip 20: Video footage helps Nikki Bridges lead her workshop on reading comprehension strategies.

Whenever educators watch video of actual teaching, we are quick to find the flaws—it's in our nature! When doing so, however, we lose sight of what was effective in that clip. When Nikki stated the question that she wanted the participants to answer while observing the clip, she was not only targeting their watching of the video: she was also guiding them to focus on the positive and not the negative. This simple act will greatly increase the learning for the participants. We learn best by watching successful practice, not by critiquing bad practice.

Nikki also kept this clip very short. Our attention spans have gradually declined as a society—note that we go only seven minutes between commercials on most television shows. Doug Lemov strengthened this vision when he chose only two- to three-minute teaching clips for his book *Teach Like a Champion*.[1] When he used longer clips, he found that he lost the audience's focused attention. The other advantage of Lemov's work is you now have access to a cache of highly effective teaching videos to use with your own teachers! The video clips of leaders used in this book adhere to the same philosophy.

> ### Core Idea
>
> Keep teaching videos short and have participants focus on the positive. Then they will be more likely to learn the skill you are presenting.

Another common type of airtight activity is a role play in which participants can watch and learn. In the following clip, I conduct a session on how to lead data analysis meetings. My objective with this role play is that leaders do not lecture teachers nor confront their belief systems during an analysis meeting (when they do, they'll lose). In this example, I role-play a leader who tries this approach and fails. See what happens.

WATCH Clip 21: By role-playing ineffective planning meetings, Paul evokes an emotional response and engages participants in his workshop.

What you will notice is that the role play is very short (less than a minute), and when I ask the participant in the role play how it felt to be the teacher being lectured, he says, "I'm angry." What is the advantage of such a role play when I could have just presented a PowerPoint slide telling participants not to lecture a teacher on their beliefs? By watching this two-minute role play, the audience of school leaders was able to have a visceral reaction. They didn't like how it looked when a leader lectured the teacher, and that emotional connection will make them far less likely to commit that error themselves.

What is common in both of these activities—the teaching video and the role play—are some key things that describe any airtight activity. Each activity has the clear big idea embedded within it, so participants can experience it and come to the right conclusions with minimal guidance from you. In each case, participants are told what to look for. Directions are clear and precise, and participants head straight to sharing and reflection without the facilitator telling them the answers.

These keys form the foundation for allowing participants to "live the learning." Gone is the classic PowerPoint lecture; in its place is participant-driven learning.

Airtight activities don't have to be long: you might have four or five in one session, or you might need only one. Once you have them, the next step is to determine what to do right after the activity finishes.

Sharing

If participants are going to do the learning themselves, they need time to process an airtight activity. Jumping right to large group is not very advisable, because then only a handful of people will raise their hands and participate—normally, the same extroverted few for the duration of the workshop. That reduces the number of participants who are doing the cognitive thinking. In nearly all of the video examples in the accompanying DVD, workshop presenters give participants a chance to write individually (see more on this in the section on reflection) or to share with a partner or small group before moving to

Keys to Airtight Activities

Overall Characteristics
- Aligned to PD objective
- Planned tightly with the objective embedded in the activity

Keys to Each Type of Activity
Video Clips

- Focus on the positive.
- Ask precise focus questions *before* showing it.
- Keep clips short.

Case Studies (Written)

- Embed every PD objective in a well-written case:
  - Type 1: Solving Problems—for participants with expertise
  - Type 2: Learn from Failure—to check for understanding and to set the stage for positive learning
  - Type 3: Success Story: build expertise by identifying the key levers to success

Role Plays/Simulations (Acted Out)

- Establish tight schedule and detailed procedures.
- Explicit guidelines for skill(s) participant will be practicing and observing during activity.
- Keep role plays short; include time for feedback.
- Use to elicit an emotional connection.

Movie Clips

- Connect explicitly to learning objective.
- Ask precise focus questions.
- Keep clips short.
- Use when you need to build buy-in.

---

large-group sharing. For example, in Aja's session on reading in-class transitions, teachers write down their reflections and then debrief the video in pairs or threes. For the final five minutes, there is a whole-group sharing. What this accomplishes is significant: every participant has a chance to engage in the content himself or herself. This is an obvious point that is made in the classroom, where small-group or partner discussions are so valued. Yet this step is often skipped with adults.

At times, no matter how airtight you have made your activities, you will discover that the participants are not identifying the key points you were expecting. In

Keys to Sharing

Large-Group Sharing
- Start from the end goal: Identify what you want participants to say.
- Volleyball, not Ping-Pong: Let multiple participants share without commenting on each of their answers.
- Use scaffolded questions that point to specific moments or data to guide them to the end goal.

Small-Group Sharing
- Have explicit protocol and precise roles.
- Group intentionally (preassign in large PD).
- Check pulse of group progress: Check for understanding and adjust times.

---

this case, effective presenters are ready with a series of scaffolded questions that keep participants doing the thinking. Take a look at how Julie Jackson does this in her session on implementing effective morning routines as part of a student culture workshop. The participants have just finished watching a video of students arriving at school and eating breakfast. After sharing with partners, they have begun large-group sharing. Julie realizes that they haven't noticed the systems the school has in place for students who arrive late. She has a choice: she can tell the participants what happened, or she can see whether she can still guide them to the right answer. Pay attention to the scaffolded questions she asks to guide the participants.

 WATCH Clip 22: Julie Jackson asks scaffolded questions to guide a large group toward previously overlooked observations about the airtight activity.

What Julie does here so effectively ensures that the participants uncover all the core learning from the activity. She could have just told them the answer, but then she would have deprived them of the opportunity to learn it more deeply.

Framing

When designed well, participants in a Living the Learning professional development session will generate almost all the right answers on their own. At this point, the leader simply has to *frame* the answers received in formal language. Framing is just that: putting a structure around participants' sharing so that everyone shares a common language about what was just discussed. Aja demonstrated this in the opening clip that we saw.

 REWATCH Clip 17: Aja's teaching of transitions.

If your activity has been well chosen and your questions were well designed, it is overwhelmingly likely that someone will produce the correct answer, an answer you can then reframe in the appropriate language. Once you have restated this key idea, it makes sense to clearly display it, such as on a PowerPoint slide. Doing so heightens the sense that the group has "discovered" the correct response and makes the ultimate message of the session clear.

Core Idea

Wait to frame until the end: let participants do the cognitive work. Limit the words: be succinct and precise.

Application

The fourth step to an effective Living the Learning workshop is to give teachers the time they need to practice what they've learned. This is the difference between an engaging afternoon and a sustained improvement in instruction. Most of the time, this practice will take one of two forms. For professional development focused around planning, such as writing more concise objectives, it will consist of modifying existing lesson plans or other written documents. For classroom techniques, such as using economical corrections to address student misconduct, practice will take the form of a role play. Leaders like Aja Settles and Julie Jackson do not end training by telling participants to simply "Go home and practice." Instead, they create a dedicated time during which participants can receive feedback on their techniques to improve at that moment.

> ## Core Idea
>
> Giving teachers time to apply their learning is the difference between an engaging afternoon and sustained improvement in instruction. Don't ask them to practice on their own; give them time to do it in the supportive setting of the workshop itself.

As an example, let's return to Aja's PD session. In the last 10 minutes of her workshop, participants take their existing routines for reading in-class transitions and rewrite them to incorporate the new techniques they learned during the workshop. Then they practice these transitions in mini–role plays with other teachers taking the roles of their students. All the while, Aja is circulating, giving tips here and there and being supportive.

On this point, it is important never to sacrifice application for the other components. Practice is essential to making sure that things are internalized. Consider the following application clip, taken from workshops on elementary reading led by Emily Hoefling Crouch.

WATCH Clip 23: Participants at Emily's workshop create "book intro-ductions" incorporating what they've learned; Emily offers individual feedback.

> ## Core Idea
>
> Make practice as directly connected to teachers' work as possible (lesson plans, teaching role play). Combine with follow-up activities post-workshop to guarantee effective implementation.

A Word On ... The Importance of Common Language

Creating a common language and vocabulary for key teaching and leadership practices is of fundamental importance in making the most of professional development. As an example, consider the practice of having students begin each class with a short written activity to get settled and set the tone for the day. If some teachers call this activity "a quick start," some call it "the worksheet at the start of class" and some call it "the morning wakeup," it is much harder to talk about the idea than if it is simply called a "do-now" by all staff members. As this brief example shows, if framing is not used correctly, there can be multiple understandings of a single topic. Moreover, we lose the ability to talk to each other effectively. Doug Lemov revealed this insight implicitly in his book *Teach Like a Champion*.[2] By naming 49 techniques for teaching and defining them precisely, he created a common language that everyone could use.

Reflection

Finally, in designing her lesson, Aja created frequent opportunities for teachers to reflect on what they had seen. The neurological research on the importance of quiet writing reflection time is noteworthy.[3] After watching the video, teachers were given one minute to silently record their first impressions. Later, before the application role play began, teachers were given four minutes to script out their role play. Leaders like Aja build in time for teachers to reflect on what they have learned. Reflection should happen throughout the workshop and should occur at strategic moments—between activities, after big insights, to break up longer session components.

Workshop leaders should use reflection time as a way to ensure the main objectives and conclusions of the workshop stick in participants' minds. Supplying a colorful sheet of paper is one way successful PD leaders ensure purposeful reflection. We have all had moments when we return to our notes and struggle to decipher words scribbled in margins and on the back of pages. By providing a sheet specifically for recording the biggest takeaways from a workshop, leaders make it more likely that participants will record all their ideas in one memorable place. These sheets can already carry the headings of the major sections of the workshop in order to help structure the participants' thoughts.

WATCH Clip 24: Emily ends her elementary reading workshop by letting participants create lesson plans based on what they've learned.

AVOIDING COMMON PITFALLS OF POOR PD

There is no doubt that to do Living the Learning well requires a great deal of planning. But to see why such work is surely worthwhile, consider the alternatives. How else might PD look?

Lecture: Sage on Stage

In its most basic form, professional development might take the form of an uninterrupted presentation or lecture. If Aja had presented her content like this, it might have focused on a long lecture with questions at the end. K–4 reading techniques would be introduced in this way. The trouble is that lectures don't stick. Extensive research and personal intuition say the same thing; when people are "talked at," they retain very little.[4]

Guided Practice (I Do, We Do, You Do)

Professional development is sometimes presented in the familiar guided practice format: "I do, we do, you do." In this set-up, a leader might start with a short PowerPoint introduction. When arriving at the slide with a sample assessment, he would begin by analyzing the difference among actual assessment questions, modeling how to analyze assessment questions to the audience. He then would invite the audience to analyze a subsequent assessment question. This is different than the lecture in that participants are doing something more than listening, but presenters are still doing the lion's share of the thinking and talking. As participants do not have a chance to identify the core skills on their own, it is less likely to stick.

Living the Learning offers the most effective approach to increasing student learning.

A Word On . . . Preparing Presentations

In keeping with the theme of this book, great professional development is about making every minute count. To get the most out of each session you lead:

Rehearse, rehearse, rehearse. Scripting and practicing the entire presentation will make it far more polished and effective. Even if it feels awkward presenting in front of a mirror or to a colleague, it will make the final performance much better.

Script for tough responses. Because Living the Learning is driven by audience participation, Living the Learning presenters need to be ready to deal with challenging audience responses, such as wrong answers during framing or confrontational reactions. Preparing scaffolded questions to guide your audience back to the topic can be invaluable at dealing with these situations. Although these will vary depending on the situation, remember that scripting in advance will help you keep your cool and remain confident even if the questions or responses are challenging.

Build time for movement. Building in more kinetic activities is a great way to keep engagement high. Movement can be built into presentations by having participants "share out" on bulletin boards, switching groups in the middle of the presentation, or building in frequent breaks.

Preplan transitions. Taking the time to script and plan for transitions between activities can make a big difference. For example, pre-positioning binder supplies rather than handing them out can save several minutes and will make the presentation feel much more dynamic.

HOW TO MAKE IT STICK: ACCOUNTABILITY

The Impact of Your Levers

How the Instructional Levers Hold Teachers Accountable

A week after her PD session, Aja conducts her weekly observation of Jacqueline, a kindergarten teacher on staff. As she does, she is watching to see how Jacqueline is implementing the PD. Jacqueline does not disappoint; as her students transition from fluency to comprehension during small-group reading, Jacqueline uses the techniques she just learned in the PD. Aja nods and writes down confirmation of implementation in her observation tracker. Jacqueline still struggles with one element of the technique—nonverbal signals—and Aja writes that down as her key action step for their next check-in.

Making Accountability One Step Easier

Additional Tips for Ensuring Teachers' Implementation

As I closely observed all of the leaders of this book, I noticed some additional strategies that they took to make it easier for them to monitor implementation. For example, North Star High School requires a reflection box at the top of the weekly lesson plans, where teachers briefly indicate exactly how they are implementing the PD, their six-week data-driven instruction (DDI) action plans, and their observation feedback. It only takes teachers a few moments to complete, and then a leader can quickly peruse the reflection box to make sure teachers integrate everything into their plans.

At other schools, teachers post their lesson plans on clipboards next to the door. Then a leader can arrive and observe with the lesson plan in hand, making it easier to see the arc of the lesson even when only observing for 15 minutes.

Other leaders added a row in their observation tracker to include the PD goal, so that they were reminded to look for it when they opened their observation tracker for the observation. This is especially helpful when you have differentiated PD and different teachers are implementing distinct PD skills.

The general principle remains constant: monitoring implementation changes PD from a theoretical, optional exercise to practical implementation.

The final key to professional development is to make sure it changes teacher practice. As we saw in the previous section, having participants practice during the PD session can go a long way toward making sure that changes are put into place. Yet on a broader level, leaders must create the systems needed to hold teachers accountable for putting PD into place.

The beauty of the instructional levers already presented in this book—data-driven instruction, observation and feedback, and planning—is that they are built-in drivers of accountability. You can look across all your observations for the week following the PD and see whether there is evidence of implementation. As Aja reaffirms, "My PD is only really successful if we can be in classrooms the next day, and a month, two months, four months from now and see the new skills at work. When that happens, and when we can make sure it happens, that's when we see real change."

Interim assessment results then let you see if these improved practices are contributing to improved student learning. And planning meetings allow you to

A Leader's Testimonial on Leading PD

Erica Woolway

As school leaders, we have all participated in countless professional development workshops. Some are painfully bad, some have a few good ideas that we can implement in our classrooms, and a distinct few actually change our practice forever. The workshop that introduced me to the Living the Learning framework in 2007 fell into this last category. I had never heard of Living the Learning before, but within the first two minutes of the session, I knew that something *different* was happening.

The difference was not so much in the workshop's content as in how the leader relayed that content. He began the workshop by showing a clip from the movie *October Sky*. That may not seem as innovative to 2011's YouTube-saturated society as it did four years ago. But what was effective wasn't just that the leader used the clip; it was that he set it up by asking a provocative question that got every person in the room to think deeply about the clip and how it related to our work. Later in the workshop, the facilitator wove the clip back into the key takeaways of his message, which really made them "stick."

What made the workshop so effective? It was planned down to the last minute. Every single PowerPoint slide had a yellow box on it, which contained a number indicating the amount of time it would take to present the slide. Timers beeped when time was up for each activity my fellow participants and I completed. The leader was presenting to an audience of about 60 school leaders for two hours. Combined, that's 120 hours—about two weeks' worth of collective work managing schools and teaching students. Time truly was of the essence, and this workshop intentionally maximized every minute of every individual's time.

Years later, as an adjunct literacy instructor at Teacher U [now Relay Graduate School of Education], I learned how to use the same Living the Learning framework that the leader I'd so admired had used to draft my own professional development sessions for adults. The Living the Learning template immediately made sense to me. This type of planning was akin to what I had done as a teacher: crafting detailed lesson plans that supported me as I led my students to achieve our objectives. I was embarrassed that I had never before thought to use a similar process when planning to lead professional development for adults. I also realized that the Living the Learning template could help me respond to some of the feedback I had previously received as a workshop leader, such as, "Erica, you have great ideas and really important things to tell us. You just need to speak with confidence." What my colleagues had perceived as a lack of confidence on my part had actually been the result of a lack of clear planning and preparation.

I used the Living the Learning template to change my entire approach to leading workshops. Instead of looking for engaging "hooks" or "ice breakers," I began developing "airtight activities" that would not just engage participants but would lead them to takeaways that were central to what I wanted them to learn.

Earlier in my career, I would have typed these takeaways into bullet points on a slide and laboriously (and nervously!) talked through them. People might have written them down out of respect, but not because they had learned something groundbreaking. If teachers in workshops mentioned my key points before I had introduced them, I worried that I was telling them something that they already knew—I was, after all, a young leader, often leading teachers more talented than I. Using the Living the Learning framework, by contrast, gave me the permission and the ability to spark insights for people. Then, I simply framed their learning with clear, concise language. Teachers remembered my workshops' conclusions better, because they were reaching those conclusions on their own.

What was most amazing about this shift in leading professional development was that it was not a drastic change in my practice. Often, all I had to do was take my original approach and flip it on its head. Many of my airtight activities were already part of my workshops; I just moved them to the beginning, so that they would guide participants to conclusions that matched my objectives. My framing now served not to present information, but to teach a common language that my participants could use to describe their takeaways.

Since I began using the Living the Learning template, I have had the incredible privilege of practicing several of my workshops in front of Paul Bambrick-Santoyo. Paul was specific and precise about the things I did well and identified several specific elements I needed to tweak: "Speak more slowly around your key points," for example, and "Change the airtight activity slightly to elicit a takeaway closer to your objective." While his feedback was method altering, the mere act of practicing over and over again also improved my workshops—and my confidence—immensely. So, what's the best way you can use your time when planning PD? Plan and practice, practice, practice.

I'm still practicing. In fact, I'm writing this on the plane back from training 70 teacher leaders from Houston Independent School District. There, once again, I found myself training teachers more talented than I; and now, thanks to the Living the Learning method, I know what to say to such teachers after they've participated in my workshops. They tell me how much they've learned from the workshop. And I tell them, "You didn't learn it from me—you learned it yourself."

---

support teachers in integrating the skills they learned during the PD into their weekly lesson plans.

In most schools where PD is less effective, the most significant place where it falls apart is in the lack of accountability. Thus I often say that PD is the weakest of the instructional levers. Yet when you Live the Learning and support PD via your other instructional levers, professional development changes from the weakest lever to a driving tool for the execution of excellence.

> ## Core Idea
>
> When PD is supported by the other instructional levers, it changes from the weakest lever in school improvement to a driving tool for the execution of excellence.

TURNAROUND: WHAT TO DO FIRST

The biggest challenge in most school settings is the lack of time: time for delivering high-quality PD. Many schools only have 40 minutes of time with their faculty on a weekly or biweekly basis. What do you do when you have such limited time?

The first thing, quite objectively and pragmatically, is to get DDI, feedback, and planning up and running before you worry about PD. PD only becomes effective when those are going well. Many a leader has devoted countless hours to PD, and without the other systems in place they did not see an increase in student learning. You can make dramatic improvements without many PD sessions.

Once you are ready to focus on PD, the most obvious strategy is creatively building in more PD time:

- Acquire a grant to offer PD stipends to be able to have teachers attend more PD sessions.

- Offer voluntary PD sessions that are so effective that many want to attend.

- Rebuild common planning blocks to include PD workshops.

The second strategy is to leverage your limited time as effectively as possible:

- Remove announcements from faculty meetings and put them in a weekly memo. Make the 40 minutes of the meeting purely PD.

- Pick the very highest leverage areas (see the section in this chapter on What to Teach).

- If you need to cut down, go through only one Living the Learning cycle—rather than three video clips on checking for understanding, just show one, frame it, and have teachers spend 15 minutes applying.

- Never sacrifice application, no matter how little time you have.

Leading Professional Development

One-Page Guide

Living the Learning Model: An Effective Approach for Leading Adult PD

AIRTIGHT ACTIVITIES: ALIGN TO OBJECTIVE, PLAN TIGHTLY, MAKE RELEVANT	
TEACHING VIDEO CLIPS • Focus on the positive • Ask precise focus questions before showing it • Keep clips short CASE STUDIES (written) Embed every PD objective in well-written case: • Type 1: Solving problems—for participants with expertise (Results Meeting) • Type 2: Learn from failure: To check for understanding and to set the stage for positive learning • Type 3: Success story: Build expertise by identifying the key drivers	MOVIE CLIPS • Explicitly connected to learning objective • Ask precise focus questions and keep clips short • Use when you need to build buy-in ROLE PLAYS/SIMULATIONS (acted out): • Tight schedule and detailed procedures • Set explicit guidelines for skill(s) participant will be practicing/observing during activity • Have as many people directly participating as possible • Keep role plays short: Include time for feedback • Use to elicit an emotional connection
SHARING	**REFLECTION, FRAMING, and APPLYING**
LARGE-GROUP SHARING • Start from the end goal: identify what you want participants to say • Volleyball, not Ping-Pong • Use scaffolded questions that point to specific moments or data to guide them to the end goal SMALL-GROUP SHARING • Have explicit protocol and precise roles • Group intentionally (preassign in large PD) • Check pulse of group progress: Check for understanding and adjust times	REFLECTION (solidify the learning) • Brief and written in one place FRAMING • Wait until the end: let participants do the cognitive work • Limit the words: Be succinct and precise APPLYING • Make it as directly connected to their work as possible (lesson plans, teaching role play) • Combine with follow-up activities post-workshop to guarantee effective implement

(continued)

- Design *airtight activities* that lead participants to the right conclusion with minimal redirecting by facilitator.
- Facilitate substantive *sharing* time that allows participants to draw the conclusion from the activity.
- *Frame* the participants' conclusions with the formal vocabulary of the associated principles so that participants share one common language.
- Provide ample opportunities for *reflection* and to *apply* the learning in simulated and real-world experiences.

Overall, *manage time well* and *inspire* by sharing a vision of success: we always want stories that show it can be done!

This list of strategies is only a starting point. The key trait of the leader in a turnaround setting is creativity: leaders are always willing to find creative ways around seemingly insurmountable obstacles.

CONCLUSION: BEYOND THE CONFERENCE ROOM

By teaching the right things, teaching them well, and implementing the leadership systems presented in previous chapters, leaders guarantee that PD sticks. We are now halfway to extraordinary results. Next up: the power of culture.

Table 4.4 Making It Work: Where It Fits in a Leader's Schedule

	Monday	Tuesday	Wednesday	Thursday	Friday
6:00am					
:30					
7:00am					
:30					
8:00am		Meet Wilson	Meet Bradley		
:30		Meet Vargas	Meet Frint		
9:00am	Observe Wilson, Vargas, Jenkins	Meet Jenkins			
:30					
10:00am			Observe Mitzia, Boykin, Devin		Observe Hoyt, Settles, Palma
:30					
11:00am					
:30					
12:00pm	Observe Henry, Bernales, Christian				Meet Bradley
:30		Meet Worrell			Meet Palma
1:00pm		Meet Christian			Meet Settles
:30		Meet Bernales	Meet Boykin		Meet Hoyt
2:00pm		Observe Bradley, Frint, Worrell	Meet Devin		
:30			Meet Mitzia		
3:00pm					
:30			Professional development session		
4:00pm					
:30					
5:00pm					
:30					

▢ Work Time ▢ School Culture ▢ Observations ▢ Meetings

Pulling the Lever
Action Planning Worksheet for Professional Development

Self-Assessment

* What percentage of the professional development you lead would you say is aligned with assessment data and meets the needs of your teachers? _____ percent
* What elements of the Living the Learning framework would most enhance your delivery of professional development?

_____

_____

_____

_____

_____

_____

Planning for Action

* What tools from this book will you use to improve professional development at your school? Check all that you will use (you can find all on the DVD):

  ☐ Leading Professional Development One-Pager

  ☐ Professional Development Rubric

  ☐ Videos of Effective PD

  ☐ PD materials for training leaders to lead PD effectively

* For what key topics do you want to use the Living the Learning framework to deliver upcoming professional development?

_____

_____

_____

_____

_____

_____

- What are your next steps for leading PD effectively?

Action	Date

Part 2

Culture

Chapter 5

Student Culture

One-on-All: Setting the Tone in the First Five Minutes

At Rochester Prep Elementary, Fridays mean a morning meeting. Principal Stacey Shells leads the student body in a 30-minute assembly centered on the school's core values: integrity, courage, and determination. Yet this is no mere "pep rally." Instead, for the bulk of the half-hour students are given an intense—and joyful—intellectual workout. Stacey starts with arithmetic.

"Ms. Shells went to the store with some coins. She had three quarters," ... the students gasp, "five dimes," ... a dramatic pause, ... "and four pennies. What was the total that Ms. Shells had?"

After hesitating a beat, Stacey calls on Tariq, a first grader:

"Tariq, show us all how strong you are!"

"Ms. Shells had $1.29."

In unison, the other kindergarten and first-grade students chant out, "*How do you know?*"

Unfazed, Tariq begins his explanation: "I know that each dime is 10 cents, and there were 5 dimes, so that is 50 cents. Three quarters is 75 cents, and the pennies are 4 more."

"That is a very precise explanation! Give Tariq the muscle man cheer!"

A hundred students flex their arms and chant "*Loo-king good.*" Tariq is beaming.

As the morning meeting ends, Ms. Miller, the music teacher, begins strumming her guitar. As the students quietly hum, the song begins: "This land is your land . . . ."

 WATCH Clip 25: Strong morning routines let Stacey Shells set the tone for the day and provide a model for teachers.

You can tell a lot about student culture just by how a school feels. Rochester Prep feels urgent—as if every second counts. In Ms. McKenzie's kindergarten, students seamlessly transition from desks to the carpet while singing a geography song. In Mr. Robinson's second grade, every student's hand is excitedly raised to answer history questions. In a thousand different ways, from morning meeting to math to reading to lunch, Rochester Prep students continually hear this message: nothing is as important—or as engaging—as learning. Learning is the means to developing a sharp mind and a strong character, and it opens doors to a brighter future.

> ## Core Idea
>
> In schools with strong cultures, students receive a continual message that nothing is as important—or as engaging—as learning.

The results? Striking. In Stacey's six years in Rochester, her leadership has produced phenomenal results in two different schools: at the middle school level (where she led her first school) and the elementary school (which she now leads). Each day, Stacey's students engage in the sorts of activities that had once been largely limited to affluent suburban schools: seventh graders critique the political symbolism of *Animal Farm*; second graders complete division problems. It is unsurprising, then, that in 2010 Rochester Prep Middle School not only had the highest results in their city in the seventh grade but also the highest in New York State. Figures 5.1 and 5.2 show Rochester Prep compared to some of the other schools in the district—including the average for New York students overall.

Given such staggering success, you might conclude that the school's remarkable energy relies on the innate, irreplicable charisma of its principal. Yet this is not the case. How do we know? Because as Stacey left her first school to lead the second, the culture she left behind has been sustained and replicated, even by very different leaders. How, then, did Rochester Prep become Rochester Prep? And how does it stay that way?

The answer lies in a single powerful idea: if you want a culture of excellence, you build it by repeated practice—performed both by children and by adults. Motivational speeches, school values, and vision statements miss the boat if they

Figure 5.1 True North Rochester Preparatory Charter School, Eighth-Grade English Language Arts (ELA)

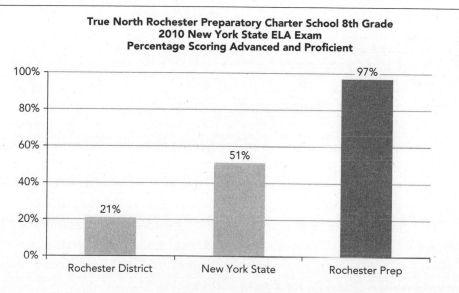

Figure 5.2   True North Rochester Preparatory Charter School, Eighth-Grade Math

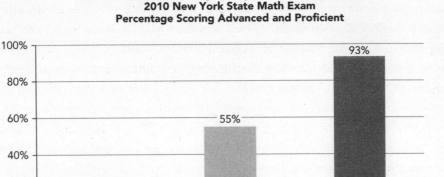

True North Rochester Preparatory Charter School 8th Grade
2010 New York State Math Exam
Percentage Scoring Advanced and Proficient

are not centered on practice that builds the right habits. As Aristotle famously said, "We are what we repeatedly do. Excellence, then, is not an act, but a habit."

Core Idea

Student culture is not formed by motivational speeches or statements of values. It is formed by repeated practice—using every minute of every day to build good habits.

Every moment our students practice the right things is a moment that builds habits of excellence, the framework for strong students and moral leaders. In contrast, in every moment in which we as adults allow our students to do less productive actions, we are unintentionally the authors of their bad habits.

This rings true for Stacey in her work as a leader of student culture. "My students learn to become moral and intellectual leaders from each action they take from the moment they come to school," she says. "We waste no time, because every second is a precious learning opportunity."

Of course, "make every second count" can seem like a vague policy. But consider the concrete consequences it carries: each minute spent away from instruction and character development is a lost opportunity. One particularly compelling example, used by Doug Lemov in *Teach Like a Champion*, involves passing papers across a room.[1] Doug begins from the assumption that a teacher might take 1 minute and 20 seconds to hand out papers individually. If you can reduce this to 20 seconds, you've made a bigger difference than you realize. Don't believe it? Let's do the math:

- Number of times a teacher might hand out or collect papers in a day: 20

- Amount of time this would take if teacher spent 1:20 minutes each: 27 minutes per day

- Amount of time this would take if teacher spends 20 seconds: 7 minutes per day

- Amount of time saved per day: 20 minutes

- Amount of time saved per week: 100 minutes (two classes)

- Amount of time saved per year (180 days): 60 hours

- If a teacher teaches 5 hours per day: 60 hours = **12 school days**

You've just added twelve days of school. Twelve days. That's 7 percent of a school year's worth of learning. The benefit of these 12 "found" days can be tremendous: it is enough time to teach a new unit on poetry, a comprehensive review of fractions, or a full discussion of World War II. Now multiply that by all of the systems and routines in a school day. When you add it all up, you have doubled or tripled the amount of learning that happens. No wonder Stacey's school has such success: their culture makes it seem like they have 360 days of school in one year! Yet it's not just about the amount of time saved. For students in an environment where every detail is focused on learning, the message is powerful: time is a precious commodity, and we should value every moment of it. That message's great worth revolutionizes the classroom—and reaches well beyond it. When nothing is as important or exciting as learning, leaders like Stacey pay exact attention to details to allow the "big stuff" to happen: poetry, dance, quadratic equations, and a mock trial of the Spanish explorers to evaluate whether they violated human rights.

If the instructional levers in Part 2 of this book help to make sure teachers are teaching as effectively as possible, student culture makes sure students build the habits of mind and heart that allow their learning to fly.

> ## Core Idea
>
> If the instructional levers help to make sure teachers are teaching as effectively as possible, student culture makes sure students build the habits of mind and heart that allow their learning to fly.

FROM VISION TO SYSTEM

Every school leader has some sort of vision of the student culture he or she wants to create: a mission or vision statement and/or an articulation of core values. What is noteworthy from looking at schools across the county, however, is that one realizes that having a vision or a set of school values was *not* a distinguishing factor of exceptional schools. What sets top leaders apart is that they transform their vision into meticulously built systems that operate across every single classroom.

Such consistency is rare. Many schools operate as sets of isolated, independent classrooms, connected only by proximity. Classroom culture varies wildly from room to room, and students can easily tell the "strict" teachers from the "doormats." Imagine this school from the perspective of a child: students have no consistency, and they do not learn that there are consistent professional expectations. The result is that children have to switch gears radically when they switch from class to class.

Building Consistency

Rochester Prep, and the ultra-successful schools like it, take a different approach. At Prep, procedures, expectations, and consequences are the same across each and every classroom. Stacey's students know that the rules in a veteran teacher's class are the same as those in the newest novice's, creating a tremendous support for faculty—and clarity for the students. Consistent expectations keep students happier because it is easier to know what to do. James Robinson, a second-grade teacher who sends his own students to Rochester Prep, explains it well: "With our consistent culture, everything becomes predictable and safe. The result is that kids are much happier and much more willing to open up and take risks." At their core, consistent schoolwide expectations create the most meaningful student freedom imaginable: the freedom to thrive.

Building Virtue

In this context, Stacey's schools are also able to build a strong moral formation in the application of a set of core values. Rochester Prep doesn't just use these as platitudes; they are living parts of the school's cultural systems. When students talk at inappropriate times, it is cited as a breach of responsibility (one of the school's core values). If a student helps a peer up stairs, it is praised as an example of responsibility. Even morning assemblies are geared toward teaching and presenting these values as essential. Time and time again, this commitment to moral values in student culture reasserts itself.

In building from these core values, top leaders make an important insight. Ultimately, a culture of making every moment count and of continually improving practice is not an end in itself; it matters insofar as it prepares students to be fully formed individuals. Stacey Shells and others know, however, that without a school that builds culture meticulously and relentlessly, students will not have what they need to fulfill this vision. Values without cultural systems can never be put into practice. Cultural systems without values are truly meaningless. Only together can they build the schools our students deserve.

Core Idea

Student culture systems are the foundation upon which students develop virtuous action.

Poke, Pull, Eat

A Simple System to Make Lunch Easier

Stacey's vision succeeds through its exacting attention to detail. The best example of this can be summed up in three words at Rochester Prep: "Poke, pull, eat." Several years ago, teachers at Prep were realizing that younger students were having trouble with their pre-wrapped lunches. Each day, kindergarten students would find themselves baffled by the thick plastic wrapping their food came in, with no idea of how to remove it, noisily complaining to peers. Seeing this, Stacey and her staff realized they would need to teach their students how to do this: poke the plastic with your fork twice, pull the plastic back with your fork, and then begin eating. Poke, pull, eat. With this simple procedure, Emily Swinson notes, the school "gained a sense of order during lunch, helped children know which plate was theirs, and avoided conflict." But consider the level of attention to detail that it took for Rochester Prep to notice this problem and find a solution. Stacey's team isn't running just to finish the race; they're working to win.

Making the System to Match the Vision

Ultimately, it takes the discipline of thinking through every small action of the school day to build schoolwide procedures that create truly transformative school cultures. Look at the following example:

 WATCH Clip 26: Rochester Prep kindergarteners learn the "poke, pull, eat" technique to deal with plastic-wrapped breakfasts.

"Poke, pull, eat" is not magic; it's just one of a thousand tiny actions that have built a fantastic school. Although every school leader's vision is different, a culture like the one Stacey helped to create at Rochester is impossible unless a few key systems have been thought through down to the meticulous level of detail of "Poke, pull, eat."

The key areas for developing consistent, schoolwide routines are:

Daily Routines
- Morning routines (arrival, breakfast, transition to class)

Dress Your Chair

Another Example of a Daily System

Another area of the day that can be very stressful is dismissal. For young elementary students, packing up their things can be very chaotic and difficult to manage. To address this challenge, North Star Elementary School came up with "Dress Your Chair." At the end of the last class period, kindergarten and first-grade students "dress their chairs." Just as they would dress dolls or themselves, the students dress their chairs—not with clothes, in this case, but with their backpacks. Then each student can put his or her books or pencil cases in the backpack one by one without the backpack falling over or everything ending up sprawled on the floor.

- Assemblies

- Lunch and recess

- Class-to-class transitions

- Dismissal and after school

In-Class Routines

- Opening procedures

- In-class transitions

- Strategies and consequences for students off task

- Bathroom signals

The only way to make this happen for every moment of the school day is to answer these four critical questions:

1. What is the leader doing?

2. What are the teachers doing?

3. What are the students doing?

4. What will happen immediately when a student doesn't comply?

Students learn from what we do, not what we say. Answering these questions, then, is how we decide what to teach them—and it's also the first step to

An Example of Setting the Vision

Planning the Transition from Breakfast to Morning Meeting

What is the *leader* doing?
- Leader signals the beginning of morning meeting.
- Leader stands at the entry to the meeting area and greets students, redirects off-task behavior, checks for uniform compliance, and reinforces smiling faces, heads up, and hands at sides.
- The performing arts teacher stands in the center of the circle, and once the leader has finished, the teacher signals students to sit (hands out, palms downturned).
- A student leader will signal the first song for circle (the core value of caring) using a sign and a verbal signal.

What are the *teachers* doing?
- Teachers signal students to stand by giving signal (palms up at waist level, raise both hands up to signal "rising").
- Teachers target students who need shirts tucked in, and so on, and pinpoint students who are having a rough start to their day and handle appropriately (words of encouragement, stand next to them, and so on).
- As students proceed into circle, teachers ensure students are walking with hands at side, spacing properly, and turning into the circle at the designated point.
- Teachers place themselves between students who need additional attention during the morning meeting.

What are the *students* doing?
- Students walk silently with hands at sides when signaled by their classroom teachers.
- Students smile, heads up, and follow the line of tape on the floor to stand in the appropriate spot in the circle.
- When students reach their stopping point in circle, they turn their bodies to face toward the circle and stay standing. When the signal is given, students sit with legs crossed and hands in their laps, looking at the leader.

What will happen immediately when a *student doesn't comply*?
- If a student is not walking silently or with hands at side, teachers use a nonverbal redirect and/or proximity.
- If a student enters the circle off task, the school leader or any teacher in school either redirects the student or sits the student next to him or her.
- For severe off-task behavior, student is removed from circle and is addressed by the teacher or the principal when meeting has concluded.

converting our visions for school culture into realities. Look at "An Example of Setting the Vision" on page 172 for simply the small moment it takes to transition from breakfast to morning meeting (a time when all students gather in a circle to sing songs and get motivated to start the day).

This is the level of detail that a vision needs to have. It is not enough to want an efficient transition to morning meeting—we need to articulate what we hope every child and adult is doing during that time.

It is one thing to have a written system; it is far more complicated to get everyone to implement it. Implementation is where you move from aspiration to mastery.

PRACTICE: MOVING FROM ASPIRATION TO MASTERY

For most marathon runners, preparing for a race follows a fairly simple course: doing practice runs of a prescribed length each week, getting enough sleep, eating right. Through these efforts, the runners get in shape, improve their form, and earn good times. For the elite marathoners, however, training looks very different. In the months before race day, elite marathoners plan *obsessively*: creating strategies for each hill, each turn, and each drink station. In the hours before the race, they don plastic bags to reflect sunlight, working to save single calories for competition. These runners aren't training to participate; they're preparing to win. And when the goal is victory, it's the details that separate contenders from weekend warriors.

Core Idea

When it comes to developing a great school culture, it's the details that separate contenders from weekend warriors.

How does this apply to school leadership? Imagine two school leaders: Ms. Smith and Ms. Jones. Smith and Jones both want to put strong school culture into place. To prepare, both lead professional development (PD) sessions for their staffs. Yet the similarities end there.

A Case Study

A Tale of Two Leaders Launching Student Culture

Leader 1: Ms. Smith

Ms. Smith begins her staff professional development with a presentation on the general principles of the culture she wants. The slideshow is elaborate, containing instructions on a variety of classroom and schoolwide norms. In pairs, Smith has her teachers read a recent article on the "achievement gap" in America before partner groups discuss how this work connects to the school's overall mission. After narrating what each procedure might look like, Smith leaves her teachers to determine how each procedure will be applied to their individual classrooms. During the two weeks that follow, leaders create templates of their student rules and make them available to the school leader for feedback and suggestions.

Leader 2: Ms. Jones

Ms. Jones, like Ms. Smith, kicks off her new culture with a full-staff training session. Yet instead of focusing on broad principles, Smith begins with video clips of master teachers, each clip showcasing an effective culture system. After each clip, teachers discuss what they have seen in small groups before sharing their findings with the whole session. From this input, Jones then presents a specific set of culture systems that every teacher in every classroom will commit to implementing. The next day, teachers role-play each system, with veteran instructional leaders offering advice to novices. But Jones isn't finished. Two days before school begins, the entire staff engages in a "dress rehearsal," a minute-by-minute walkthrough of the school's entire day, from morning breakfast to detention dismissal. Teachers finish the exercise by rehearsing their systems in pairs, offering critiques and suggestions as they refine their systems. Scarcely a detail seems to have been overlooked: teachers perform role plays of every aspect of their classroom routines—other teachers act as the students during this practice, or they practice simply by imagining the students' presence. For example, they stand in the hall outside their classrooms watching students enter, teaching students to sharpen pencils and how to put away books. By the time the real students finally arrive two days later, every teacher knows exactly where he or she is supposed to be and exactly what he or she is supposed to be doing at all times.

WATCH Clips 27 and 28: The week before classes begin, North Star Elementary teachers rehearse the entire first day to ensure a smooth start.

In the marathon that is building strong student culture, Ms. Smith is a weekend warrior. She has good ideas, works hard, and may make a positive impact. But she will not build an extraordinary school. What makes culture builders like Stacey Shells so exceptional is that they, like the elite marathon runners, train down to the smallest details. They set a meticulous vision and work relentlessly to achieve it. In short, leaders like Stacey Shells do not leave learning to chance.

Seeing Is Believing

Once Stacey identified the vision and built her systems, she made sure that professional development for teachers would make them stick. Stacey had her teachers carefully watch and take notes on video clips of effective cultural systems, such as transitions to the "reading carpet." After allowing teachers to share their findings, Stacey recorded their conclusions as the schoolwide rationale for particular systems.

The core point to remember is that seeing is believing. It is very difficult to make effective culture happen without being able to see that it works. This is why videos of real teachers getting real results are so important. As Stacey says, "Systems and routines can seem daunting or even unnecessary to some teachers. They need the video to help highlight the importance and to truly transfer the vision. You can describe it all day, but until they've seen it, they don't know the expectation, how to make it happen, or that there can be joy involved in something that seems so mundane." The good news is that people have captured very effective systems that can be used for teachers to follow: *Teach Like a Champion* features many clips of classroom routines. Alternatively, you could videotape the best teachers in your own building—or even yourself![2]

Practice, Practice, Practice

You can set up a beautiful vision for student culture, but if you don't practice, it will only last a week. As you have probably noticed, practice is a consistent theme across many of the levers. Student culture is no different. Stacey makes her staff practice the systems of culture from the opening professional development, but as seen in the opening vignette, that is only the beginning. The highly effective school leaders take it even further with full dress rehearsals of the entire day's procedures in the week before school starts. A piano player wouldn't dream of not rehearsing before a major recital; why should teaching be any different? The success of day 1—and each day after that—is founded on the successful practice of every aspect of the day. During these rehearsals, new teachers can get feedback from veteran teachers, and school leaders can identify and solve problems before a single student enters the building. Muhammad Ali was famous for saying that "the fight is won or lost far away from witnesses—behind the lines, in the gym and out there on the road, long before I danced under those lights." Before the "lights" come on for the school year, Stacey and her team are hard at work to guarantee their students' success.

 REWATCH Clips 27 and Clip 28: The week before classes begin, North Star Elementary teachers rehearse the entire first day to ensure a smooth start.

MAINTAIN AND MODEL: KEEPING CULTURE ON TRACK

As you've seen, Stacey Shells views "sweating the small stuff" as the key to culture. Yet once leaders like Stacey put their systems into place, they work relentlessly to maintain them. The task starts early: "When buses arrive I'm usually the person that gets people off the bus. I ask the bus driver how behavior was, to let kids know that our culture starts from before you enter the building." This sends a strong message to students: they are accountable for every moment of their day, from the time they board the bus until they return home. Indeed, at each major student culture moment—breakfast, lunch, dismissal—Stacey (or another school leader) is present, continually enforcing every school expectation. This is particularly true at the start of the year, when culture is first being set.

At these times, a leader's presence can transform student behavior and set a high expectation for the year.

Yet a less obvious benefit of Stacey's high visibility is that it allows her to lead her staff by example. Stacey knows that if she doesn't sweat the small stuff, she can't ask her teachers to do the same. The result, as one teacher noticed, is that Stacey is "constantly modeling, showing us how to interact with kids and with each other." When leaders like Stacey model the highest standards for culture expectations, her teachers do the same.

 WATCH Clip 29: Stacey Shells catches small details to maintain Rochester Prep's strong culture.

Locking It into Your Schedule

Strong culture doesn't stop in September. To keep cultural systems strong, Stacey is continually on the lookout for how expectations and procedures are in play. As in every other chapter, we've seen that these exceptional leaders don't just hope to do this sort of monitoring; they lock it into their schedules. Monitoring student culture is as important as any meeting or observation. This is why, in Chapters 1 to 3, our leaders avoided planning observation or meetings in time periods where the monitoring of culture is so important. In Table 5.1, we've now placed student culture (from 6:00 to 7:30) into the original schedule we've been following since the first chapter.

A couple of important points should be noted in this schedule. Student culture has the risk of being the "black hole" that sucks up all of a leader's time. Here the leader identifies the times when student culture issues are most pressing and when her presence makes the biggest impact. This allows the leader to be maximally effective, and it also keeps him or her from scheduling meetings when student culture issues are likely to arise. "Trying to have a teacher meeting at dismissal doesn't work," commented Stacey, "because you'll constantly be interrupted."

By having a schedule like this one, Stacey can monitor culture via schoolwide moments and via her observations.

Table 5.1   Making It Work: Where It Fits in a Leader's Schedule

	Monday	Tuesday	Wednesday	Thursday	Friday
6:00am					
:30	Greet Students				
7:00am	Morning assembly	Morning assembly	Morning assembly	Morning assembly	Morning assembly
:30					
8:00am		Meet Wilson	Meet Bradley		
:30		Meet Vargas	Meet Frint		
9:00am	Observe Wilson, Vargas, Jenkins	Meet Jenkins			
:30					
10:00am			Observe Mitzia, Boykin, Devin		Observe Hoyt, Settles, Palma
:30					
11:00am					
:30	Lunch	Lunch	Lunch	Lunch	Lunch
12:00pm	Observe Henry, Bernales, Christian				Meet Bradley
:30		Meet Worrell			Meet Palma
1:00pm		Meet Christan			Meet Settles
:30		Meet Bernales	Meet Boykin		Meet Hoyt
2:00pm		Observe Bradley, Frint, Worrell	Meet Devin		
:30			Meet Mitzia	Dismissal	
3:00pm					
:30					
4:00pm	Dismissal	Dismissal	Dismissal		Dismissal
:30					
5:00pm					
:30					

■ Work Time   ■ School Culture   ■ Observations   ■ Meetings

*a*NOTE: In this example, the principal has chosen to have an abbreviated day on Thursday in order to have time for a weekly staff meeting and/or professional development session (a concept we explore in detail in Chapter 6).

EVALUATING STUDENT CULTURE

Even with observations, however, leaders like Stacey realize they can be blind to gaps in their culture. Think of it as the wear and tear on your tires. On a day-to-day basis, the slight damage to the tires will be invisible to the untrained eye. Over time, though, even this slight warping adds up, to the point when, months down the line, a car may be markedly slower or brake more poorly than in did when the tires were new. Paradoxically, the more your culture is developed, the easier it can be to overlook creeping problems. Think of it this way: on a giant 18-wheel truck, if one tire blows out, the driver may not even notice since the ride appears to be smooth; only a trained mechanic could recognize that a blowout had, in fact, occurred. Similarly, in schools where culture is relatively strong, more systematic and nuanced analysis is needed to ensure that new problems are not developing. The key point here is that culture is seldom a night-or-day proposition; usually it's a shade of gray.

To ensure that her culture is not eroding from her original vision, Stacey and leaders like her create objective tools to assess their culture and create opportunities to produce feedback. There are two parts to this:

1. Create a tool to measure your culture.

2. Create systems to use it.

First, evaluating student culture depends on the creation of an effective rubric or benchmark. At Rochester Prep, Stacey has focused heavily on identifying and quantifying student behavior, such as "percentage of students on task," to help determine when culture is meeting expectations and when it is not. In Table 5.2 we include a small slice of the culture rubric to show how leaders can systematically monitor and repair their own school cultures.

A leader's second task is to establish times to evaluate culture in accordance with the rubric. For relatively quick checks of schoolwide culture, Stacey looks to a team of instructional leaders and veteran teachers to conduct "culture walkthroughs," using the rubric shown in Table 5.2. As an added benefit, including experienced teachers as part of the observation team goes a long way toward building greater investment in a school's systems and culture.

Table 5.2 Student Culture Rubric: A Sample Row from a Tool to Evaluate Your Culture

Student Culture Area	Advanced	Proficient	Working Toward	Needs Improvement
Student Joy and Engagement	Students seem to be joyful and excited to be in school. 90–100% of students are engaged in classroom activities. Older students internalize and model behavioral expectations without teacher supervision.	Most students seem to be joyful and excited to be in school. 80–90% of students are engaged in classroom activities. Older students internalize and model behavioral expectations with minimal teacher supervision.	While many students seem joyful, there are notable instances of student arguments and/or lack of joy. 70–80% of students are engaged in classroom activities. The older students have not internalized behavioral expectations.	Students generally seem disinterested in school. Fewer than 70% of students are engaged in classroom activities. The older students have not internalized behavioral expectations and are more resistant to those expectations than younger students.

Note: For a full student culture rubric, see DVD.

In the longer term, finding external observers, such as leaders at successful area schools, is also a key source of objective perspective. Of course, asking another leader to take a day out of her schedule could be a daunting request. Recognizing this, Stacey and other leaders have formed a sort of reciprocal "co-op," all members agreeing to visit and evaluate one another's schools. This means that on several days each quarter, Stacey is observing at other nearby campuses. Yet it also means that she has guaranteed quality insights into her own school. Outside observers can greatly improve the quality of culture-based feedback, because their insights are often far more detached and objective. "When leaders from other schools evaluate Rochester Prep, it really takes down the walls," Stacey explains, "allowing us to see our own culture in a whole new light."

Living the "Rochester Prep Way": Two Parents' Testimonials on Student Culture

Robin Gulley and Jessica Rosario

We are two mothers, Robin Gulley and Jessica Rosario, who each enrolled a son in Rochester Prep Middle School's founding fifth-grade class in 2006. Five years later, each of our sons is a successful tenth grader planning to go to college, and our younger children are proud members of Rochester Prep Elementary School's founding class. We'd like to share with you what's so special about Rochester Prep—what made us so certain that sending our children to a brand-new school was a decision worth repeating.

Robin's Story

I first met Stacey Shells, the principal of Rochester Prep, at a festival during the summer of 2006. She was promoting her new school, and I walked up to her because I was looking for a more extensive education for my son Damion.

"Send your son to my school," Stacey told me, "and I'll make it worth your while."

Stacey kept her promise. Damion is talking about college now, and Rochester Prep is what got him on that level. The people at this school care so much about their students. Teachers work with the kids individually and take extra time to help kids who are struggling with their material. I really think that it is good for students to know their teachers are right there with them. They climb up the ladder that way.

Rochester Prep is a very structured school, which is also good for the kids. When you look at their test scores, you see right away how much they learn in this environment. The more time you spend working in school, the more you learn—and the more you succeed. I wanted to be at a school where you could be worried not about a lack of rigor but too much. Damion loved it, and his younger sister Heaven loves it now. They talk all day about Ms. Shells and Rochester Prep. I even hear them teaching their neighborhood friends the chants they learn at school, like, "Story! Story! S-T-O-R-Y!"

Damion loves Rochester Prep so much that he got a summer job there, reading with younger kids and talking with them about going further with education. His school has taught him to love learning, and it's also taught him to give back. I'm so grateful to Stacey and the rest of the teachers for showing my children the value both of school and of community. Stacey's been a great leader for our kids since that festival in 2006, but she's not just a principal: she's our friend.

Jessica's Story

My eldest son, Xavier, had been having some trouble at his old school, so I was a little worried about how he would do at Rochester Prep Middle School. A couple of weeks into the school year, I nervously asked Xavier's new teachers if they were having any difficulty with him.

(continued)

"What do you mean?" they asked. "No, we haven't had any problems with him. He's a really smart kid!"

Sure enough, Xavier was learning, and fast—just like his classmates. The kids in Rochester Prep's founding elementary school class are already the same way. My younger son, Jazario, is in that class. It's a first-grade class, but a lot of what they do is more like second-grade work. That's because the teachers at Rochester Prep want their students to accomplish great things in life. They look out for your kids.

The high test scores students get here show that Rochester Prep is a good school, but what really proves to me how much my kids' teachers care about their students is the way they treat them. Every time I walk into the building, I see teachers talking to students with a combination of kindness, familiarity, and discipline that almost makes the teachers seem like parents. It's not just one teacher that does this—it's every one of them. They really show that love and that care to each and every student.

My kids, too, know they're loved at their school. I thought at first that Rochester Prep might be too strict for them, but they're always excited about waking up and going to school there every morning. I once asked Xavier if he wanted to go to a different school, just to make sure, and he said, "No, Mommy, I want to stay here!"

Stacey has taught both of my sons so much. I know she'll teach my two-year-old daughter, too, in a few more years. My advice to anyone who wants to build a school where students learn and feel loved would be to call Stacey. She'll tell you how she did it. She'll probably even show up at your school to help you in person.

TURNAROUND: FIXING A BROKEN CULTURE

Sometimes, a school culture faces more serious problems. If normal wear and tear in culture can reduce performance, sometimes—when the culture becomes seriously worn down in spots—a school experiences a "blow-out": a full collapse. Even without such a collapse, some schools were just never in good shape to begin with. Just as a blown-out tire is very difficult to repair, a culture that has deteriorated to the point where there is a serious breach will face daunting challenges. It is for this reason that leaders like Stacey place so much weight on getting it right the first time.

If culture has been seriously damaged, or if you have come into a new situation where culture is already "blown out," you have to make a plan to reset the culture. Given her success as a culture leader, Stacey has been called on many times to support school leaders in turning around a broken culture. A number of these schools ended up being successful in rebuilding their student cultures. Stacey's experiences with them can reveal the difference between desire to change and results.

Facing the Brutal Facts

In *Good to Great*, management guru Jim Collins famously says that we must face the "brutal facts" of our situation before we can improve it.[3] What might these look like? In many schools, these could include:

- Mass student apathy
- Students violent or off task
- Students not engaged

The first key step to resetting a seriously damaged culture comes in carefully assessing the "brutal facts." Stacey describes one of the schools she supported on her first visit:

> It was an environment no one would want for their child. In more than half the classrooms, we couldn't find more than one or two students on task. Children were running around, screaming, kicking, hitting, getting up, walking away from adults. No one was paying attention to the teacher. I watched as a six-year-old child blatantly defied a teacher and walked away right in front of the principal. The principal didn't do anything because she considered discipline the job of her assistant principal. ("I am the instructional leader," she said. "He manages the discipline.") In short, a catastrophe.

Yet while knowing the scope of the problem is doubtless necessary, it is only the first step to turning around a culture.

Model, Intervene, Wean

Stacey followed a six-step process to turning around the culture with the principal:

1. *Set an agreement for "all hands on deck."* A root problem in most schools with failed cultures is a lack of support from one staff member to another. To start, the leadership team of the school has to make a commitment to address this equally. If an assistant principal walks down the hall and ignores the culture

issues, it sends a message to the students that school culture is dependent on the individual. The leadership team needs to commit to everyone taking the same actions if they ever want the teachers to do the same. Note, too, that all hands on deck means that people are paying close attention to culture at critical times of the day and have key look-fors to ground the work in a common set of things they are looking at.

2. *Start with the staff who are most invested in change.* It is next to impossible to address the issues going on in every classroom at once. Stacey sat down with the school leader and went staff member by staff member. They identified the faculty members who would be most invested in making a change, and that's where they devoted their energy in the first days. They sat down with those teachers and talked through routines and procedures they would reset in the classroom.

3. *Train invested staff by modeling, intervening, and weaning.* Stacey and the principal then went into the classrooms of those teachers and took over the classes for a moment to model the resetting of classroom procedures. "We just had students do certain routines over and over again until they got it right, while building in lots of challenges to keep the students motivated." As soon as the students were starting to turn the corner, the teacher would join Stacey in leading the class. By the end of a few days, the teacher was leading the students independently, and Stacey and the principal were only observing. "This was simply classic I-Do, We-Do, You-Do training," Stacey recollected. During this entire time period, they videotaped the transformation: Stacey modeling, and then the teacher leading. Given a leader's incredibly busy schedule, this may seem very challenging to put into place. However, it is worth the effort.

4. *Deliver professional development for the rest of the staff.* Now the principal was ready to launch these changes schoolwide with the rest of her staff. Stacey worked with her to design the PD session. At the heart of it was Living the Learning (see Chapter 4 on professional development): they watched the video of the transformation of their peers' classrooms. Then they practiced and role played to prepare to make those same changes happen in their classrooms. "Watching video of their peers was key. We could have shown video from *Teach Like a Champion* or another school, but then they would have said it doesn't apply or won't work here. Belief begins when you see it happening right next to you."

A Word On . . . Buy-In to a Culture Change

Building a strong culture is hard work, especially if you are changing a broken one. One of the most challenging issues is dealing with the backlash that can occur with a significant change in school practices. Should you take it slowly, one thing at a time? Leaders who have consistently succeeded at turnaround say "No."

Jarvis Sanford and Brian Sims are managing directors for the Academy of Urban School Leadership in Chicago, one of the most successful organizations in the country at urban school turnaround. They have successfully turned around the culture in dozens of public elementary and high schools. What are their lessons learned on this issue?

"When a culture is dysfunctional, you need a marked change, not gradual release," commented Sims. Sanford concurred: getting elementary students to line up and enter the school building quietly on day 1 of school cannot be done halfway. "If you don't start to change habits completely, you won't be successful later on." This is the number one error they see in leaders who don't make turnaround stick. "They remain content with the students acting 'better' than before, but because they didn't push for 100 percent compliance, it slowly unraveled later."

There is a consequence to this approach: leaders will get tons of challenging pushback from students, parents, and even some staff members. Weathering this storm, however, is what will make October far more successful. "Leaders and staff have to prepare themselves for the challenge of the initial shift. If they stay the course, the rest of the year will be significantly better," remarked Sims.

---

5. *Put aside instruction for one or two days and reset.* Teachers spent the next two days of class retraining all of the routines and procedures established in the PD session. Most importantly, the principal spent all day in their classrooms, observing and providing support wherever necessary. Note that in some cases this is essential, even though it is not a decision to be taken lightly.

6. *Evaluate your progress.* The power of a school culture rubric is the ability to have a more objective measure of whether the student culture is improving. The principal shares the results with the staff so that everyone is participating in the process. One month after the beginning of the turnaround, it can be helpful to have an external assessor to continue to support the growth process.

Staying the Course

Before the principal began the turnaround process, Stacey and her peers evaluated her student culture as 7 percent proficient on the rubric. By the end of the semester, the school had jumped dramatically to 70 percent. Still room to grow? By all means. But the process of self-improvement had begun. As Stacey notes, "Unless we make progress a priority, culture will not change."

CONCLUSION: SMALL DETAILS, BIG RESULTS

Stacey Shells is an exceptional leader, but she's also replicable. She has successfully transferred her implementation of school culture across multiple campuses and from situations that were both start-up and turnaround. Like the other leaders highlighted in this book, she turns dreams into reality, and it's how she spends her time that makes the difference.

Four Keys to Student Culture

1. *Establish a vision.* What do you want students and adults doing in school?
2. *Turn vision into minute-by-minute systems.* Build the minute-by-minute routines that will make the vision a reality.
3. *Practice.* Give multiple opportunities to practice and rehearse before stepping into the classroom.
4. *Monitor and maintain.* Evaluate your progress with a measurable tool.

Table 5.1   Making It Work: Where It Fits in a Leader's Schedule

	Monday	Tuesday	Wednesday	Thursday	Friday
6:00am					
:30	Greet Students				
7:00am	Morning assembly	Morning assembly	Morning assembly	Morning assembly	Morning assembly
:30					
8:00am		Meet Wilson	Meet Bradley		
:30		Meet Vargas	Meet Frint		
9:00am	Observe Wilson, Vargas, Jenkins	Meet Jenkins			
:30					
10:00am			Observe Mitzia, Boykin, Devin		Observe Hoyt, Settles, Palma
:30					
11:00am					
:30	Lunch	Lunch	Lunch	Lunch	Lunch
12:00pm	Observe Henry, Bernales, Christian				Meet Bradley
:30		Meet Worrell			Meet Palma
1:00pm		Meet Christan			Meet Settles
:30		Meet Bernales	Meet Boykin		Meet Hoyt
2:00pm		Observe Bradley, Frint, Worrell	Meet Devin		
:30			Meet Mitzia	Dismissal	
3:00pm					
:30					
4:00pm	Dismissal	Dismissal	Dismissal		Dismissal
:30					
5:00pm					
:30					

☐ Work Time   ☐ School Culture   ☐ Observations   ■ Meetings

[a]NOTE: In this example, the principal has chosen to have an abbreviated day on Thursday in order to have time for a weekly staff meeting and/or professional development session (a concept we explore in detail in Chapter 6).

Pulling the Lever
Action Planning Worksheet for Student Culture

Self-Assessment

- Look at the student culture rubric (located on the DVD). Select the sections you think are valuable for evaluating your school. For those that you selected, on what percentage of them is your school proficient? _____ percent
- What items on the student culture rubric are your biggest areas for improvement?

_____

_____

_____

_____

_____

_____

Planning for Action

- What tools from this book will you use to lead student culture at your school? Check all that you will use (you can find all on the DVD):

☐ Student Culture Rubric

☐ Student Culture Planning Template

☐ Videos of Effective PD

☐ PD Materials for leading student culture

- What are your next steps for improving your student culture?

Action	Date

Chapter 6

Staff Culture

Brett Peiser

One-on-One: A Teacher's Perspective

Neal Teague is a stellar teacher. For years, his history class has been joyful, rigorous, and focused. He also works tremendously hard. Walking through his classroom, surrounded by exemplary student work and detailed activities, one might think that Neal has found his true calling—that he was simply "born to teach."

Talk to Neal, however, and a different story comes out. "Honestly, teaching is incredibly demanding work. When I first started, I can't tell you how often I wondered whether it was all worth it." Ask him why he stayed, though, and a giant grin crosses his face. "This culture, this staff, this school ... I wouldn't want to work anywhere else in the world. Even though things were tough, being part of a team like this is what keeps me going."

As founding principal of Williamsburg Collegiate Charter School—the flagship school of Uncommon Schools' New York City region—Julie Kennedy has created one of New York's most successful middle schools. Despite coming from significantly disadvantaged backgrounds, Julie's 300 students have become well known for their place among the top performing in the city, leading Williamsburg Collegiate to be the number one ranked school in all of New York City on the NYC Department of Education (DOE) Progress Reports since the DOE began issuing reports in 2006. What made this success possible? Ask Julie, and she'll cite the hard work of dedicated, driven, and experienced teachers like Neal as a great part of the answer. Recognizing the value of her teachers has motivated Julie to spend a tremendous amount of time building a workplace where teachers can do their best work—and do it for a long time. "Invested, happy teachers are force multipliers," Julie Kennedy explains. "When people want to do this work, anything is possible."

Although a strong staff culture is important in any organization, it is particularly crucial to a great school. Closing the achievement gap is a demanding, long-term marathon, not a short-term sprint. But doing this work does not mean that your happiness or your teachers' happiness needs to be jettisoned as a result. It also does not mean that you need to sacrifice your school's core operating principles, or that you can't hold teachers accountable because you'd prefer to avoid conflict with them. In fact, it means the opposite. When leaders create a vibrant and joyful culture, teachers are *more* willing to be held accountable and *more* willing to do the hard work that makes a school work because there is a level of respect, trust, and appreciation for the work that they do. Even if building culture seems to be one of the "softer skills" for a school leader to master, it is one through which leaders can make a profound impact on how well their students can learn.

Of course, many school leaders claim to focus on building a strong staff culture. What makes Julie Kennedy's commitment so special—and so effective—is the concrete actions she takes to ensure that her staff are fully invested and that kids come first. As important, these actions are consistent: Julie works throughout the year to ensure that a strong staff community is not a one-time exercise but rather a habit of excellence. The results are transformational: new teachers improve faster, returning staff work smarter, and veteran teachers stay longer. "It may be obvious to say, but when people are happy at what they are doing, they will be more likely to do amazing work with our students," Julie says. Business writers

Gretchen Spreitzer and Christine Porath agree. As they cited in the *Harvard Business Review*, happy, or thriving, employees exhibit:

- 16 percent better overall performance
- 125 percent less burnout
- 32 percent greater commitment to the organization
- 46 percent greater satisfaction with their jobs
- Lower rates of absenteeism[1]

The good news is that "one's general sense of well-being is surprisingly malleable. The habits you cultivate, the way you interact with coworkers, how you think about stress—all these can be managed to increase your happiness and your chances of success."[2]

On the surface, building a great staff culture may seem incredibly complicated—and incredibly personal. In short, it may seem "unlearnable." Fortunately, while there is no one system for creating a joyful school, there are key principles that can make any staff community stronger. Leaders like Julie drive teachers to do their best by focusing on several key areas. Each, by itself, is small. Together, however, they build a community that keeps teachers like Neal coming back—and keeps students learning. Most important, each of these steps relies not on some intangible, irreplicable charisma but on clearly identifiable actions and choices. Through careful and consistent practice, these actions become the habits that build a strong staff community.

Core Idea

Great staff cultures don't come from irreplicable charisma; they come from the careful development of habits that build a strong staff community.

FIVE STRATEGIES FOR A SUCCESSFUL STAFF CULTURE

Julie Kennedy created a dynamic school culture by focusing on five key areas. Each of these areas centers on a set of concrete, observable actions. Building a great staff culture is not about being a born "inspiration"; it's about making purposeful choices that will enable you to realize the staff culture you want and need. The five most important places to focus are

1. *Set the vision.* Wisely design a clear and palpable vision for the work environment in your school.

2. *Get the right people on the bus.* Without great people, little else matters. Ensure your vision helps drive your hiring.

3. *Put a stake in the ground.* Reflect your commitment to developing a strong staff culture by prioritizing it from the first interactions of the year.

4. *Keep your ear to the rail.* Look and listen for negative culture warning signs that are coming down the tracks.

5. *Lather, rinse, repeat.* Staff culture is fragile. If you're not intentional about building, maintaining, or communicating your staff culture, someone else will define it for you.

Set the Vision

To build a great staff culture, leaders like Julie must start from some very fundamental questions: What is my personality? What are my values? What can I genuinely implement and create at my school? What will feel artificial or disingenuous? It is at this initial stage that too many leaders fall into the trap of trying to be someone they aren't. Great staff culture builders draw on different strengths: fiery oratory, quirky senses of humor, quiet and steady consistency, or on any number of other qualities. Can a leader who is more comfortable discussing English literature with a colleague than enlisting her staff to sign up for an adult kickball league create a strong staff culture? Absolutely! The first step is just knowing and owning who you are as a leader and what you do (and do not) feel comfortable with.

Beyond honest self-reflection, the next key step is setting a clear and concise vision for your school. When leaders fail to create this vision for themselves, they are trapped in the pit of trying to analyze why their staff culture is "bad" or "good" without knowing exactly what that means for their school. Realizing this, leaders like Julie Kennedy begin from a core question:

• *What is the staff culture you want to build?*

A Word On ... Setting the Vision

In understanding (and accepting) the role their personalities play in supporting their visions, school leaders can (and should) draw on others to help them. In her first year at Williamsburg Collegiate, Julie Kennedy worried about her ability to prioritize the "fun" with all of the other urgent demands on a new principal's time and energy. She planned for this by appointing a "director of fun" on the staff and tasking her with doing whatever was necessary to create a workplace that teachers looked forward to coming to each day. Julie prioritized meeting with this staff member regularly to ensure that this priority stayed alive even in the most stressful moments of the first year. If leading the staff step dance or holiday party is not your strong suit, letting a teacher on staff take the lead can greatly build investment and ensure a richer community.

Or, as Julie puts it, "When teachers are out with friends or family, what do you want them to say about your school? How do you want them to feel? How would you want teachers to talk about school culture when they're not in school? How would staff events feel? How, specifically, would teachers respond to disagreements with each other? With me?" In other words, your vision should be able to create a concrete picture in people's heads: it's palpable.

Core Idea

The core questions for setting a vision for staff culture are, What do you want teachers to say about their school? How do you want them to feel?

Leaders need to be as strategic about building culture as they are about building curriculum or instruction. To do this, you might consider using the planning template in Table 6.1 to clearly articulate the vision for your school culture: writing out how you want your staff to describe your staff culture, how you will measure whether you've achieved your vision, and what you need to do to get there.

Based on this process, Julie built a staff culture around three core ideas: she wants her staff to feel like they are (1) on a team; (2) supported by and

Table 6.1 Plan Strategically to Build Your Culture: Template for Creating a Vision for Staff Culture

Your Ideal Staff Culture	Measures	Action Steps	
Ideally, how do you want your staff to describe the culture at your school? List one to three sentences that describe what you would hope they would say.	How will you know whether you are meeting these staff culture goals, that staff is indeed describing your school culture in your ideal ways? What will it look like? How will you measure it if you can?	For each ideal staff culture goal or sentence, what are the five to ten actions you will take during the year to accomplish each goal and help foster the culture you described?	When will each happen?
1			
2			
3			

supporting their colleagues to improve student achievement; and (3) having fun while getting results. As important, she had considered everything from how staff would communicate with each other during summer training to winter holiday gifts, thinking as deeply and specifically as possible about the community she wanted to create.

Get the Right People on the Bus

In the long run, the most effective step you can take in ensuring a positive culture is to make sure that the teachers you hire are, to the greatest extent possible, the right fit for your school—or, as business theorist James Collins noted in *Good to Great*, making sure "the right people are on the bus."[3] Although this is important to any field, in education, which hinges so heavily on intense interpersonal interaction, it is essential.

Although there are many paths to an effective school culture, a few are non-negotiable if leaders are to build the sort of success that Julie has enjoyed. What are these?

Mission Alignment

The core vision you established for your school is one that prospective teachers must understand and embrace as their own. At Williamsburg Collegiate, this means committing to work in a challenging environment while maintaining a fierce focus on college preparatory rigor. To ensure candidates are aligned with this vision, Julie asks probing questions about why candidates are interested in teaching and, in particular, why they want to teach in an urban school.

Openness to Feedback

At Williamsburg Collegiate, which uses the data systems outlined in Chapter 1, and the feedback, observation, and planning systems described in Chapters 2 and 3, feedback is a fact of life. For Julie Kennedy, the ability to accept such feedback openly and sincerely, and to act on it conscientiously, is non-negotiable. Julie always looks for a chance to see the teacher in action, in a sample lesson, before hiring. Knowing that the individuals she is adding to her team are not trained in the team's practices nor accustomed to the level of feedback she gives, Julie focuses less on the skill of the teacher in the classroom at that specific moment and more on his or her enthusiasm to grow. Sample lesson feedback gives her a sense of a teacher's willingness to join her professional learning environment. "It's important to make the distinction between candidates who eagerly take the feedback versus those who may seem uninterested or even defensive," Julie explains. Rigorous follow-up questions are critical as well. For example, there's a big difference between asking, "Are you okay with getting feedback?" and "What kind of feedback do you *not* like?" or "Are you okay with a structured academic environment?" and "At our middle schools, students line up before entering class, students don't use the bathroom during class, and they always raise their hands to participate in class. Why does this structure appeal to you?" These sorts of questions can help separate candidates who "Yes" you from the reflective teachers your school will need to make each of the other core levers work.

Fit on the Team

Beyond the two points mentioned, it is important to determine whether an applicant is a good fit for your school. With your staff culture vision in mind, ask questions, develop scenarios, or create role-play opportunities to determine whether he or she will improve your staff culture. "Candidates are often so practiced and rehearsed during interviews that it can be difficult to discern their real personality," Julie notes, "so I prefer to focus in on informal opportunities that reveal much more about who they are." For example, in looking to hire individuals who share a team mentality, Julie may have the candidate interview with several other teachers during his or her visit to the school. She does this to look for individuals who bring their "interview A-game" to every interaction, because that seems to reveal their respect for their potential future colleagues. Because she values positivity, enthusiasm, and optimism, Julie Kennedy zeroes in on those traits in her interactions—both formal and informal—with candidates.

Getting the right people on the bus certainly isn't easy. As former chief executive officer of General Electric Jack Welch and former *Harvard Business Review* editor Suzy Welch write in their book *Winning*, "Hiring good people is hard. Hiring great people is brutally hard. And yet nothing matters more in winning than getting the right people on the field. All the clever strategies and advanced technologies in the world are nowhere near as effective without great people to put them to work."[4] The upshot, for leaders like Julie, is that time invested in very careful recruitment and selection will pay enormous dividends in building a strong culture, while time "saved" by neglecting these concerns is penny-wise, pound-foolish.

Core Idea

Let your vision drive your hiring.

Put a Stake in the Ground

As we've seen in data-driven instruction, feedback, planning, and student culture, our priorities are defined by how we spend our time and how we ask staff to spend theirs. To create a powerful school culture, great leaders "put a stake in the ground" and mark out the time and space that they will claim for building a strong staff community. Most importantly, they do so early, building a strong first impression, both for new hires and for returning veterans. The first interactions of the new year—which can even be the communication you have post-hire but pre-start—are vital to ensuring that the message of staff culture resonates—particularly in the case of a turnaround culture or one in need of significant repair. Starting strong means taking the opportunity to prioritize two key times: the first interactions that new teachers have with the school, and the first weeks of the school year.

1. The Interview and Hiring Process

Starting strong means being purposeful about how your culture feels to candidates who come to visit your school. Teachers carry their first impressions of a school along with them into their first days and weeks of teaching (and sometimes longer). In fact, their first impression during their first visit might even be the primary factor that prompts them to choose your school over another. With your vision for school culture in mind, think through the experience that candidates have as they interview, and ensure that the two are aligned. Details to consider as you do this work:

- Who will greet the candidate when he or she arrives?

- What kind of introductory tour will you give the candidate? Who will give it?

- Whose classes will you take the candidate to observe?

- What questions will you ask to help convey your workplace culture and determine whether the candidate is a fit?

- Who else will you invite to meet with the candidate after the sample lesson?

- How will you follow up with the candidate after the lesson?

In the event that a candidate is hired, setting down the culture early will pay off in a big way.

2. The First Weeks of the Year

According to Julie Kennedy, "Ninety percent of a school year is determined in the first few weeks of school." At some schools, such as Williamsburg Collegiate, these first weeks take place during summer training—a time when teachers can work without students in the building, which creates a distinct opportunity to instill staff culture. During these weeks, training in instructional best practices and school systems plays a big role, but Julie also makes sure to build in daily time for creating and training staff community. The activities she devotes to this task may be small, like starting afternoon sessions with ice breakers, sharing a school-bought lunch together, or wrapping up the day with team-building activities. Or, they may be large, like a weekly chunk of time spent defining team work, discussing the difference between dialogue and debate, and building team communication skills. Julie also sets aside several hours during one day to get staff out of the school for a team-building activity—a citywide scavenger hunt, cooking class, Go Kart racing—that is disguised as a fun outing. Small, large, or one-time, it is essential to think back to your vision for staff culture and be purposeful in how you plan and frame such activities.

Julie also devotes summer training time to discussing how staff will interact with one another in formal and informal settings, something often overlooked as seemingly more critical topics—the school's mission, human resource logistics, and so on—get prioritized. "I use seating charts for faculty meetings," Julie Kennedy explained, "ensuring that for partner discussion activities, new staff talk with veterans and teachers talk across departments." Seating teachers strategically in this way carries important benefits: it allows new teachers to feel welcome and helps create a unified culture. Moreover, orientation can be a time for leaders to see how newer teachers are fitting in to the culture. "If a teacher isn't participating or interacting with colleagues, there's a fair chance that an issue might be there," Julie observes. "It's something to look out for."

Lauren Vance, former principal at Kings Collegiate Charter School and one of Julie's New York City peers, spent time during summer orientation discussing the school's mission in an even more structured way. Because frustration often comes from the gap between expectation and reality, she created a document—"What It Means to Be a Kings Collegiate Staff Member"—to close this gap. By getting the surprises out of the way before the year began, she realized she'd have smoother sailing the rest of the year.

Keep Your Ear to the Rail

During the early days of railroads, people would put an ear to the rails to hear the train rumbling along the tracks long before it was in sight. For many leaders, negative staff culture can feel quite similar: like a train zooming toward you with such momentum and force that you're powerless to stop it. Leaders of powerful staff culture don't wait to hear the train whistle or see it in the distance to act. They continually keep an ear to the rail, listening for rumblings and warning signs that the train might be coming sooner rather than later.

Mission Alignment

Excerpts from
"What It Means to Be a Kings Collegiate Staff Member"

1. We do whatever it takes.
2. We are positive and optimistic.
3. We believe good work comes from hard work and hard work pays off.
4. We sweat the small stuff.
5. We are both caring and strict.

What is the culture of the school like?

- We realize that as members of a start-up school, there will be hundreds of *odd jobs* that pop up unexpectedly. We realize that the success of our school is a *collective responsibility*, and we willingly take on the myriad of unexpected tasks that present themselves—stapling report cards and cover sheets during a planning period, getting an ice pack for a student who twisted her ankle during enrichment, photocopying something for a colleague who forgot to make copies before class, answering questions from a visitor to the school, un-jamming the photocopier, covering classes for an absent colleague, etc.—these things are all parts of our job! Basically, we share an attitude of doing what it takes to make our students and our school as successful as possible.

- We want to build a culture of open, honest, and productive dialogue with one another. We are expected to share our ideas, thoughts, and concerns. We are also expected to buy into and own group decisions, even if we originally expressed disagreement. The leaders' doors are *always* open to discuss anything and everything. We don't put our heads in the sand to avoid a problem.

- This will not be a school where teachers close their doors and teach in isolation. We realize that we will share space with one another and that our classrooms are always open. We observe one another and have honest and constructive conversations about what we see happening in our classes.

- We know how essential it is that we are all true team players, that we keep a positive outlook (even on our most exhausting days), that we share our passion for teaching and learning with our colleagues, our students, and our families.

- We respect all members of the staff, in both teaching and non-teaching roles. We recognize and value the contribution that each person makes in supporting our individual and collective success.

- Perhaps most importantly, we believe in our school values (THINK), and they will pervade our interactions with each other and with our students:
  - *Tenacity.* We are resourceful, work hard, and always strive to do our best. We show persistence and "grit" in overcoming obstacles and in working towards achieving our mission of preparing our students for college.

(continued)

- *High expectations.* We are mission-driven, highly motivated, and maintain the highest expectations for ourselves, our students, and our colleagues. We believe all children will learn and succeed, that all of our students deserve to go to college, and that closing the achievement gap is an issue of social justice.
- *Integrity.* We are honest and ethical in our words and our actions. We do the right thing, even when no one is watching, because we know it is the right thing to do.
- *No excuses.* We accept no excuses from our students, their families, or ourselves. We will each do what it takes to achieve our shared goals. As part of this attitude, we each take initiative when we see opportunities to help others or help our school improve. We step up in large and small ways on a daily basis and get the job done.
- *Kindness.* We genuinely care about and respect all people. We are willing to help those in need, and we show compassion and generosity. We treat others as we would want to be treated. We care about our students deeply, and though we may be strict and "sweat the small stuff," we also try to bring a sense of joy and humanism to the classroom.

Look for Warning Signs

One way Julie Kennedy systematically keeps her ear to the rail is through her weekly staff meetings. Every Wednesday, Williamsburg Collegiate has an early release day when students get out early to ensure ample time for staff meetings and teacher professional development (PD). That time sustains staff culture, because it gives the staff a weekly chance to come together, working as a team to make the school and each other stronger. Schools are busy places, and in elementary schools especially, a teacher can go an entire day without seeing his or her peers. As a result, it's critical that a school devote regular time for colleagues to just be in the same room with one another, celebrate their successes, share their thoughts on topics that matter to them, and work together to improve their classroom teaching and school operations. It is here that Julie can put her ear to the rail: Is staff arriving on time? Is there a good buzz in the room? Does staff make small talk before the meeting? Are individuals engaged and participatory?

Beyond providing opportunities to observe and address the staff as a whole, the weekly staff meeting is an important time to create the vital expectation that you are open to regular feedback and input. At Williamsburg Collegiate, this input comes in the form of weekly surveys that are targeted to collect feedback and opinions on a variety of parts of the school. Standard each week are four questions:

1. What's going well?

2. What's one thing that could be going better?

3. What's one thing any of the school leaders could do to make your life easier?

4. A fun question, such as, What is your favorite costume from a past Halloween, or What singer would you most like to sound like?

Through the first three questions, Julie and her school leaders can get an ongoing pulse check on what's on her staff's mind. Through the fourth question, Julie keeps the meeting joyful, and by sharing the results with her teachers, staff can get to know each other a little better. By administering this weekly survey—in addition to a more comprehensive one in the middle of the year—she sends a message of transparency—that there is no subject, data, or feedback she is not willing to hear or discuss.

Julie and her fellow school leaders also schedule standing meetings with their teachers, as has been described in Chapters 2 and 3 (on observation and feedback and planning). These standing meetings build staff culture immediately by sending the message that face-to-face communication is valued and is a priority. They are also an opportunity to stay ahead of any potential frustrations or more complicated staff and school issues and head off any potential miscommunication about expectations or priorities. As discussed in Chapters 2 and 3, these meetings are "sacred": they are locked in to calendars and prioritized. By making sure you are focused on and emotionally present for each teacher, you can gather any warning signs that might suggest that your school is veering off track.

Remember, formal surveys and direct questions only take you so far. Julie Kennedy's number one tool is simply checking on the nonverbal or subtle signs that teachers give every day as they move throughout the building. Are they unusually quiet or stressed one day? Are they talking animatedly with colleagues in the staff workroom or do they go quiet when Julie enters? Are cliques forming? When she engages teachers in small talk, do they respond differently than they usually do? Julie uses these warning signs to intervene early. She is reaching out to get information from a teacher who shows signs of stress—sometimes even before that teacher realizes he or she is doing so. These little but important warning signs give Julie and her team the information they need to act and be proactive so they're not stuck on the tracks.

Acting on Warning Signs

Every leader knows that some negativity and tough times are normal components of a work environment. There is a biorhythm to a school year—between Thanksgiving and the winter holidays, for example, is one of the toughest stretches in the calendar—and it is the job of the school leader to know which data to ignore and which data require a response. And a leader's response to the warning signs he or she sees ultimately builds, or breaks, the staff culture he or she envisions. When Julie Kennedy confronts a warning sign, she resists the urge to ban the behavior. Early on, she learned that responding to a warning sign with phrases like "We don't do that here" drove the negativity further underground and made it more difficult to address. In contrast, Julie first looks to see what caused the behavior and attempts to learn from that. For example, as a school leader, Julie might hear secondhand that a teacher is frustrated with a requested task, a decision that was made, or a schedule change and is responding negatively to peers in the teacher office. Julie's first response is to quickly meet with the teacher yet resist the urge to reiterate the teacher office norms to the teacher and the need to tell teachers that "we're positive here." Instead, Julie lets the teacher know that she heard about the teacher's frustration and she asks for feedback about why the teacher didn't come straight to Julie when she got frustrated. She asks if there is anything in her tone or style that makes it difficult to express disagreement and listens carefully to whatever the teacher has to say. Finally, she thanks the teacher for her feedback and reiterates the expectation that at Williamsburg Collegiate, concerns are brought to her rather than vented in the teacher office. This response does two things: (1) it provides Julie with feedback on her communication and management, and (2) it underscores the expectations that support a powerful staff culture.

It's imperative that a leader confront warning signs as they come. Initially, if a teacher seems disengaged during professional development, a leader may be tempted to let it go; perhaps the teacher's having a bad day or it's a one-time event. Yet unless it is addressed immediately, it is likely to weaken your culture. As the leader of the school, you have the moral and managerial authority to act. If you are hesitant to do so, you are only delaying the need to address the problem. A preemptive action is always better than a reactionary one. Note that confronting such problems should not be aggressive; usually, a calm question to help understand the individual and the situation is enough. Asking "I noticed that you didn't seem yourself in PD today. Is there anything going on?" opens up the situation to get feedback and better understand your staff and school and also works to show your staff that you notice and care. On this point, the fact that there are regularly scheduled teacher check-ins is crucial because they create an ideal forum to consistently engage in this type of dialogue. Unless you act on and seek to understand the root of the warning signs, they are likely to spread and weaken your culture.

> ### Core Idea
>
> Great leaders maintain strong staff cultures by remaining continually on the lookout for warning signs. They look for signs of stress before those signs become larger problems.

The way leaders handle these types of interactions can be the difference between a culture that thrives and one laden with resentment. Fortunately, there are a few steps that can be taken to ensure these conversations are productive:

- *In person.* Challenging conversations should occur face to face, not by email or phone. Emails are too easy to misread and too time consuming to draft the way they would need to be written.

- *Private and with time.* Difficult conversations should occur in private, and you should allow yourself more time than you think you'll need. This provides the space and time to have an honest conversation.

- *Targeted.* Dig deeper into the action in question, nothing more. Keep in mind, for many teachers, who they are and what they do are one and the same, so when you criticize their actions, they may feel like you're criticizing them as people, which is obviously not the case.

- *Immediate.* New leaders often take a long time to say anything, practice their speeches, and talk the next day. Highly effective leaders follow up right after to dig into the issues they're seeing. It might not feel natural at first, but the quicker the feedback loop, the more likely you'll nip the problem in the bud and get useful data—and, over time, the more natural it'll feel to do so.

Lather, Rinse, Repeat

Staff culture is incredibly fragile. If you don't actively and regularly work to build and mold your staff culture toward your vision, then the habits your staff develops will be very different from your expectations. Indeed, the key to each of the steps listed is that they're not done once. You don't train your staff on communication norms once and expect that every conversation will then go smoothly. You can't have one conversation about negative behavior on staff and expect that the problem is now solved. As a result, you have to be as intentional and relentless in building and maintaining culture as you are about any other system in your school. Maintaining a strong culture through the year means focusing on the daily actions of excellence—whether by checking in face to face with a teacher who is struggling or by taking the time to craft the right words of inspiration for the next staff meeting or all-staff email—to enrich your staff community.

Day-to-Day Excellence

The core of an effective school culture is not in grand gestures or big events. In fact, building staff culture should never be thought of as a few happy hours or trust falls. Rather, it comes from the steady and continual deepening of habits of excellence. Keeping these expectations up throughout the year begins with strong communication between school leaders and teachers. One day in the early years of Williamsburg Collegiate, a newly hired teacher approached Julie Kennedy to apologize for wearing a denim skirt. Confused, Julie asked why this teacher was apologizing; the teacher quickly explained that she had been told by other staff that Julie frowned on denim skirts as "too casual." Knowing that she had no opinion one way or another on denim skirts, Julie went to the source and asked where this idea came from. The original teacher explained that one day several years earlier she had worn a jean skirt to school and she thought she saw Julie give a disapproving look in the hallway. This single look (which Julie to this day can't recall doing but is confident was related to something other than denim skirts) was extrapolated over several years into a "No denim skirts" rule at the school. Amazed, Julie noted the power of both verbal and nonverbal communication. With both, leaders build and maintain effective staff culture through purposeful communication.

When it comes to school leadership, potential sources of trouble—beyond denim skirts!—often seem endless. As a leader, it is critical that you accept this stress and not convey it to your staff. The stakes are high. As Julie notes, "Teachers need to believe that you have a vision and you have a plan, so sending the message that you're not panicking in tough times is crucial." This requires thoughtfulness and purpose in your verbal and nonverbal communication. Fortunately, there are several key steps leaders like Julie can take to consistently and effectively communicate their expectations and maintain a strong culture.

Keep an open face

Bill Graham, of Graham Corporate Communications, specializes in coaching leaders how to communicate effectively. He has worked with everyone from governors, executives, and actors to educators. When he studies the most effective leaders, he notices a common physical trait, which he calls "the open face." When inexperienced leaders are confronted with something they didn't anticipate—stress, conflict, tough interview questions, and so on—something often occurs on their face. They subtly "close" the face: lower the eyebrows, frown, and/or close the eyes just slightly. "We are attracted to exactly the opposite," Graham says. "The leaders who make it to the top in every field have an open face that rarely wavers—eyebrows naturally up, eyes wide, and a subtle positive look on their face." The good news is, this is coachable. Simply videotaping yourself in stressful moments can allow you to check for subtle signs that send the wrong message to your staff. Or, hang a mirror in your office so you can "check your face" before walking the hallways and classrooms. You may think you look one way, but sometimes your self-perception may be off, and you wouldn't want staff to see something different (especially stress that can easily and negatively spread). As for Julie Kennedy? You guessed it: she is a master of the open face. As one of her teachers writes, "Julie works incredibly hard and somehow is able to shoulder whatever bulk of the work needs shouldering without anyone else in the building being aware that she's got a lot on her plate and could potentially be stressed out."

Listen first

Many leaders show stress when hearing ideas or information with which they disagree. The stress damages staff culture because it discourages your staff from coming to you regularly. Julie shares, "It's natural to shake your head, scrunch up your face or look stressed when you disagree with what someone is saying. You lose out on information by doing that, though. And that hurts your staff culture." It is important to train yourself out of this habit of showing stress. First, simply slow down and refrain from responding. Use the energy you usually use to craft your rebuttal or pick apart the argument and focus it on listening instead. If you don't have time to really listen and be emotionally present when the person might share this kind of information, reschedule the conversation for another time. Second, train yourself to ask questions as your first response. This will help you develop a deeper understanding of the ideas presented and also continue to give you time before responding. Finally, exercise your right to not respond in the moment. Have in your pocket a standard set of responses that you use when you find yourself surprised or when you know you will need to vehemently disagree.

Wait before sending emails ... or just don't

Email—the current predominant form of communication—has some major drawbacks over face-to-face conversation: your words can be misinterpreted, and you have no control over when or where the emails you send are read. Plus, by its very nature, email conveys stress and hostility in a particularly clear way. Julie Kennedy always waits a few minutes, or even hours, before sending an email. Sometimes, after 24 hours have passed, she may not send it at all. Additionally, whenever possible, she avoids sending emails and seeks out the individual first in person. She finds it is too time consuming to try to craft the words so she's heard perfectly right. When sending emails, leaders miss the opportunity to learn more about their staffs, themselves, and the effectiveness of their communication because they are not there to see how the information is received.

Use we instead of I or you

Running a school is a team sport. You would never want to hear the coach of a football team say, "I prepared for the game this week by doing x, y, and z" or "You need to do better if you want to win the game." What you would want to hear—especially if you were on the team—is "We prepared" or "We need to do better." The same is true for a principal and his or her teachers. The team is greater than the individual and using *We* in all verbal and written communications reinforces that organizational attitude and helps unifies staff culture.

Have a bias toward Yes

Teachers should be comfortable approaching school leaders about problems they see in the school or potential areas for improvement. If a teacher brings up a problem that needs to be fixed, invite him to suggest a solution and provide him with the time and resources he needs to follow through with his suggestion. At Williamsburg Collegiate, Julie Kennedy reserves 15 minutes of a weekly staff meeting for whole-school solution groups—round-robin, results-driven discussions with teachers to collectively brainstorm a solution to a pressing whole-school problem. By giving teachers this freedom to problem-solve, you provide them with the opportunity to be leaders in a small but meaningful way and prepare them to take on larger roles in the future. Similarly, when teachers come forward with new ideas, or looking to start a new project, always have a bias toward saying *Yes*. Seriously investigate the benefits of a teacher's proposal, and never dismiss it offhand. When possible, find a way to make your response a *Yes*. By giving teachers the opportunity to innovate in this way, leaders like Julie harness the collective wisdom of dozens of dedicated educators. They let the teachers be the school's greatest resource, an idea engine driving the school's success. As one of her teachers wrote about her, "Julie truly believes in and respects the power of other people's ideas, seeks out others' opinions, and encourages them to start stuff, be involved and try new things (with constant support and an ability to rein folks in if something's gone awry)."

Revisit the mission often

Beyond communicating effectively, it is vital that school leaders connect their messages back to the school's overall vision, to continually reinforce just why the habits being developed are so important. Great staff culture feeds off a strong sense of mission. When the going gets tough, leaders refer teachers back to the cause, and everyone can then draw motivation from being part of something larger than himself or herself. For Julie's school, this mission is about making learning joyful while maintaining a high level of rigor. To emphasize this goal, especially when the going gets tough, great leaders look to positive framing. Consider the following email from one of Julie Kennedy's principal peers—Jessica Simmons, founding principal at Brownsville Collegiate Charter School—sent in the challenging final month of the school year:

> We have 3 awesome weeks left to close out our 09–10 school year, of those days, we have 12 instructional days to make sure our students are one step closer to college, 3 days until our Enrichment Potluck

and Celebration, 8 days until FINALS, 10 days until Field Day and just 15 days until we all head out to Vegas and Hawaii and ATL (and yes, that is all for one person!), camping and wine tasting in California, hiking and camping in Yosemite, hanging out in Texas, watching a sister get married, hiking in New Hampshire and reading, hiking in the mountains of Washington state, and just hanging out with friends and family.

Leaders like Jessica know that June is only "June" if you allow it to be.

This sort of positive reinforcement can refocus staff on the importance of a very challenging few weeks. But this sort of reinforcement does not just happen occasionally; it is connected to every action we take. Consider Julie's experience In "Bagels Don't Talk, I Do."

> ## Core Idea
>
> It's not the decision you make that matters, but how you message your response.

By emphasizing a common mission, the leader creates an internal motivation to work harder rather than imposing yet another external incentive to perform. Great leaders use the mission they share with their staff as a source of motivation during particularly trying times.

Keep it up

Finally, on any given day, there are dozens of opportunities to model and build the staff culture you want to see. These small leader actions, when sustained, make a staff's culture grow and thrive much more than large events do. Julie notes, "As a leader, it's important to engage on a less formal level to show that teachers are valued. Handwritten notes of praise, participating in teacher-driven class- or schoolwide events or simply taking the time to get to know the teacher as a person can play this role. Whenever teachers bring visitors to the school, I make it a priority to spend time with the visitor because it helps me to both get to know the teacher better and to reinforce how much I value that member of our team."

Bagels Don't Talk, I Do

An Example of Strategic Messaging

Along with making time and space, the strategic messaging that goes around this is critical. Julie recounts one story:

It had been a long week at Williamsburg Collegiate. We'd had a family event one night, an afternoon field trip that returned late another night, and we were rounding the corner to our next set of interim assessments. People were dragging and seemed to have low spirits. They were giving a lot of time and not necessarily feeling like that time was being acknowledged or valued. We decided we wanted to remind our staff that we valued them. The next morning, I picked up four dozen bagels and a variety of cream cheeses, knowing that nothing lifts spirits like food. I set up the bagels in the teacher workroom and sent a quick email that just said, "Enjoy the bagels!" I happily watched people sprint to the office to get their bagels before class and watched as people continued to enjoy them throughout the day.

As the day wore on, I started getting emails like, "Hey, could you give us a heads up the night before you get bagels so I don't get a bagel in the morning before school and then end up eating two bagels?" and "I feel like I've really been carb loading. Do you think you could get fruit instead?" followed by "Do you think the school could just have a supply of low-fat cream cheese that we can use when we get bagels?" It suddenly became clear that my purchase of bagels didn't translate to people feeling valued. It translated to something else entirely.

I retraced my steps to try to figure out where our plan when awry and found my way back to the email. My e-mail simply said "Enjoy the bagels." It gave no indication of why we were giving them bagels or anything that showed the connection to "We value you." I quickly jotted down some other ways I could've written the email, like "You've worked a lot of hours this week. We really value you and your time. We're getting bagels for everyone tomorrow morning to we hope simplify your life just a little bit and give you one less thing to do in the morning! Thank you for all you do!" I also jotted down my takeaway from this moment that "bagels don't talk, I do."

While it's certainly important for leaders to be thoughtful about the "thing" that they do for teachers, it's as important that they strategically message the "thing" so staff understands the connection between what has been observed and what they decided to do as a result.

The key, though, is to be systematic and prioritize sustaining staff culture over other commitments. If you don't, the work it takes to keep staff culture strong may get pushed aside. There'll always be something seemingly more important than the day-to-day tasks described here. But never forget that nothing is more important than your people. A teacher standing in front of you is the most important business you can take care of—not your email, not a phone call, not anything else. The most hectic days are also the most important days to be informally connecting with the individuals on your team. As Julie says, "When I was first developing this habit, I scheduled in time to circulate at different stress points each day. Some days I would be available and present after lunch, some days after school during particularly stressful times like testing periods or building up to vacations. I would block out my schedule to be sure that I was present and engaged with staff when they needed me."

MONTH-TO-MONTH EXCELLENCE

There is no doubt that the consistent, daily actions to build and reinforce a strong staff culture are the core of building a great professional community. Yet leaders like Julie also recognize the value of creating larger cultural events to build greater cohesion among teachers, parents, and students. At Williamsburg Collegiate, Julie Kennedy documents staff, student, and parent events, traditions, and rituals via a culture tracker. This simple tool allows Julie and her fellow school leaders to know exactly what they do, when, why—and what is missing. If you don't track such things formally, they are likely to get lost in the shuffle of a busy school day, week, month, and year. For example, it's not enough to randomly remember to send one teacher one handwritten note one time. But, if you track it, you'll remember that you wrote these teachers this month and can plan to write those teachers next month. Or if reading achievement is your big theme of the year, you have to figure out how you're going to keep such a theme alive culturally beyond its introduction during orientation. A sample excerpt from a culture tracker appears as Table 6.2.

A tracker such as this is great for strategically planning events so that they're neither overloaded in one month nor missing in another. For example, here is where you can decide how often to buy staff breakfast or lunch; which standard snacks the school will have on hand; what tokens of appreciation to give to and parties to hold for teachers for the winter holidays or at the end of the school year; what school "swag" to purchase to instill school pride; how you'll celebrate staff birthdays; what talent you'll perform during the staff talent show; where your staff outings will be; and any other planned or surprise celebrations and activities you plan to hold.

Table 6.2 Sample Culture Tracker

What Do We Do?	Value	Why Do We Do It?	Date/Month	Who Does It?	Who Is it For?
Midyear evaluations	Achieve	Set goals and show grit	Annually		Teachers
Model lessons for teachers	Achieve	Love of Learning	As needed		Teachers
Cover classes so teachers can observe one another	Achieve	Love of Learning	As needed		Teachers
Themed August orientation (*The Incredibly Book Eating Boy* to highlight school focus on literacy?)	Achieve	Love of Learning	August		Teachers
Reading-based PD: Teachers can select content areas for schoolwide growth and choose books to read	Achieve	Love of Learning	Biannually		Teachers
Teacher check-ins	Achieve	Set goals and show grit	Biweekly		Teachers
Send in updates to alumni newsletter for each teacher's alma maters	Achieve	Love of Learning	February		Teachers
T-shirts: "Scholar"	Achieve	Love of Learning	January		
Picture of student who inspires on teacher PD binders	Achieve	Love of Learning	January		Teachers
TerraNova celebrations to acknowledge everyone's hard work	Achieve	Set goals and show grit	June		Teachers
T-shirts "Add"	Achieve	Love of Learning	March		Teachers

(continued)

Table 6.2 (Continued)

What Do We Do?	Value	Why Do We Do It?	Date/Month	Who Does It?	Who Is it For?
T-shirts: "Read"	Achieve	Love of Learning	October		Teachers
Pay for certification expenses	Achieve	Love of Learning	Ongoing		Teachers
Pay for outside PD	Achieve	Love of Learning	Ongoing		Teachers
Set SMART instructional goals and track growth	Achieve	Set goals and show grit	Ongoing		Teachers
Send out Marshall Memo every week	Achieve	Love of Learning	Ongoing		Teachers

Building culture is more than just hosting periodic happy hours. It's about *consistently* giving honest feedback to teachers on their instruction. It's about *consistently* emailing the entire staff to acknowledge the great signs of progress you see in the hallways and classrooms. And it's about *consistently* saying thank you to teachers, in myriad different ways, for going above and beyond.

Whether it's from day to day or from month to month, the key for leaders is to remember to periodically revisit and retrain culture throughout the year. Julie does this all year long: by sending encouraging all-staff emails, by dedicating staff time weekly to gather data around staff morale, by publicly reviewing the results of the school's annual midyear staff survey. These touch points not only provide the entire team with time to build and refine staff culture but, more important, they consistently send the message to staff that staff culture is a priority.

Keep Your Culture on Track

Leaders can take a subjective area like staff culture and quantify it, allowing them to narrow their focus on particular aspects of the culture that they'd like to improve. Table 6.3 presents some sample criteria that a leader can use to evaluate his or her progress.

Data create a sense of urgency around instruction and foster the belief that student learning is the primary concern. Planning spreads the message that

Table 6.3 Staff Culture Rubric (excerpt)

Leader Tone	Principal is upbeat, motivational, and inspiring. Principal is present throughout the school. Principal celebrates real and meaningful progress and results, large or small.
Staff Culture-Building Events	School develops events and traditions. Events and traditions are warm, thoughtful, frequent, and joyful. Events and traditions (as well as new ideas) are staff driven as much as they are school driven.
Principal–Teacher Communication	Principal embraces feedback from throughout organization. Teachers and staff members feel their opinions count. Principal knows how teachers are currently feeling about their work.

preparation is the key to success. Observation and feedback fosters the belief that everyone is part of the team and that collaboration drives results. Frequent professional development creates a culture in which teachers know that they come to work not only to use what they already know but also to grow themselves and learn new skills. But for these systems to work, teachers must feel supported and driven to succeed. By developing your staff culture in a way that supports these systems, you make your instructional efforts even more powerful. If your staff culture is weak, having the right tools will mean little. To ensure lasting success, you need to be as deliberate about culture as you are about instruction.

TURNAROUND: FROM CRISIS TO COHESION

Even the most successful schools can face serious challenges when it comes to building a rich and supportive staff culture. At schools where negativity has prevailed, and where teachers have become factionalized, politicized, or otherwise disengaged, the challenge of fixing "adult culture" seems very daunting. Brian Sims, director of high schools for the Academy for Urban School Leadership (AUSL), has seen this firsthand. Over the past ten years, AUSL has transformed fourteen of Chicago's least successful district schools into solid community bedrocks. Improving staff culture was one of the critical components to their success. To transform staff culture during turnaround, Brian looks to two key steps.

A Colleague's Testimonial on Staff Culture

Stephanie Ely

I worked with Julie Kennedy for five years at Williamsburg Collegiate. Over the course of those years, I transitioned from math teacher to dean of curriculum, but I never forgot what it was like to be a teacher under Julie's leadership. That experience revolutionized not only my definition of a team, but also my sense of myself as team player.

I still remember the year that Julie kicked orientation off by showing us a picture of a Great White Buffalo. "White buffalo are extremely rare," Julie began, referencing a popular movie. "It's estimated that they appear only once in every 10,000,000 births." On this team, she went on, each of us was a white buffalo: unique, awe inspiring, and irreplaceable.

Julie intentionally develops our team so that we all see the Great White Buffalo in each other. During orientation, she highlights why she hired everyone on the team. She has shared the exact same reason she hired me on every first day of orientation for five years. To this day, I can remember why she hired every person on our staff: from the teacher who used the same line graph as another teacher and announced to the students, "This is like showing up to a party in the same shirt as someone else"; to the one who hung out in the main office after his interview as if he were already on staff. All of the other stories are just as precise and heartfelt as these.

Many leaders talk about the importance of "having the right people on the bus," but Julie *shows* her people the bus. From that first day of orientation onward, she outlines our school's culture and mission clearly. She also makes sure we sprinkle our own "secret sauce" into the mix, encouraging us to share our own goals and experiences. We all understand that whether we are new or returning to WCCS, we are valuable.

When I transitioned from teaching math to serving as dean of curriculum, I gained a new, firsthand appreciation for Julie's ability to develop staff culture from the perspective of a teacher-leader. Those orientation sessions always end with our leadership team sitting together and debriefing. We reflect on the key messages that have been presented, the responses we get from our staff, and the way we've framed our culture. We ask each other questions like "What did you notice?" "How did people do during independent time today?" "Did anyone get a chance to talk to Sarah after she seemed disengaged during the morning session?" Julie consistently challenges herself and her fellow leaders to listen to our teammates and to ask ourselves how we can lead them most effectively. Remembering how Julie's techniques shaped me as a teacher is what makes me so passionate about using them myself as a leader.

Throughout the year, we revisit our staff culture to make sure we stay true to our vision. It's a tough task: teaching is personal work, which makes it difficult to maintain trust and communication lines as the school year unfolds. But the good sportsmanship our team established at the beginning of each year stems from one source: the coach behind the team.

1. Get on the Same Page

The core principle of a staff culture turnaround is that teachers need to know the school's core mission . . . and be unified in putting it into practice. "What most undermines failing schools is that everyone on the staff is doing his or her own thing," Brian explains. "Turning a failing school around demands a culture where everyone is on the same page, supports the school's mission, and accepts what is needed to get back on track." To set this expectation, each of Brian's turnaround schools holds a three-week training before school starts to set the new culture's expectations and to teach the common language that students will be responsible for during the year. Perhaps the most important part of these weeks comes during role-play exercises, where staff practice the responses they will give to students and to each other. "Getting teachers used to a culture of positivity, of high expectations for students and of respectful interaction with peers is the most important work we do over the summer," Brian notes. "If we don't build a strong expectation and shared culture early in the turnaround, it's extremely difficult to build it later."

2. Leverage Your Presence

A strong start isn't enough to turn a culture around. Just as turning around student culture means becoming more present for students at key moments, building a positive staff culture means becoming highly visible to your staff at key moments. For Brian, this means explicitly and immediately recognizing when teachers are meeting the new culture's expectations and addressing problems on the spot when teachers do not meet the new expectations. "It's about sweating the small stuff," Brian notes. "If the expectation is that student uniform violations will be corrected, and if a teacher doesn't correct them, the time to deliver that message is immediately." By creating a tight feedback loop around actions and by continually acknowledging when teachers are on the right track, leaders can go a long way toward turning around a toxic culture.

CONCLUSION: GETTING TO TEAMLYNESS

Staff culture is notoriously difficult to describe, but we've all experienced its effects. Every group of people has a unique fingerprint—a style of work and a set of attitudes and philosophies that define the organization. Staff culture does not

A Word On . . . Resistant Staff

In the vast majority of situations, keeping your "ear to the rail" and openly addressing challenges early will resolve staff culture problems. Teachers genuinely want to do what is best for students, and most will respond to the less confrontational approaches outlined here. Sometimes, however, teachers will behave in ways that are entirely out of bounds or will repeatedly resist meeting basic expectations in ways that stem not from misunderstandings but from deeper disrespect or a lack of commitment to the mission. This is particularly likely to happen in turnaround situations when teachers may have developed a very different set of habits, attitudes, and expectations for approaching school and the principal's role. In many situations, it is very difficult to dismiss such a teacher.

In the long term, the best way to deal with this sort of challenge is often to change the culture *around* the resistant teacher rather than confront him or her head on. As Brian Sims notes, "The more unified a culture is around core ideas and values, the more likely it is that 'holdouts' will begin to feel that the culture is simply not for them, leading them to look elsewhere." Indeed, the more consistent a culture is, the more isolated such negativity becomes, ultimately leading the negative to move on.

Five Strategies for Successful Staff Culture

1. *Set the vision.* Wisely design a clear and palpable vision for the work environment in your school.
2. *Get the right people on the bus.* Without great people, little else matters. Ensure your vision helps drive your hiring.
3. *Put a stake in the ground.* Reflect your commitment to developing a strong staff culture from the first interactions of the year.
4. *Keep your ear to the rail.* Look and listen for negative culture warning signs that are coming down the tracks.
5. *Lather, rinse, repeat.* Staff culture is fragile. If you're not intentional about building, maintaining, or communicating your staff culture, someone else will define it for you.

Table 6.4 Making It Work: How It Will Fit in a Leader's Schedule

	Monday	Tuesday	Wednesday	Thursday	Friday
6:00am					
:30	Greeting and breakfast	Greeting and breakfast		Greeting and breakfast	Greeting and breakfast
7:00am					
:30	Staff culture check	Morning assembly			Morning assembly
8:00am		Meet Wilson	Meet Bradley		Staff culture check
:30		Meet Vargas	Meet Frint		
9:00am	Observe Wilson, Vargas, Jenkins	Meet Jenkins			
:30					
10:00am			Observe Mitzia, Boykin, Devin		Observe Hoyt, Settles, Palma
:30					
11:00am		Staff culture check			
:30	Lunch	Lunch	Lunch		Lunch
12:00pm	Observe Henry, Bernales, Christian				Meet Bradley
:30		Meet Worrell			Meet Palma
1:00pm		Meet Christian			Meet Settles
:30		Meet Bernales	Meet Boykin		Meet Hoyt
2:00pm		Observe Bradley, Frint, Worrell	Meet Devin		
:30			Meet Mitzia		
3:00pm					
:30			Professional development session	Staff culture check	
4:00pm	Dismissal	Dismissal		Dismissal	Dismissal
:30					
5:00pm					
:30					

☐ Work Time   ☐ School Culture   ☐ Observations   ☐ Meetings

exist independently of instructional systems. The systems you intentionally put into place help define your culture, and your culture determines the efficacy of the systems you use.

To boost achievement, we need to follow Julie Kennedy's lead: be proactive and craft the right staff culture for the job. Choose key moments during the day, week, month, and year to insert culture-building elements. As you add these elements together, a coherent culture will quickly emerge. Public praise during staff meetings, mission-building messages in all-staff communications, and a regular schedule of social events are all simple changes that can produce big results.

As one Williamsburg Collegiate teacher puts it, the wonderful thing about working at her school is the "overarching feeling of 'teamlyness' that is always present, [that] it just always feels that even though everyone is working incredibly hard, people are always happy to help each other out—and that is invaluable."

Pulling the Lever
Action Planning Worksheet for Staff Culture

Self-Assessment

• Review the checklist on the staff culture rubric. Where are your biggest areas for improvement?

_____

_____

_____

_____

_____

_____

Planning for Action

• What tools from this book will you use to improve staff culture at your school? Check all that you will use (you can find all on the DVD):

☐ Staff Culture Rubric

☐ Culture Tracker

• What are your next steps for improving your staff culture?

Action	Date

Chapter 7

Managing School Leadership Teams

All-on-One: Feedback on Feedback at a Leadership Team Meeting

The lights have been dimmed in the classroom as a video is shown of a teacher and his department chairman.

"What was the goal of the Do-Now sheet?" asks the department chairman. The teacher responds, "It was to make sure class got off to a strong start, as far as management was concerned."

The video pauses. Mike Taubman, chair of North Star High School's English department, has just watched himself giving observation feedback to a novice teacher. He's not the only one watching. On this Friday, the high school's department chairpersons are meeting to review each other's success at giving feedback and to hone in on what will make their coaching more effective. Art Worrell, chair of the history department, refers to the six steps of feedback and praises Mike's use of a probing question, but he wonders if more concrete examples might have helped. Shana Pyatt, chair of the science department, suggests that Mike should have moved more quickly to identify the problem, allowing more time to work with the teacher on planning his upcoming do-nows. Mike silently records these observations for reference at his next check-in. Then it's Art's turn: the laptop is set back up, and the next clip starts playing.

Chapters 1 through 3 clearly laid out two of the highest-leverage actions that can drive quality of instruction: a 15-minute weekly observation and a standing weekly meeting between the teacher and an instructional leader in which leaders can give feedback, hold data analysis meetings, and plan upcoming lessons. Chapter 2 (Observation and Feedback) demonstrated that one leader can effectively observe and give feedback to 15 teachers every week. It also showed that if we count every possible leader in a school, most public schools have a 15:1 ratio of teachers per leader. In quick summary:

- Teacher-to-leader load in most public schools (when all leaders are counted): 15:1

- One classroom observation per week: 15 minutes

- Total minutes of observation per week: 15 teachers × 15 minutes = 225 minutes = less than 4 hours

- One feedback and planning meeting: 30 minutes

- Total minutes of feedback/planning meetings: 15 teachers × 30 minutes = 7.5 hours

- Total hours devoted to teacher observation and feedback: 11.5 hours

- Percentage of a leader's time (assuming 7:00 a.m.–4:00 p.m. school day): 25 percent

The premise in Chapter 2 was that this was feasible if principals effectively distributed the instructional leadership work across all other leaders in their schools: assistant principals, coaches, department chairs, special education chairs, and so on. Chapter 2 addressed this premise head-on: What does it look like to distribute instructional leadership in this way, and how do you manage those leaders so as to make them effective in their work?

For starters, thinking this way about instructional leaders will signify a change in priorities for many school leadership teams. Ask yourself the following questions about your school leadership teams: How much time do you spend . . .

Giving and receiving feedback on the quality of your observational feedback, data analysis meetings, and coaching of teachers in their planning?

Practicing or role playing the meetings you have with teachers?

Planning and practicing upcoming professional development (PD)?

Evaluating and improving school culture?

Just as teachers are rarely observed in most schools, leaders are rarely coached around what matters most: the quality of their meetings with teachers. We've just mentioned the highest-leverage actions that affect student achievement. Highly successful schools make sure that their leadership teams are focused on those same actions.

Core Idea

Leaders are rarely coached around what matters most: the quality of their meetings with teachers. Change your leadership team's purpose, and you'll change your results.

It's not enough to simply select leaders or even to train them. Instead, effective leadership teams are built by continually receiving "feedback on feedback" and by critically evaluating the skills of guiding others. Simply put, forming a successful team means ensuring that leaders like Mike Taubman and Art Worrell are continually honing their ability to guide teachers to greatness.

Building a strong instructional leadership team is the core task of leaders who want to build successful schools. In large schools, it is the instructional supervisors and coaches on such a team who ensure that data meetings, observations, and planning all occur with the same level of focus, and that as a result change can occur beyond any one classroom (or, indeed, beyond any one campus). The key to building such systems requires four tasks:

1. *Identify* instructional leaders.

2. *Train* initially and follow up throughout the year.

3. *Give feedback and practice* to leverage face-to-face meetings to develop leadership.

4. *Evaluate* leaders on what matters most: the quality of their instructional leadership.

When a principal knows the levers of student achievement and has the tools to see whether these levers are in place, he or she will have an impact that extends well beyond any one classroom—or school.

Core Idea

Identify your leaders, train them in instructional leadership, and give them plenty of feedback: that's the formula for success.

CHOOSING LEADERS

The first step is identifying who your instructional leaders will be. Some leaders, Julie Kennedy among them, have designated leaders like a dean of curriculum or assistant principal. Others, like Julie Jackson, select strong teachers to take on instructional leadership for a few teachers in addition to their teaching duties. Regardless of how leaders are chosen, a number of core principles must be kept in mind:

• *Remember 15:1—The Golden Ratio.* As noted previously, even the most diligent school principal usually cannot serve as instructional leader for more than 15 teachers. Fortunately, principals need not (and, indeed, should not) be the sole instructional leaders. Members of the administrative team, such as vice principals or deans of instruction, also take on this instructional role. At many successful schools, each veteran teacher serves as instructional supervisor for at least one novice teacher. External coaches are also aligned to the same instructional leadership model. Through the creative use of such personnel, virtually any school can meet this 15:1 threshold to ensure that every teacher is observed and receives key feedback.

- *Leverage teachers as additional leaders*. Highly successful schools also leverage strong teachers in their building to coach one or two teachers each. In order to plan how much time it will take, Julie Jackson refers to a 3-hour rule: "For a new instructional leader who will also be teaching, we assume it is a 3-hour weekly time commitment for each teacher they will lead. While the 15-minute weekly observation and 30-minute check-in take up less than an hour, we build in 2 additional hours for the preparation work and lesson plan support that occur." Based on these calculations, as a lead teacher takes on a teacher for instructional leadership, the principal reduces the lead teacher's other responsibilities (for example, by cutting back that teacher's lunch duties) or provides a stipend that is similar to what others would receive for a 3-hour weekly commitment. When that teacher takes on more than two teachers, his or her course loads may need to be reduced or modified.

- *Reliability and receptiveness matter*. Just as there is no one "principal personality" there is no one "instructional leader personality." That said, these leaders need to be reliable. Julie Jackson notes, "You will have tools to monitor each leader's work, but it is far more challenging when a leader isn't committed to implementing the steps of effective instructional leadership." Additionally, in choosing instructional leaders, receptiveness to the systems presented in this book is essential. For the instructional leadership model to work, it is essential that the team be committed to the practices of data-driven instruction, regular feedback, and systematic planning. Teachers or administrators who cannot make this leap will not be good choices for this role.

TRAINING YOUR TEAM

Implementing this model of instructional leadership involves a shift in thinking for everyone in the school. Teachers will be receiving much more systematic instructional support, but in turn that means they will be held more accountable to their own development. Making this transition work requires introducing the new model to teachers—making sure to clarify the role of the instructional leader who will be working with each teacher—and training each instructional leader to lead data, feedback, and planning effectively.

Start with the Leader's Schedule

Shifting to the kind of team leadership we've just described starts with building schedules for the leadership team, just as the work we explained in the previous chapters began with the creation of a re-envisioned principal schedule. Each instructional leader needs to lock in observation time and weekly standing check-ins on his or her calendar. What might this look like in practice? For a full-time instructional leader, it can look very similar to a principal's schedule. For someone who also teaches, it will look slightly different. Consider the schedule of Mike Taubman, the English department chair we met at the start of the chapter, who teaches three-quarter time and leads three teachers, in Table 7.1.

As you can see from Table 7.1, the instructional leader's role is, in important ways, a microcosm of the school leader's. By delegating these responsibilities, large-school leaders can ensure that every teacher in the building is observed, receives feedback, and conducts data analysis with an instructional leader.

Launch the Initial Training

Once the schedule is in place, each instructional leader needs to be thoroughly trained in the core instructional systems outlined in this book. Carrying out such training would normally be a daunting task. The purpose of this book, however, is to take away that burden. Parts 1 and 2 of this text are devoted to making each necessary principle clear to you. Meanwhile, the chapters in Part 4 offer *all the materials, scripts, videos, and PowerPoint presentations* you will need to train your instructional leaders in those same principles. (See Table 7.2.)

These are far more materials than you'll likely have time to use! Prioritize the training that matches the needs of your school and instructional leadership team. Remember: data-driven instruction and student culture are the super-levers. However, if you have instructional leaders who don't have to lead student culture, then you can choose data-driven instruction and observation and feedback as a starting place.

Training does not have to occur in one setting. When you don't have a full day or a half-day to train your leadership team, you can implement the training piece by piece in your leadership team meetings. Like every school leader, you'll have to find creative ways, specific to your school's circumstances, to implement the training—but at least you won't have to invent it!

Table 7.1 Instructional Leader's Schedule

	Monday	Tuesday	Wednesday	Thursday	Friday
6:00am					
:30		Morning Greeter Duty			
7:00am					
:30					
8:00am	Teach 9th-grade English	Teach 9th-grade English	Teach 9th-grade English	Teach 9th-grade English	Teach 9th-grade English
:30					
9:00am		Obs. 10th-grade English: Kayliss		Lead feedback/ planning mtg: Souter	
:30					
10:00am	Teach 9th-grade English	Teach 9th-grade English	Teach 9th-grade English	Teach 9th-grade English	Teach 9th-grade English
:30					
11:00am		Lead feedback/ planning mtg: Kayliss	Obs. 11th-grade English: Sanders		
:30					
12:00pm	Teach 12th-grade English	Teach 12th-grade English	Teach 12th-grade English	Teach 12th-grade English	Teach 12th-grade English
:30					
1:00pm		Receive feedback/ planning mtg from principal	Obs. 9th-grade English: Souter	Lead feedback/ planning mtg: Sanders	
:30					
2:00pm					
:30					
3:00pm					
:30			Cover detention duty		
4:00pm	Instructional leader mtg with principal				
:30					
5:00pm					
:30					

■ Work Time   ■ School Culture   ■ Observations   ■ Meetings

Table 7.2   Guide to Training Materials: All the Resources for Training Leaders (Part 4 of this Book)

Leadership Lever	Training Materials (found in Part 4 and on DVD)
Data-Driven Instruction (Chapter 1)	Videos of leaders in action (training materials can be found in my previous book, Driven by Data[1])
Observation and Feedback (Chapter 2)	7 hours of training materials and video of leaders in action
Planning (Chapter 3)	4 hours of training materials and video of leaders in action
Leading PD (Chapter 4)	5 hours of training materials and video of leaders in action
Student Culture (Chapter 5)	4 hours of training materials and video of leaders in action
Finding the Time (Chapter 8)	4 hours of training materials

Offer Refreshers Throughout the Year

Everyone forgets the details of an initial training, and you may well need to revisit whatever training you provide over the course of the year. Luckily, the help of some of the other videos that accompany this book will make it easy for you to offer refresher sessions.

LEVERAGING LEADERSHIP TEAM MEETINGS: IRON SHARPENS IRON

Chapter 4 on leading professional development taught us that professional development is not effective unless it is embedded within the cycle of data analysis and regular feedback and planning meetings with teachers. These meetings support teachers and hold them accountable to implementation. The development of your leadership team follows the same tenets. Your initial training can be extraordinary, but without effective follow-up, it will not bear fruit.

Most schools that I have encountered have some sort of leadership team meeting. In a small school, it might be just the principal and a lead teacher. In larger schools, it is all the instructional leaders with the principal or individual check-ins of each instructional leader with the principal. Regardless of the size, these meetings represent a golden opportunity to develop instructional leadership. Unfortunately, they most often fall short. Here are the most common errors of leadership team meetings.

Common Errors of Leadership Team Meetings

The following actions *do not* meet the goal of enhancing the quality of instructional leadership:

- *More announcements than instruction.* Peruse the agenda for your leadership team meeting. How many items on the list are directly connected to student learning and teacher development? More importantly, how much time of the meeting do those announcements and logistics take up? Honing instructional leadership takes time, and it requires prioritizing.

- *More talking about teachers than talking about feedback.* Now look more closely at the agenda items that are centered around teachers. How often do they simply involve talking about teachers' development? There is a real danger to a principal simply listening to an instructional leader talk about a teacher's development. First, you are assuming that the instructional leader's beliefs about what the teacher is struggling with are correct. Second, you are assuming that the leader's feedback to the teacher is sound, and that the only remaining issue is that the teacher is not following the leader's advice. Yet we know well that identifying the right lever, giving effective feedback, and holding teachers accountable to that feedback are three of the four core principles to effective observation and feedback. None of those is addressed by simply talking about the teachers.

- *Walkthroughs, and little more.* Walkthroughs are a step better than talking about teachers. During a walkthrough, at least, you and an instructional leader can observe together and discuss what the best action step to focus on for the teacher's immediate development. But if we use these as our only tools for developing leadership, we are still missing two of the four key components of observation and feedback: giving effective feedback and holding teachers accountable to that feedback. Walkthroughs have their place in leadership team development, but it should be a much smaller place than it currently holds for many teams.

- *More reading about leadership than doing.* Another trend in leadership team meetings is a book club or reading articles about leadership. If all you do is read this book, I can pretty much guarantee it will have little impact. What changes practice is when we practice, putting those ideas into action. Practicing reaches beyond leaders sharing their big takeaways from reading: it means role playing or acting on the spot.

> **Core Idea**
>
> If you want to develop high-quality instructional leadership, talking about teachers is not enough. You need to give feedback on a leader's feedback.

Redefining the Leadership Team Meeting

This book has given you all the tools you need to redefine a leadership team meeting with little work required. Simply use the tools given to you in each chapter and the videos on the DVD that accompanies this book. On page 231, the highest-leverage actions you can use with a leadership team are drawn out of each instructional lever.

All of these agenda possibilities are available to you if you use the tools and guides in this book. Each action gets you closer to the real work of instructional leadership. Note that video is a particularly helpful tool to use for this type of observation, because often, when the principal steps into a room to observe, he or she changes the dynamic of the class. Admittedly, the presence of a video camera changes the dynamic as well, but you'd be amazed by how quickly people forget about the video camera—not so the principal! A video may, in these cases, give you a more accurate image of how instruction is going than your own vision would.

So what might this look like? If you build a weekly leadership check-in into your schedule (either with individual leaders or with the team as a whole), you can build a cycle of development that hits one of these topics at each meeting. Turn to Page 232 to read the meeting cycle for Mike Mann with his instructional leaders.

Think about the implications of following a meeting cycle like this with every instructional leader in your school. The principal will have an in-depth understanding of the quality of instructional leadership provided by each individual. He or she will be able to track—and drive—the progress that will create real change, regardless of the size of the school. The whole system also guarantees much more consistent support for every teacher in the building.

Leveraging Leadership Check-ins

Highest Leverage Actions for Principals and Instructional Leaders

Data-Driven Instruction

- *Analyze data* from an interim assessment of one of the teachers the leader supports: plan out the analysis meeting the leader will have with that teacher.
- *Observe the assessment analysis meeting* (in person or watch video of it).
- *Role-play* the analysis meeting.

Observation and Feedback

- *Review the observation tracker.* Has the leader observed enough? Are the action steps measurable, actionable, and bite-sized (can be accomplished in one week)? Is the teacher making progress based on the pattern of action steps over the past month?
- *Observe the teacher with the leader* and compare your sense of the most important action steps with what the leader has written in his or her observation tracker. Do you agree on the best action steps?
- *Observe the feedback meeting* (in person or watch video of it). How well is the leader implementing the six steps to effective feedback?
- *Role-play* the feedback meeting.

Planning

- *Review a teacher's curriculum plan or lesson plan together.* Is the teacher proficient on the rubric for effective plans?
- *Review a leader's feedback to a teacher's curriculum or lesson plan.* Is it the right feedback? Do teachers seem to be implementing the feedback?
- *Role-play* leading a planning meeting.

Leading Professional Development

- *Plan a PD session* together using the Living the Learning template.
- *Observe the PD session* (in person or watch video of it): Where can they improve in their delivery of PD?
- *Rehearse* the PD session.

Putting It into Action

A Sample Meeting Cycle for a Principal's Meetings with Instructional Leaders

Week 1

- *Review the observation tracker*. Has the leader observed enough? Are the action steps measurable, actionable, and bite-sized (can be accomplished in one week)? Is the teacher making progress based on the pattern of action steps over the past month?

Week 2

- *Observe the teacher with the leader* and compare your sense of the most important action steps with what the leader has written in his or her observation tracker. Do you agree on the best action steps?
- *Role-play* the feedback meeting.

Week 3

- *Observe the feedback meeting* (in person or watch video of it). How well is the leader implementing the six steps to effective feedback?
- *Role-play* the feedback meeting.

Week 4

- *Review a teacher's curriculum plan or lesson plan together*. Is the teacher proficient on the rubric for effective plans?
- *Review a leader's feedback on a teacher's curriculum or lesson plan*. Is it the right feedback? Does the teacher seem to be implementing the feedback?

Weeks 5–7

- Repeat weeks 1–3.

Week 8

- *Analyze data* from an interim assessment of one of the teachers the leader supports. Plan out the analysis meeting the leader will have with that teacher.
- *Role-play* the analysis meeting.

Table 7.3   Evaluating Instructional Leadership: Sample Column from Instructional Leadership Rubric

Rating	Observing Teachers and Providing Feedback
Advanced	Observes teacher every week and maintains observation tracker consistently during the year; Recommendations in the tracker are actionable, measurable, and the right levers for driving student achievement; Consistently monitors growth toward PD goals and identifies new goals as necessary
Proficient	Observes teachers three times per month and maintains 90% of observations in observation tracker; 90% of recommendations are actionable, measurable, and the right levers for driving student achievement; Consistently monitors growth toward PD goals and identifies new goals as necessary
Working Toward	Observes teachers two times per month and maintains 50–90% of observations in observation tracker; Recommendations are periodically actionable, measurable, and the right levers for driving student achievement; Inconsistently monitors growth toward PD goals and identifies new goals when previous ones are met
Needs Improvement	Does not maintain regular observations of teachers and/or record in observation tracker; Recommendations are not actionable and measurable nor are they the right levers for driving student achievement; Does not monitor growth toward PD goals nor set new goals when previous ones are met

EVALUATE WHAT MATTERS MOST

Leading meetings with your leadership team in this manner also makes evaluation so, so simple: the principal will know the quality of work leaders are doing! Mike Mann uses a succinct "instructional leadership rubric" to track progress on a host of skills, such as giving actionable feedback and responding to submitted lesson plans in a thorough and timely manner (see Table 7.3).

When you monitor instructional leadership as we've just described, filling out this column takes a maximum of a few minutes. The total rubric takes about 10–15 minutes, giving you time to write down overall strengths and weaknesses and still be done in 30 minutes. And with those 30 minutes, you have a more accurate, influential evaluation of what matters most: how instructional leaders are directly leading their teachers.

CONCLUSION: LEADER SUPPORT, STUDENT SUCCESS

Being a principal can be a very lonely job: it can feel impossible to support all the teachers in your school well. Leveraging your leadership team can change that: it enables you to delegate the management to many of your teachers, and in doing that, it enhances your ability to monitor their growth. You also send a clear message to everyone that teaching matters, and that supporting teachers in the work they do to drive student learning matters most.

Four Keys to Leadership Team Development

1. *Identify* instructional leaders.
2. *Train* initially and follow up throughout the year.
3. *Give feedback and practice* to leverage face-to-face meetings to develop leadership.
4. *Evaluate* leaders on what matters most: the quality of their instructional leadership.

Sample Instructional Leadership Rubric: Advanced Column

Category	Advanced Score
Lesson Plans	100% of lesson plans are reviewed weekly and sent on to principal. Lesson plans are highly effective in answering the following three questions: 1. What do my students need to know or be able to do by the end of the unit or class? 2. What is the most effective way for me to teach students these important concepts? 3. How do I make sure that students have really learned the concepts that I wanted them to learn? 90% of recommendations on lesson plans are actionable and represent the most important feedback for driving student learning (as evaluated during bimonthly reviews by campus principal or supervisor). Teacher has made dramatic gains toward proficiency in the lesson planning process, requiring much less critical feedback later in the year.
Observation and Feedback	Observes teacher every week and maintains observation tracker consistently during the year. Recommendations in the tracker are actionable, measurable, and the right levels for driving student achievement. Instructional leader consistently monitors growth towards PD goals and identifies new goals as necessary.
Results: Effectiveness of Feedback	Teacher(s) meet all three PD goals established at the beginning of each semester. Teacher(s) implement 90% of leader feedback (as recorded in observation tracker and measured in bimonthly review of teacher progress with campus principal or supervisor).
Data-Driven Instruction	Teacher adeptly uses data outside the interim assessment cycle collected from in-class assignments to adapt instruction. Interim assessment analysis is teacher-owned and deep. 100% of teacher's postassessment action plans drive future lesson planning.
Professional Development (When Applicable)	All observed PD sessions achieve rating of "Proficient" or "Advanced" on PD rubric. Teachers rate presenter as "Highly effective" on PD survey (when applicable).

Note: Full instructional leadership rubric can be found on the DVD.

Table 7.4   Making It Work: Where It Fits in a Leader's Schedule

	Monday	Tuesday	Wednesday	Thursday	Friday
6:00am					
:30	Greeting and breakfast	Greeting and breakfast		Greeting and breakfast	Greeting and breakfast
7:00am					
:30	Staff culture check	Morning assembly			Morning assembly
8:00am		Meet Wilson	Meet Bradley		
:30		Meet Vargas	Meet Frint		
9:00am	Observe Wilson, Vargas, Jenkins	Meet Jenkins			
:30					
10:00am			Observe Mitzia, Boykin, Devin		Observe Hoyt, Settles, Palma
:30					
11:00am					
:30	Lunch	Lunch	Lunch		Lunch
12:00pm	Observe Henry, Bernales, Christian				Meet Bradley
:30		Meet Worrell		Instructional leader's check-in	Meet Palma
1:00pm		Meet Christian			Meet Settles
:30		Meet Bernales	Meet Boykin		Meet Hoyt
2:00pm		Observe Bradley, Frint, Worrell	Meet Devin		
:30			Meet Mitzia		
3:00pm					
:30			Professional development session		
4:00pm	Dismissal	Dismissal		Dismissal	Dismissal
:30				Staff Meeting	
5:00pm					
:30					

■ Work Time   ■ School Culture   ■ Observations   ■ Meetings

Pulling the Lever
Action Planning Worksheet for Managing Leadership Teams

Self-Assessment

- What percentage of your leadership team meetings are devoted to the seven levers of leadership? _____ percent
- What percentage of the individuals on your leadership team would score as proficient on the instructional leadership rubric? _____ percent
- Which of the seven levers are your leadership team's key areas for improvement?

  _____

  _____

  _____

Planning for Action

- What tools from this book will you use to improve staff culture at your school? Check all that you will use (you can find all on the DVD):

☐ Observation Tracker Template

☐ Instructional Leadership Rubric

☐ Six Steps of Effective Feedback

☐ Planning Meetings One-Pager

☐ Leading Effective Analysis Meetings One-Pager

☐ Videos of Leadership (all videos could apply)

- What are your next steps for developing your leadership team?

Action	Date

Part 3

Execution

Chapter 8

Finding the Time

One-on-One: Getting Ready for the School Day

It's early in the morning, and Julie Kennedy is ready for the day ahead. A pair of walking shoes sits under her desk, and on the desk itself is a turtle picture frame with a note from the family of one of her first students. These are surrounded by hand-scrawled notes from various previous students.

Julie opens her Outlook calendar and her task list and confirms her plan for the day. The night before she noted open spots and planned out the major and minor tasks to be accomplished. She also notices the moment that is likely to be stressful for her, which she anticipated last night. The rest of the day will be filled with activity: the schedule includes observations, feedback meetings, and monitoring lunch. Most striking, though, is what it doesn't contain: Julie will be spending no time on building management, technology, or the upcoming fundraiser. At 7:15 a.m., with the arrival of the first students, she closes her laptop and heads downstairs.

Kim Marshall wrote a powerfully accurate critique of the lives of most principals that he entitled the "Hyperactive Superficial Principal Syndrome."[1] The job of a principal is arguably one of the most interrupted jobs anywhere. You are continually bombarded by students, parents, staff, and the mini-crises that occur each day. Because of this, a principal can invest a tremendous number of hours—and heart and soul—into the work of the school without even stepping foot into a classroom. Is the intensity and nature of the job too difficult to overcome?

The principals and leaders highlighted in this book offer an emphatic "No" to that question—along with the systems to back it up. They will not tell you that school leadership is easy—it is very, very hard. Yet in the previous seven chapters, we've outlined the choices these leaders make in investing their most precious commodity: time. Each of the systems presented is an investment that offers a tremendous return: hours that change weeks. And each of these systems is replicable. How? By nailing down your use of time.

Although many people have written about school leadership, few have offered a concrete path of how to put all the pieces together on a daily, weekly, and monthly basis. Leaving this information out of the equation is a serious mistake. Ultimately, even the best solutions are meaningless if you cannot feasibly put them into practice.

So how does this apply to you? Your school, like any other, is unique: you have your own strengths and challenges, be they the size of your staff, the number of additional instructional leaders, or the particular needs of your students. This chapter will help you adapt the lessons learned to meet the context of your own school. If you make a serious commitment to using the tools and strategies in this chapter, you will be able to lock in instructional and cultural leadership—and lock out most everything else. Results will follow.

Core Idea

By intentionally planning the use of your time, you can lock in instructional and cultural leadership—and lock out most everything else.

To make this feasible, this chapter offers three key tools for putting the vision we've outlined into practice:

1. Lock in your weekly schedule.

2. Defend your time from distractions.

3. Manage your daily and monthly tasks.

Keys to Finding the Time for Quality School Leadership

1. Lock in your weekly schedule.
2. Defend your time from distractions.
3. Manage your daily and monthly tasks.

LOCK IN A WEEKLY SCHEDULE

Throughout this book you have seen the building of a weekly schedule that includes all of the levers—data-driven instruction (DDI), observation and feedback, planning, professional development (PD), student culture, staff culture, managing school leadership teams—that build excellent schools. You are going to take that model and build a schedule for your own school. There is no doubt that embracing this calendar represents a significant change in how principals (or other school leaders) allocate their time. Fortunately, although the changes required by this shift are significant, they are entirely feasible. Not every leader will allocate his or her time in the exact same way, but as long as your schedule adheres to the core tenets listed here, it will work.

How can leaders find the time they need? Let's revisit Julie Jackson and watch, step by step, how she builds her schedule. Here is the order for building the schedule:

1. Prework: Determine your leader-to-teacher ratio.

2. Block out student culture times (Chapter 2).

3. Lock in professional development and other group meetings (Chapter 2, Chapter 6).

4. Lock in time for standing weekly individual teacher–leader meetings (Chapters 1 to 3).

5. Lock in time for class observations (Chapter 2).

6. Lock in work time.

What does this look like? Let's walk through it piece by piece:

Prework: Teacher-to-Leader Ratio

The number one variable that will influence your schedule is how many teachers you manage directly and the number of other instructional leaders you supervise in the management of the rest of the teachers. Here are the two core questions to get this started:

1. How many teachers are in your school? _____ teachers

2. How many in your school are or could be instructional leaders? _____ leaders

   - Formal instructional leaders: Assistant principals, coaches, department chairpersons, and so on

   - Others who could be leveraged this way: Special education coordinators, lead teachers, and so on

   - Ratio of teacher to leader (divide teachers by leaders): _____ teachers per leader

If your school is like most, you will come up with a ratio of 15:1 or less. That is the Golden Ratio: if it applies to your school, you can make the principles in this book work as written.

Your next step is to distribute the teachers across your leadership team: Which teachers will you manage directly and which will you delegate to others? In most cases, you should distribute teachers according to each of your instructional leader's strengths: her content expertise, his strength at working with novice teachers or teachers with management problems, and so on. If you are leading a very large school and you have a large number of instructional leaders to lead yourself, you might decide to distribute all your teachers among them and focus on managing the leaders only.

Once you have made this choice, every other decision flows naturally. We're off!

Step 1: Block Out Student Culture Times

As one of the super-levers, management of student culture is the thing to put on your schedule first. As mentioned in Chapter 4, there are a few critical moments when you have the biggest impact on student culture, and when crises or challenges are most likely to happen. For every school this is slightly different, but almost everyone would identify breakfast and arrival, lunch, and dismissal as key moments. Because these events occur at set times, they are the least flexible of the scheduling constraints and so should be pinned down first. Let's look at Julie Jackson's schedule in Table 8.1 as a guide.

Note that here Julie has left Wednesday morning and afternoon, as well as Thursday lunch, free. This means that she will designate another leader to cover those moments. Remember, for a school that needs a student culture turnaround, your calendar will need to be filled with a lot more "green" to manage the challenge

Table 8.1 Julie's Weekly Schedule with Just Culture

	Monday	Tuesday	Wednesday	Thursday	Friday
6:00am					
:30	Greeting and breakfast	Greeting and breakfast		Greeting and breakfast	Greeting and breakfast
7:00am					
:30		Morning assembly			Morning assembly
8:00am					
:30					
9:00am					
:30					
10:00am					
:30					
11:00am					
:30	Lunch	Lunch	Lunch		Lunch
12:00pm					
:30					
1:00pm					
:30					
2:00pm					
:30					
3:00pm					
:30					
4:00pm	Dismissal	Dismissal		Dismissal	Dismissal
:30					
5:00pm					
:30					

☐ Work Time   ☐ School Culture   ☐ Observations   ■ Meetings

of making significant improvements to a struggling culture. (See Chapter 5 for a turnaround leader's schedule.)

Step 2: Lock In Your Group Meetings

The next set of events to schedule is regular group meetings: PD and staff meetings, leadership team meetings, and so on. Be careful about too many meetings. Planning to attend all grade-level meetings every week—on top of your feedback meetings—won't work. See what Julie's schedule looks like in Table 8.2.

Table 8.2 Julie's Weekly Schedule: Student Culture + Group Meetings

	Monday	Tuesday	Wednesday	Thursday	Friday
6:00am					
:30	Greeting and breakfast	Greeting and breakfast		Greeting and breakfast	Greeting and breakfast
7:00am					
:30		Morning assembly			Morning assembly
8:00am					
:30					
9:00am					
:30					
10:00am					
:30					
11:00am					
:30	Lunch	Lunch	Lunch		Lunch
12:00pm					
:30				Leadership team meeting	
1:00pm	Meeting with principal supervisor				
:30					
2:00pm					
:30					
3:00pm					
:30			Professional development session		
4:00pm	Dismissal	Dismissal		Dismissal	Dismissal
:30					
5:00pm					
:30					

☐ Work Time   ☐ School Culture   ☐ Observations   ☐ Meetings

Note that she has kept her meetings to a minimum: one check-in with her principal supervisor, a leadership team meeting, and her weekly staff PD session.

Step 3: Lock In Your Teacher–Leader Meetings

Now it is time to add the highest-leverage drivers of your work: your standing weekly meeting with teachers to give observational feedback, review lesson plans, and do data analysis. Here you should take out your school schedule and look for the prep periods of each of the teachers you will manage. Pick a standing half-hour window when they are not teaching. Julie has 15 teachers to manage, so she locks in 15 half-hour check-ins, as shown in Table 8.3.

Julie likes having back-to-back meetings, because that gives her larger open chunks of time to spend on other tasks. If you need a break between each check-in, schedule accordingly. Remember the power of scheduling these meetings: you lock the time into the teacher's weekly plan as well, and then there is no need to chase down the teacher to find time to give him or her feedback! This routine and its consistency save significant time for everyone.

Step 4: Lock In Your Observations

Now it is time to lock in your observations. Remember our core principle: weekly 15-minute observations are far more valuable than twice-yearly full-length observations, and they are also more substantive than five-minute walkthroughs. Julie planned for three observations in each hour time period, budgeting for time to get from one classroom to the next and complete her observation tracker on the spot, as shown in Table 8.4.

These observations are placed strategically before the weekly meetings so that the observation is fresh when you're going into the meeting. If you need more time to prepare for your feedback meeting, then you might leave a larger gap between the observation and meeting.

Step 5: Build In Time to Check on Staff Culture

You have almost finished your schedule—just a few more things remain to be added. The next will be a periodic check on staff culture. This is time to simply walk the building and check in informally with staff: see how they're doing, sense the vibe in the faculty room, and be present for the staff. Nothing instructional occurs during this time: just building a stronger connection with your staff. See Julie's schedule in Table 8.5.

Over time, checking in on staff culture will become natural and won't need to be scheduled. But if this is something that doesn't come naturally to you, putting it on your schedule is a great way to start.

Step 6: Build In Time for Big Projects

Your final piece is to pick a block of time when you'll work on larger, non-daily projects. In reality, for most principals, this time will occur outside of the school

Table 8.3 Julie's Weekly Schedule: Student Culture + All Meetings

	Monday	Tuesday	Wednesday	Thursday	Friday
6:00am					
:30	Greeting and breakfast	Greeting and breakfast		Greeting and breakfast	Greeting and breakfast
7:00am					
:30		Morning assembly			Morning assembly
8:00am		Meet Wilson	Meet Bradley		
:30		Meet Vargas	Meet Frint		
9:00am		Meet Jenkins			
:30					
10:00am					
:30					
11:00am					
:30	Lunch	Lunch	Lunch		Lunch
12:00pm					Meet Bradley
:30		Meet Worrell		Leadership team meeting	Meet Palma
1:00pm	Meeting with principal supervisor	Meet Christian			Meet Settles
:30		Meet Bernales	Meet Boykin		Meet Hoyt
2:00pm			Meet Devin		
:30			Meet Mitzia		
3:00pm					
:30			Professional development session		
4:00pm	Dismissal	Dismissal		Dismissal	Dismissal
:30					
5:00pm					
:30					

■ Work Time   ■ School Culture   ■ Observations   ■ Meetings

Table 8.4 Julie's Weekly Schedule: Student Culture, Meetings, and Observations

	Monday	Tuesday	Wednesday	Thursday	Friday
6:00am					
:30	Greeting and breakfast	Greeting and breakfast		Greeting and breakfast	Greeting and breakfast
7:00am					
:30		Morning assembly			Morning assembly
8:00am		Meet Wilson	Meet Bradley		
:30		Meet Vargas	Meet Frint		
9:00am	Observe Wilson, Vargas, Jenkins	Meet Jenkins			
:30					
10:00am			Observe Mitzia, Boykin, Devin		Observe Hoyt, Settles, Palma
:30					
11:00am					
:30	Lunch	Lunch	Lunch		Lunch
12:00pm	Observe Henry, Bernales, Christian				Meet Bradley
:30		Meet Worrell		Leadership team meeting	Meet Palma
1:00pm	Meeting with principal supervisor	Meet Christian			Meet Settles
:30		Meet Bernales	Meet Boykin		Meet Hoyt
2:00pm		Observe Bradley, Frint, Worrell	Meet Devin		
:30			Meet Mitzia		
3:00pm					
:30			Professional development session		
4:00pm	Dismissal	Dismissal		Dismissal	Dismissal
:30					
5:00pm					
:30					

■ Work Time   ■ School Culture   ■ Observations   ■ Meetings

Table 8.5 Julie's Weekly Schedule: All Culture, Meetings, and Observations

	Monday	Tuesday	Wednesday	Thursday	Friday
6:00am					
:30	Greeting and breakfast	Greeting and breakfast		Greeting and breakfast	Greeting and breakfast
7:00am					
:30	Staff culture check	Morning assembly			Morning assembly
8:00am		Meet Wilson	Meet Bradley		Staff culture check
:30		Meet Vargas	Meet Frint		
9:00am	Observe Wilson, Vargas, Jenkins	Meet Jenkins			
:30					
10:00am			Observe Mitzia, Boykin, Devin		Observe Hoyt, Settles, Palma
:30					
11:00am		Staff culture check			
:30	Lunch	Lunch	Lunch		Lunch
12:00pm	Observe Henry, Bernales, Christian				Meet Bradley
:30		Meet Worrell		Leadership team meeting	Meet Palma
1:00pm	Meeting with principal supervisor	Meet Christian			Meet Settles
:30		Meet Bernales	Meet Boykin		Meet Hoyt
2:00pm		Observe Bradley, Frint, Worrell	Meet Devin		
:30			Meet Mitzia		
3:00pm					
:30			Professional development session	Staff culture check	
4:00pm	Dismissal	Dismissal		Dismissal	Dismissal
:30					
5:00pm					
:30					

■ Work Time   ■ School Culture   ■ Observations   ■ Meetings

day. Julie chooses to work on big projects on Monday evening, but she gets some help on Friday afternoon to free up an additional block. When we polled the exceptional leaders in this book, they were very realistic about the fact that they normally only have about three to five hours of weekly time for big picture work—their jobs consume everything else! We'll see how you keep that big project work focused on the right things in the next section of the chapter. For the time being, lock in the planning time, as in Table 8.6.

Take a Moment to Reflect on What You've Accomplished

Take a moment to consider what this schedule accomplishes. First, half of your schedule is still open, allowing for daily issues and unforeseen challenges to arise. Thus, if a student issue occurs during your observation window on Monday, you can move your observations to Tuesday. This is what makes the schedule feasible. If, when you build your schedule, you don't leave at least 30 percent unscheduled, the weekly schedule won't work. You'll need to cut down on some of your group meetings (that's the one variable that will make it untenable if you've limited yourself to managing 15 teachers directly on a weekly basis).

Look at what you've accomplished:

- *Every teacher in the building is observed every week.* For schools that formerly observed once a year, this is a twentyfold increase!

- *Every teacher is getting feedback every week.* You've moved from one or two pieces of feedback in a year to forty.

- *Every teacher is getting explicit support on his or her lesson plans via the weekly check-in.* An ounce of prevention is worth a pound of cure.

- *Staff are regularly receiving high-quality professional development.*

- *Interim assessments are substantively and deeply analyzed.* Once every eight weeks, observation feedback gets replaced by data analysis. With locked-in teacher meetings, you don't need to reschedule anything to make this happen.

- *You or another leader is present to drive student culture at each key moment of the day.*

Most importantly, you have taken the critical step that each top-tier leader in this book has taken: you have taken control over your time. The seven previous

Table 8.6 Julie's Weekly Schedule: Everything

	Monday	Tuesday	Wednesday	Thursday	Friday
6:00am					
:30	Greeting and breakfast	Greeting and breakfast		Greeting and breakfast	Greeting and breakfast
7:00am					
:30	Staff culture check	Morning assembly			Morning assembly
8:00am		Meet Wilson	Meet Bradley		Staff culture check
:30		Meet Vargas	Meet Frint		
9:00am	Observe Wilson, Vargas, Jenkins	Meet Jenkins			
:30					
10:00am			Observe Mitzia, Boykin, Devin		Observe Hoyt, Setles, Palma
:30					
11:00am		Staff culture check			
:30	Lunch	Lunch	Lunch		Lunch
12:00pm	Observe Henry, Bernales, Christian				Meet Bradley
:30		Meet Worrell		Leadership team meeting	Meet Palma
1:00pm	Meeting with principal supervisor	Meet Christian			Meet Setles
:30		Meet Bernales	Meet Boykin		Meet Hoyt
2:00pm		Observe Bradley, Frint, Worrell	Meet Devin		Large-project work time
:30			Meet Mitzia		
3:00pm					
:30			Professional development session	Staff culture check	
4:00pm	Dismissal	Dismissal		Dismissal	Dismissal
:30					
5:00pm					
:30					

▢ Work Time   ▢ School Culture   ▢ Observations   ▢ Meetings

chapters have outlined the investments that make a school extraordinary. With this schedule, we've given you the tools to make it yours.

> ## Core Idea
>
> For seven chapters, we have offered the investments that make a school extraordinary. With this schedule, we've given you the tools to make it yours.

Make Your Own!

Table 8.7 is a blank template onto which you can copy the same exercise presented here. Alternatively, the DVD has a simple Excel document that can be used as your schedule. Other leaders make their schedules directly in Outlook. Whatever your choice, take the time and rebuild your schedule right now.

Exceptional school leaders thrive not by working more hours than other school leaders but by making their hours count. So what is next? Defending your schedule so you can follow it.

DEFEND YOUR TIME

If time is a leader's most precious resource, then it is not enough to know how it should be spent; leaders also need to know how to protect it. In this section, we provide the tools to show how one might pursue this. First, though, let's look to the pitfalls: How might a principal lose control of his or her calendar?

The Well-Intentioned Firefighters

Let's consider a school leader: Mr. Reynolds. Mr. Reynolds wants to transform his school, to conduct weekly observations, analyze data, and forge a strong student culture. Today he hopes to conduct a schoolwide culture walkthrough, observe three teachers, and finish analyzing the first math interim assessment. His day starts out well enough. After getting to school early and working in his office until 7:30 a.m., he walks downstairs to the cafeteria to monitor breakfast and deliver morning announcements.

When he returns to his office, he sees 25 emails in his inbox and immediately starts to respond. As he works, a secretary shares the four phone calls he's

Table 8.7 Blank Schedule Template

	Monday	Tuesday	Wednesday	Thursday	Friday
6:00 am					
:30					
7:00 am					
:30					
8:00 am					
:30					
9:00 am					
:30					
10:00 am					
:30					
11:00 am					
:30					
12:00 pm					
:30					
1:00 pm					
:30					
2:00 pm					
:30					
3:00 pm					
:30					
4:00 pm					
:30					
5:00 pm					
:30					
Evening					

received: two vendor requests, a call from a prospective visitor, and a parent asking directions for the school field trip. After calling each party back, Reynolds returns to his inbox, continuing to write. After two hours, he still has not watched a single teacher, analyzed a single data point, or observed classroom culture.

By the day's end, things are only marginally better. Reynolds' inbox is empty, he was able to monitor lunch and dismissal, and all phone requests have been dealt with. Yet Reynolds never stepped into the classrooms to observe or support his teachers. If a school leader's main role is to drive student learning, then Reynolds did not do his job today. Despite his best intentions, he was only fighting fires.

Core Idea

If a school leader's main role is to drive student learning, then *not* observing and meeting with teachers means a leader did *not* do his job today. Despite his best intentions, he was only fighting fires.

Mr. Reynolds means well: he knows what a schoolwide transformation requires, and he's willing to work hard to achieve it. Yet without a serious change, he will not be able to bring his vision to fruition. Without careful planning and systems, the tide of distraction will wash away any of the systems in this book. Fortunately, the leaders profiled here built systems to overcome these challenges and to give themselves the time they needed to transform their schools.

This book argues that a school leader's main role is in two places: instruction and culture. Every minute that a leader spends outside of these is a minute when the core levers of school success are not being advanced. Of course, it is easier to say than to put it into practice. In the moment, "firefighting" can seem compelling and urgent. Yet even when your help could extinguish those fires, your attention is likely more needed elsewhere. Minimizing the time that leaders spend on "everything else" is a vital priority.

Defeating Distractions: Building Your Offensive Line Against "Everything Else"

Schools, as principals know all too well, are about far more than learning: communications, technology, compliance, food service, transportation, safety inspections—the list goes on and on. These tasks, which can be dubbed "operations," are vital components of the very foundation of any school. Nevertheless, they are not where school leaders will make their impact on student achievement, and thus they are not the areas where school leaders should be investing their time. To the greatest extent possible, leaders must delegate these tasks to others to focus on the core work of instruction and culture. There are a number of strategies you can pursue to deal with these tasks, regardless of the type of school you are in or the constraints you face. Here are some of the strategies most used by successful instructional leaders that have allowed them to focus on culture and instruction:

• *Designate an operations leader.* An ideal solution to operations is the designation of one leader position solely to address these tasks. Whether the person is an assistant principal, a dean, or even a secretary, this leader is in charge of managing each of the operation systems. Beyond saving time, there is a more subtle advantage to creating an operations leader: specialization. As North Star Elementary's director of operations Christian Sparling notes, "The skills needed to succeed as an instructional and cultural leader are often very different than the skills needed as a building manager." All too often, the result is principals who are overwhelmed with unfamiliar tasks exactly when they could do the most instructional good.

• *Build an operations team.* If a separate operations leader cannot be assigned, an alternative solution is an operations team made up of teachers, office managers, assistant principals, or others. Each member of the operations team would be assigned a set area of operations; for example, a veteran teacher might be responsible for all field trip logistics, while a head custodian might be responsible for building logistics. To facilitate this process, school leaders must meet with the operations team at the start of the year to record every major operations event (for example, closing down the school for winter break; see Table 8.8) and then assigning an "owner" to it.

Note, however, that this team approach does have drawbacks; spreading out operations functions across multiple individuals can dilute accountability. More fundamentally, if you're introducing this system, it will be important to select trusted individuals who are very good at managing their time and won't let these new tasks trump their instructional responsibilities.

Table 8.8 Shutting the School Down for the Holidays: Sample Operations Plan

Task	Who Owns It	Complete By
Turn off boiler	Maria Valdez	12/15
Monitor dismissal	Cassandra Jensen	12/15
Call lunch delivery to cancel	Jeff Liu	12/16
"Deep clean" of all desks and hallways	Mike Warner	12/17
Create flyer to send home with students	Carl McManus	12/17

Table 8.9 Whom to Go To for What: Sample Guidance for Staff on Operations Support

Questions and Requests	Examples and Notes	Contact
Attendance (students)	Each morning, teachers should enter student absences into the computer database	Office manager
Transportation and dismissal	Notify office manager and copy director of operations of any messages received regarding student transportation or dismissal changes	Office manager and director of operations
Certification	Letters, questions, requirements, and so on	Director of operations
Extracurricular programs	Afterschool, sports, summer internships, and so on	Community engagement coordinator
Facilities and maintenance	Maintenance requests, cleaning requests, and so on	Custodian for immediate and low-cost maintenance requests Director of operations for larger requests

Whom to Go To for What

Whatever system is chosen for operations, it will save time only if it is clear and readily understood. At the start of the year, several of the schools studied distributed a document to each staff member on "whom to go to for what." This document contains clear contact information and instructions for whom to contact. For example, if Jon, a science teacher, is in charge of special projects, then the chart would list him as the contact. If the guidelines are unclear, people will email you. I've included a brief example of such a document in Table 8.9.

Getting Them to Block and Tackle

Once operations are taken care of, the next crucial step in defending time comes in setting clear expectations and guidelines to streamline and reduce one-off requests. School leaders are continually bombarded with nonroutine events, whether teacher questions, technology issues, or visitor requests. On its own, each of these events is innocuous; three minutes here, two minutes there. Unfortunately, they add up. Imagine if each day, one person has one question for the principal and there's a parent who has one question per principal per day. For a staff of 30, if it only takes two minutes to answer every question, this is an hour a day. In "investment" terms, the cost is enormous: three observations, or two data conferences, or a lunch and a morning assembly spent supervising. Throw in 300 students, 600 parents and guardians, support staff, and visitors, and leaders may soon be entirely overwhelmed, sprinting from one fire to another, but never moving forward. To defeat distraction:

• *Lock in time to check in with teachers.* The quickest way to reduce the number of questions teachers have is to make sure teachers know there's a time when they'll be able to ask those questions. The beauty of the weekly check-in is that with them, you've scheduled a moment to answer questions that don't fit elsewhere in the schedule. You can do the same for parents by just locking in certain times when parents can come to you with questions. Weekly check-ins are sacred for teachers. If they know they'll have time to ask you any questions they have, then they'll hold their questions until that time. This applies to email, too. Use weekly check-ins to reduce "pop-in" distractions: set an expectation that teachers should hold nonemergency questions (for example, field trip ideas, project proposals) until their scheduled weekly check-ins. Doing so will allow questions to be addressed much more efficiently.

• *Block and tackle.* Almost anyone with a question about a school—parent, teacher, or guest—will want to talk to the principal. At the schools we've seen in this book, leaders trained officer staff and others to "block and tackle," working to ensure that nonessential requests did not eat into the leader's time. Note that the use of a "whom to go to for what" document, as outlined, will make this easier (for example, guests with questions about facilities can be directed to a member of the operations staff or the operations team of staff members, not the school leader). There will, of course, be some meetings with school leaders that can't wait, but 95 percent of the meetings principals need to have do not need to happen in the moment, so you've reduced the 5 percent here.

- *Avoid pet projects.* Often, school leaders will be drawn to particular aspects of school management that are unrelated to the core priorities of instruction. For example, a principal may be personally interested in student fundraisers and may spend a great deal of time micromanaging. This is a serious mistake. As Christian Sparling, director of operations at North Star Elementary, notes, "Though it's always tempting to go with your personal interests, the best leaders are the ones who are able to stick to their core strategic priorities and not be distracted."

- *Plan blocks for communication.* Answering emails or calls as they come in is vastly disruptive; it breaks the flow of a sustained task and can naturally pull leaders away from their core tasks. Setting aside a solid block of time to address all emails is a much better approach. Even if it takes up an hour a day, it's vital that your schedule determines your email and that your emails don't determine your schedule.

- *Say it once.* Giving announcements to individual teachers multiple times quickly adds up. Leverage your time more effectively by saying it once in a staff meeting or weekly memo.

THE FINAL STEP: MANAGE TASKS

You're in the home stretch. You've scheduled your weekly routines and protected your time. The last piece is to manage your tasks: your daily tasks and your monthly tasks. To keep track of these tasks, leaders need a way to map their actions and to build a plan beyond the daily and weekly level.

The Monthly Map

To do so, many of the leaders we've seen used a tool called the monthly map. The monthly map is effectively a task list of the most important things that you should be doing, with each task separated by month. Maia Heyck-Merlin, author of *The Together Teacher,* notes that setting up a monthly map is imperative for keeping your eyes on what matters most.[2] You don't want your data-driven analysis meetings to sneak up on you, or forget to schedule the dates of your interim assessments. (Important note: Data-driven instruction is much more a set of monthly tasks than weekly tasks. Thus, it is the lever that most needs a monthly map.)

Table 8.10 Principal Monthly Map: On My Radar

Month	Task
September	1. Launch reading intervention/guided reading (*Data-Driven Instruction*). 1. Assess curriculum plans for rigor and alignment and return to teachers (*Planning*). 2. Quarterly leadership team meeting (principal, dean, instructional leaders) (*Leadership Team*). 3. Videotape planning meetings of all instructional leaders (*Leadership Team*). 3. Make a student and staff culture walkthrough (*Student Culture, Staff Culture*). 4. Co-observe teachers with instructional leaders (*Feedback and Observation, Leadership Team*). 4. Set yearly PD goals for all new teachers in observation tracker (*Feedback and Observation*).
October	1. Design PD session on classroom pacing (*PD, Student Culture*). 1. Give teachers curriculum planning update and revision time (*Planning*). 2. Ensure instructional leaders are reviewing video clips with novice teachers (*Leadership Team*). 3. Administer interim assessment # 1 (*Data*). 4. Evaluate school on data-driven instruction Rubric (*Data*). 4. Coordinate grade-level culture walkthroughs (*Student Culture, Staff Culture*).

There are a few different ways to build a monthly map. The longer, more thorough way is to launch a full strategic planning process: set core goals for each lever or leadership, smaller objectives and major tasks to accomplish. Maia Heyck-Merlin's work is a perfect source of information about how to complete this process systematically.[3] Realistically, however, many of us don't have the time to do that. To simplify the task, we've included sample monthly maps for elementary, middle, and high school on the DVD. Table 8.10 presents a small sample so you can see what it looks like.

You'll notice that each task is labeled 1 to 4: that represents the week of the month the action should take place. This doesn't just help you see your tasks clearly; it also makes monthly maps easier to carry over from year to year.

To prepare monthly maps in the short version, take the sample monthly maps on the DVD, eliminate what is not relevant, add what's unique to your school, and make sure the dates work for your calendar. After you have your maps, you can refer to them throughout the year.

The Daily and Weekly Action Plan

A daily action plan gives you a way to organize tasks and hold yourself accountable for getting them done. The action plan coupled with a weekly schedule gives you

A Leader's Testimonial on Finding the Time

James Verrilli

Being a principal means having a thousand little things to do at any moment of the day. Whenever you sit down to deal with one conflict, you're likely to be distracted by another one popping up. It's like having a thousand fires to put out, all at the same time.

When I first became a principal, one of the hardest lessons I had to learn was how to prioritize those fires. Trying to extinguish them as they came at me wasn't always effective. Worse, it left me with very little time for instructional leadership. I needed to observe teachers and give them feedback in order to make sure instruction was happening in their classrooms, and that wasn't really happening. I usually knew which teachers I wanted to see, but I would give myself an impractically flexible schedule for doing so, and I would let it slide altogether if other tasks came up.

I knew I had to develop a better time management system; instructional leadership was too important to be this sporadic. I needed to hold it sacred, and in order to do that, I needed to schedule it firmly, every single week.

I began marking out the time I would spend observing teachers, giving them feedback, and helping them plan lessons and curriculum. It helped to do it visually—with colored Post-it notes on a calendar, or on Microsoft Outlook. Whichever calendar I used, though, I didn't just stick observation time blocks on it—I also put the names of each teacher I needed to observe into each block. Scheduling weekly feedback meetings with those specific teachers helped me stay accountable to my new observation schedule, since I couldn't very well lead a feedback meeting with a teacher whose classes I hadn't observed. My new system put all the pieces of instructional leadership together at the beginning.

As I adjusted to the new system, I still had fires to put out. There were still days when I didn't get through all my observations. In that sense, my job didn't change. But I became much more effective at *doing* my job. Planning every week with this level of detail made it easier for me to keep instructional leadership a priority, even if a parent or another colleague came to me with a problem during that time. Saying, "I can't help you right now, I need to see the teachers," is always hard, but it's a lot harder when you haven't scheduled the time you need to spend observing teachers.

Now, when instructional leadership tasks slip by me, I know what they are, and I know to reschedule them. I also always know what each teacher at my school is teaching, and which instructional teams are successful in which ways. I'm better at avoiding double booking, because I have an agenda that tells me when I'm available to make a new appointment. I interact with my fellow staff on a more personal level. Best of all, I get to put my classroom expertise, as well as my leadership expertise, into practice.

Admittedly, I also have to be more strategic now on completing larger projects than I did before I committed to my instructional leadership schedule. When I have a special project to work on, I'll often end up needing to complete it before or after school, or on a weekend. To me, though, it's clear that the benefits of my new system outweigh the costs. After all, shouldn't we be doing instructional leadership during the day, when instruction is happening?

---

everything you need to ensure that time and task management never gets in the way of your school's success.

While the typical to-do list groups together all of your various tasks, the action plan organizes entries into separate buckets. (See Table 8.11.) You can customize these buckets to fit your needs, but the general model should work for any school leader. On the first page of the action plan there are six buckets: today, this week, this month, next month, leadership team agenda topics, and faculty memo topics. The first four buckets explain themselves. Use the leadership team agenda bucket to jot down ideas for your group meetings with instructional leaders. The faculty memo section gives you some brainstorming space as you think of important messages to send out to the staff during the week.

TURNAROUND: SCHEDULE FOR SUCCESS

The most important turnaround you can make, and the one that you have the most control over, is changing your own use of time. Your schedule is the key to finding the time you need to put the other systems into place and to begin changing your school. Yet as we have noted throughout this book, the first core steps to change must come from student culture and data-driven instruction. As Brian Sims observed, "It doesn't matter if it takes a month, three months or a year: without a safe and stable student culture, nothing else will matter." As a result, during a turnaround, the ways in which a principal uses his or her time will carry a different emphasis. What might this look like? Placing more time on student culture and less on other components.

Be careful, however, about skipping observation and feedback altogether. When leaders do not do observation and feedback from the beginning, they find it very difficult to incorporate it later. Without a cycle of data-driven instruction supported by observation feedback, turning around student culture will not be sufficient to increase student achievement.

Table 8.11 Daily and Weekly Action Planning Template

To Do	New Topics to Capture
Today	This Week
This Month [May]	Next Month [June]
Leadership Team Agenda Topics	Faculty Memo Topics

CONCLUSION: EVERY MINUTE MATTERS

If this book offers a single message, it is that the central question school leaders must confront is how they use their time. Answering this question requires focus, determination, and hard work. Yet as this chapter shows, it does not demand

Weekly Schedule Creation for School Leaders

Summary How-to Guide

Prework

- Determine the number of instructional leaders you will need to manage directly (assistant principals, coaches, and so on).
- Determine the standing meetings you want to occur at least once a month (leadership team meeting, faculty PD).
- Determine the total number of teachers in your school and which people will lead which teachers directly. Determine the number of teachers you will manage directly (ranging from zero for a large-school leader to potentially all teachers for a small-school leader). *Note: Between leaders and teachers, you should have no more than 15 to 20 people you will lead personally.*
- Get out your school's weekly schedule that shows when teachers are teaching and when they have prep periods.

Weekly Schedule

- Create a simple grid for the week in half-hour or hourly segments 7:00 a.m. to 6:00 p.m. (modify the grid to match your school class schedule).
- Create the grid so that each hourly block is the size of the Post-its you will use.

Green Post-its: Student Culture

- Place green Post-its wherever you are likely to be focused on student culture and parental issues (likely breakfast or start of day, lunchtime, and at dismissal).

Yellow Post-its: Meetings

- Make a decision: Do you work best with back-to-back-to-back meetings, or do you need breaks between meetings to stay focused? Use this criterion to complete the following tasks.
- Each yellow Post-it represents a one-hour meeting.
- Label Post-its for each of your team/large-group meetings: leadership team, faculty PD, and so on. Place them on the schedule. If they only happen every other week, note that on the Post-its.
- Write the names of the one to three teachers you will lead on yellow Post-its and place them on the schedule where teachers have prep period.
  - Two teachers per Post-it for 30-minute planning and feedback meetings
  - Three teachers per Post-it for 20-minute feedback check-ins

(continued)

- Place on the schedule your check-ins with any other individuals.
- Depending on your preferences, place these meetings as close together as possible or spread out.

Orange Post-its: Observations
- Plan three or four observations for every hour (15-minute observations).
- Place one orange Post-it for every three to four teachers you will be observing.
  - If you have 16 teachers to observe, you need four or five Post-its.

Blue Post-its: Uninterrupted Work Time
- Select three blocks of two to three hours of *uninterrupted* time and place blue Post-its on those areas.
- Unless you can get out of the building and have someone cover for you, these times have to be in the very early morning, very late afternoon, evenings, or weekends.
- Designate one of those planning times for no email: just large tasks from your monthly map.

---

the impossible. On the contrary, the leaders studied succeeded because they continually worked to have the greatest impact in the *least* amount of time: the 15-minute observation that can change a teacher's career; the 30-minute data conference that changes a month's worth of achievement; the hour-long PD session that bulks up your school's skill base. The result is a commitment that is significant but manageable. Yet there is a broader point at stake, too: the same measures that are outlined here will save you time in the long run. A stronger school culture means less firefighting; stronger instruction means less time spent on emergency remediation; effective and well-aligned planning means fewer chaotic midyear turnarounds. Ultimately, then, the question is not whether it is feasible for leaders to pursue these systems, but whether they can afford not to.

> ## Core Idea
>
> Ultimately, the question is not whether it is feasible for leaders to pursue the systems presented in this book, but whether they can afford not to.

Pulling the Lever
Action Planning Worksheet for Finding the Time

Self-Assessment

- What percentage of your teachers currently gets feedback more than twice a month? _____ percent
- What percentage of your time is currently devoted to instructional or cultural leadership? _____ percent
- What are the biggest improvements you could make to your weekly schedule in order to increase the time you spend on instructional and cultural leadership?

  _____

  _____

  _____

Planning for Action
- What tools from this book will you use to manage your time? Check all that you will use (you can find all on the DVD):

☐   Model Schedule

☐   Sample Weekly Schedules

☐   Monthly Map Template

☐   Sample Monthly Maps

☐   Action Plan Template

- What are your next steps for finding the time for instructional and cultural leadership?

Action	Date

Chapter 9

The Superintendent's Guide

Managing and Developing Principals for Results

One-on-One: Principal Coach to Principal

It's November, and Dana Lehman, superintendent of the Uncommon Schools Boston network, is holding her weekly meeting with Debbie Previna, principal of Grove Hall Prep. Prior to arriving at the school, Dana consulted her superintendent's dashboard (see section later in chapter) and noticed that sixth-grade science scores on the previous interim assessment were notably lower than those of other grades and subjects. Dana and Debbie pull out that teacher's preliminary data action plan and dive in.

"Look," noted Debbie. "Her action plan states that she has to reteach all aspects of the sun and moon. But on questions 21 and 25, it's clear that the issue is really about confusing rotation and revolution." Dana and Debbie brainstorm the teaching actions that could address this standard, and then they rehearse the analysis meeting that Debbie will have with the teacher that week.

This done, the pair moves on to Debbie's observation tracker and review her feedback to the science teacher in question. This teacher, like three others, is struggling with managing independent practice. Dana and Debbie spend the last 15 minutes of their meeting discussing the professional development that could best address this area.

The previous chapters have discussed the core levers—data-driven instruction (DDI), feedback and observation, planning, professional development (PD), student culture, staff culture, and leadership team management—that a school leader can use to build exceptional schools. What does it take to lead multiple schools to this level of excellence?

For principals, superintendents, and principal managers alike, the rule is the same: how school leaders use their time is the single greatest determinant of whether their schools will succeed. Consider the opening vignette about Dana Lehman. In one 90-minute meeting with her principal Debbie Previna, Dana is able to leverage the tools in this book to review data-driven instruction, observation feedback, and professional development. Over the course of a month of meetings, every one of the levers will be addressed. In the course of that month, Dana and her principals will not only have deeply explored every key principle of what makes schools effective—they will also have practiced repeatedly. Based on the data provided by interim assessments, culture walkthroughs, and school site visits, Dana knows the pulse of each of her schools, right down to the individual classroom level. As a result, she knows the ways in which schools are struggling or succeeding well before any state test scores come in. More importantly, she knows what levers need to be pulled in order for each leader to improve those results.

Core Idea

By using tools that monitor the seven levers, superintendents can know much more quickly how each of their schools is struggling or succeeding. They also know which levers need to be pulled in order to improve those results.

The work of a superintendent merits a book in and of itself. Superintendents are uniquely placed to build transformational schools. As multiple school leaders, they have the ability to transform instruction beyond any one classroom—and, indeed, beyond any one school. Yet to realize this potential, superintendents need to re-envision the role of principal management: the way they spend their time and what they prioritize. If the key to effective school leadership is prioritizing the seven levers we've presented in this book, then the key to effective district leadership is to develop principals who can—and will—put those levers into practice. Essentially, this means three key tasks:

1. *Train the leaders.* Train aspiring and current principals in the core levers.
2. *Coach continuously.* Utilize face-to-face activities to coach principals on the seven levers in real time.
3. *Monitor progress.* Build and use tools to monitor progress on what matters most: the seven levers.

Prioritizing these actions means putting instructional quality at the core of the superintendent's role. In too many districts, this is not done. Just as principals often find themselves fighting fires, superintendents often find themselves bogged down by a daily parade of non-instructional tasks. While shifting a leader's focus to instructional work may require significant reconfiguration, it offers an unparalleled chance to drive student success.

Core Idea

If we want all school leaders to succeed, we need to develop them intentionally—just as we propose for teachers:

- *Train the leaders.* Train aspiring and current principals in the core levers.
- *Coach continuously.* Utilize face-to-face activities to coach principals in real-time on the seven levers.
- *Monitor progress.* Build and use tools to monitor progress on what matters most: the seven levers.

Table 9.1   Guide to Training Materials: All the Resources for Training Leaders (Part 4 of this Book)

Leadership Lever	Training Materials (found in Part 4 and on DVD)
Data-driven instruction (Chapter 1)	Videos of leaders in action (training materials can be found in the book *Driven by Data*[1])
Observation and feedback (Chapter 2)	7 hours of training materials and video of leaders in action
Planning (Chapter 3)	4 hours of training materials and video of leaders in action
Leading PD (Chapter 4)	5 hours of training materials and video of leaders in action
Student culture (Chapter 5)	4 hours of training materials and video of leaders in action
Finding the time (Chapter 8)	4 hours of training materials

TRAIN YOUR PRINCIPALS

The first key step to ensuring that your principals can put the core levers into place is to show them what these levers are. The chapters in Part 4 offer *all the materials, scripts, videos, and PowerPoint presentations* you will need to train your instructional leaders in these principles. (See Table 9.1.)

The heart of these trainings is that they show exemplary practice in action: real leaders leading feedback conversation, data analysis meetings, or student culture rehearsals. For the participants, seeing it in action is the first step; practicing it in the moment of the workshop solidifies the learning. All these workshops follow those precise steps, leaving participants with the tools to take the results of the training into their schools.

Yet none of this training will matter without follow-up. Without follow-up and accountability, leading PD becomes the weakest instructional lever. The same holds true for leader development.

COACH CONTINUOUSLY

School leadership is one of the most challenging—and important—jobs in our community. Yet it is also one of the least supported. Today, many districts are trying to respond to this reality by building systems to support their principals more effectively. Unfortunately, many of those activities fall prey to one of the following errors.

Errors in Coaching Principals: What *Not* to Do

Here are the three most common errors superintendents and their leadership teams make in managing principals.

Error I: Walkthroughs Without Purpose

The classic superintendent walkthrough involves being led around the building by a principal, who narrates what the superintendent sees. More conscientious superintendents may travel with a rubric or checklist to gauge each classroom's effectiveness. But without an explicit link to data-driven instruction, you cannot observe for genuine rigor—at best, you can observe for the technique that looks rigorous. Of course, walkthroughs do play a key role in looking at school culture, a process described at length in Chapter 4. When the process is conflated as one that also ensures understanding of academic performance, however, it is problematic. Walkthroughs have another fundamental flaw: they don't show teachers' progress—only snapshots in time. Was the principal effective in developing his or her novice teachers? A walkthrough won't tell you that story. If you lack the tools to monitor principal actions that contribute to teacher development over time, your walkthroughs will fall flat.

Error II: School Reviews

As an alternative to walkthroughs, some have suggested that superintendents should use elaborate two- or three-day school reviews. In many ways, these days are massive document reviews: principals must produce a host of paperwork showing they are in compliance, while multiple-school leaders focus in on whether all school standards are aligned with state standards. These reviews are doubly problematic.

First, while such data might be important, they are still only a single snapshot. Just as students and teachers benefit from continuous and regular feedback, school leaders must also receive guidance as they grow, not annual information dumps. Relying on once-a-year school reviews is like coaching tennis players for two days a year and expecting them to compete at the U.S. Open: no matter how great those two days of coaching were, the tennis players would have no chance. In preparing our own leaders for their "big games," a school review approach is similarly problematic.

Yet school reviews are even more problematic for a second reason: they're looking at the wrong things. Go back to the seven levers: When do school reviews watch principals give teachers feedback? When do they check the quality of the action steps listed in an observation tracker? When do they evaluate the quality of data analysis meetings and the implementation of data-driven action plans? When do they monitor whether a principal is spending his or her time on the highest-leverage activities possible? You don't learn these things by watching classrooms or reviewing papers—you learn them by observing a principal's work with a teacher.

> ### Core Idea
>
> School reviews and building walkthroughs don't drive real change because they're looking at the wrong things: they focus on classrooms and paperwork rather than on the leader levers that make the difference.

Error III: Leading from Afar

A final, opposite misstep is to attempt to lead schools without visiting them, instead relying on school leaders to report their own data and their own compliance with each lever. Having received interim assessment reports, culture walkthrough rubrics, and observation trackers, multiple-school leaders may assume they already have everything they need to see how a school must improve. Unfortunately, this approach prevents multiple-school leaders from ensuring that their leaders are effectively using these systems—and that their self-assessments are accurate. You can look over a leader's observation tracker, but if you don't see the classes of struggling teachers, you will not know whether the principal has given them appropriate steps for improvement. You can review interim assessment data, but if you're not seeing individual quizzes, you won't know whether reteaching is truly occurring. At the end of the day, improvement must be driven from the school itself, not just from the paper.

Coaching Principals One on One: Leverage from the Seven Levers

The most important first step to re-envisioning principal support is to rebuild your schedule: allocate your time in a way that prioritizes the coaching of principals.

As is true for principals with their school leadership teams, a superintendent's face-to-face time with principals can have the biggest impact. Why? For the same reason as for teachers: we learn best from repeated practice and face-to-face feedback on the parts of our jobs that matter most. Yet principals get less of this practice and feedback than leaders in almost any other profession. What might this practice and feedback look like? It depends on the number of schools you manage.

A Word On . . . District Size

Districts vary vastly in size. Can the methods outlined in this book work in a large district? How large? The most important ratio is the number of principals per principal supervisor. In a small district, the principal supervisor and the superintendent are the same person. In a large district, the role of the principal supervisor has many different titles.

According to conversations with principal coaches and supervisors across the country, most of these school leaders can meet in-depth with their principals at the following rates:

- 7 leaders per supervisor: One on-site meeting or school visit *per week*
- 15 leaders per supervisor: One on-site meeting or school visit *every other week*
- 30 leaders: One on-site meeting or school visit *every month*

These numbers only matter if the time in those meetings and school visits is well spent.

As even a quick glance at Table 9.2 shows, 50 percent of this multiple-school leader's time is spent interacting directly with school leaders. If a multiple-school leader's goal is to directly improve schools, then this is entirely appropriate. School leaders show what they value by how they use their time: if you are a multiple-school leader, and if your goal is driving principals to lead great schools, then you must ask yourself a crucial question: What part of your week is devoted to working directly with the principals who will make a difference in your schools? Are you spending between 40 and 50 percent of your time directly working with leaders in ways that will make a difference? If not, who is? Ultimately, as Harrison, Colorado, Superintendent Mike Miles notes, we have the time for whatever we

Table 9.2 Superintendent's Weekly Schedule

	Monday (DTMS/HS/NSA)	Tuesday (CH/ES2/USI/NSA)	Wednesday (ES3/Vailsburg/USI)	Thursday (USI)	Friday (Work)
8:30am	Phone Calls	Phone Calls	Recruitment	Phone Calls	Phone Calls
9:00am	MS #1	ES #1	MS #4 (+ MS fellow)	District-wide school meetings, inspections, and others	Work time and makeup meeting day
:30					
10:00am					
:30					
11:00am	HS	ES #2 (+ ES fellow)	ES #3		
:30					
12:00pm					
:30					
1:00pm		PD Staff			
:30	MS #3		Campus walkthroughs: Observe classes, staff PD, leader-teacher check-ins		
2:00pm		Week 1: All-principals meeting Week 2: Compliance Week 3: MS/ES principals Week 4: Superintendent-business administration			
:30					
3:00pm					
:30	District Staff				
4:00pm					
:30					
5:00pm	Phone Calls		Phone Calls	Phone Calls	Phone Calls
:30					
Evening					

■ Work Time   ■ Walkthroughs / Inspections   ■ Meetings

prioritize. If you make working directly with leaders a priority, you will find the time to do it; you just need to remember how vital it is that this work take priority.

As was true for principals' meetings with instructional leaders, the main focus of these check-ins is on the implementation of the seven levers, because that is what drives school success. You cannot cover all seven levers in any one meeting, but the emphasis could shift on a regular cycle to ensure all key areas are reviewed. What might this look like?

Putting It into Action

A Sample Meeting Cycle for a Superintendent's or Principal Manager's Meetings with Principals

Week 1
- *Review the observation tracker*. Has the principal observed enough? Are the action steps measurable, actionable, and bite-sized (can be accomplished in one week)? Based on the pattern of action steps over the past month, is the teacher making progress?
- *Observe teachers with the leader*. Do the key action steps written in the observation tracker match the areas of difficulty you see in the classroom? Where are there gaps in the principal's ability to identify the highest leverage action step for a teacher?

Week 2
- *Review the observation tracker*. Has the principal observed enough? Are the action steps measurable, actionable, and bite-sized (can be accomplished in one week)? Is the teacher making progress based on the pattern of action steps over the past month?
- *Plan and role-play* the feedback meeting with teachers in upcoming meetings.

Week 3
- *Observe video of the principal's observation feedback meeting*. How well is the leader implementing the six steps to effective feedback?
- *Observe video of the leadership team's observation feedback meetings*. How well are the members of the leadership team implementing the six steps to effective feedback?
- *Role-play* improving the feedback meeting.

Week 4
- *Observe school culture walkthrough*. When you look at the school culture rubric, where do you see the school succeeding? Where does it need to grow?
- *Observe PD*. What is the quality of the PD? How does the leader make sure teachers implement what they learn during the PD?

Week 5
- *Review a teacher's curriculum plan or lesson plan together*. Is the teacher proficient on the rubric for effective plans?
- *Review a leader's curriculum and lesson plan feedback*. Is it the right feedback? Do teachers seem to be implementing the feedback?

Week 6
- *Analyze data* from an interim assessment of one of the teachers the leader supports. Plan out the analysis meeting the leader will have with that teacher.
- *Role-play* the analysis meeting.

What do you notice about this cycle? It ensures that you hit every major lever:

- Data-driven instruction (week 6)
- Observation/feedback (weeks 2–3, 5)
- Planning (week 5)
- Leading PD (week 4)
- Student and staff culture (week 4)
- Leadership team (week 3)

Even more significantly, it prevents your merely talking about these levers: it gets you to observe them, give real-time feedback, and have teachers practice with you. This is the power of high-leverage leadership: principals are spending time participating in what will make the biggest impact in their schools.

> ### Core Idea
>
> Effective principal managers don't just talk about the seven levers: they observe them, give real-time feedback, and get principals to practice them. Effective feedback and practice change results.

LEVERAGE PRINCIPAL TEAMS

Many of the actions we've described can also be carried out in meetings with teams of principals. Doing so can be a superb way to bring leaders out of their "silos" and to hold leaders accountable to each other. The key is to *do* the work of leadership, not just talk about it: share videos of observation conferences and get peer feedback from peers, review a sampling of lesson plans, role-play data analysis meetings, and so on. Activities like these get leaders more feedback and more practice—and that's the best use of their time.

Build Tools to Monitor Progress: The Superintendent's Dashboard

In his book *Blink: The Power of Thinking Without Thinking*, Malcolm Gladwell speaks of the power of looking at the right slice of information to make important judgments and take action.[2] Tachi Yamada, president of the Gates Foundation's Global Health Program, recently set out his own perspective on leadership: "I don't micromanage, but I have microinterest. I do know the details. I do care about the details."[3] So, if a superintendent's goal is to assess the quality of the leaders in his or her district—and thus the quality of learning in his or her schools—what is the right slice of information for him or her to look at?

The best place to focus is on the levers. Assess the most powerful components of each one, and you won't just be able to diagnose the future success of each school—you'll also know what actions to take to improve that outcome.

Core Idea

If you want to assess the quality of a leader, evaluate the seven levers. Not only will you be able to predict the future success of the leader's school, but you'll also know what actions to take to improve that outcome.

Each previous chapter laid out these core components in detail, but let's take a quick look at some of the most powerful measurements for each one. Each district could choose its own measures for each lever; use the ones listed here as a starting point.

What to Measure
Data-Driven Instruction (Chapter 1)
The two key measures are:

1. Interim assessment results

2. DDI implementation rubric score

Data-driven instruction is a super-lever for many reasons. One of the most powerful reasons is that it measures student learning in a way that can allow teachers to improve their teaching. As such, interim assessment results are the ultimate during year assessment of student learning. By assembling data on a school- or department-wide level, superintendents can quickly analyze broad trends or dive deep to find out where schools can improve. The complement to these interim assessment results is the ability of a school to implement all the key drivers of data-driven instruction as measured by the data-driven instruction implementation rubric. Having trained thousands of school leaders on this lever, I have yet to observe a school that implemented all aspects of the DDI rubric and did *not* get results. (If that ever does happen to a school, we'll change the rubric!)

Observation and Feedback (Chapter 2)

The two key measures can both be taken from the observation tracker (see samples in Chapter 2 and the DVD).

1. *Observation tracker:* Average number of observations per teacher
2. *Observation tracker:* Percentage of action steps that are bite-sized, measurable, and actionable

Note the power of the simple observation tracker. Without such a tool, a superintendent is powerless to know whether or not a principal is doing weekly observations and whether she is clear and precise in her feedback. This is game changing.

Planning (Chapter 3)

The key measures can be one or both of the following:

1. *Curriculum plan rubric:* Percentage of plans that are proficient
2. *Lesson plan rubric:* Percentage of lesson plans in a spot check that are proficient

By using a curriculum plan or lesson plan rubric, superintendents can look at a sampling of these plans and quickly assess the quality of planning. The simplicity of the one-page rubrics makes it easy to evaluate a lesson plan in just a few minutes.

Professional Development (Chapter 4)

The key measure is:

• *PD rubric:* Proficiency when delivering PD

The power of the rubric used in this book is that it measures the value of the PD based on its ability to change teacher practice. A superintendent could never observe all PD delivered by a school leader, but observing a few sessions with the included rubric would give her at least a snapshot of PD quality.

Student Culture (Chapter 5)

The key measure is:

- *Student culture rubric:* Percentage of categories proficient on a school walk-through

Monitoring school culture requires walkthroughs—there is no other way to assess culture. Fortunately, when leaders know what they are looking for, these walkthroughs are extremely efficient. Based on these walkthroughs (outlined at length in Chapter 4) superintendents can produce a school culture rubric that can quickly indicate strengths and areas of school growth in student engagement, joy, compliance, and consistency.

Staff Culture (Chapter 6)

The key measure is:

- *Staff culture rubric:* Percentage of categories that are proficient

Staff culture is the hardest lever to measure. Brett Peiser's staff culture rubric gives us a way to make culture observable and more measurable. Brett comments, "The best way for me to assess a staff culture is to sit in the faculty room, long enough for some teachers not to notice me in there. You learn a lot just by observing how teachers interact with each other."

Leadership Team (Chapter 7)

The key measure is:

- *Instructional leadership (IL) rubric score*

What is the best way to evaluate instructional leaders? By assessing their ability to implement the instructional levers. That is precisely what the instructional leader rubric measures: a leader's effectiveness at leading data, observations, planning, and (where applicable) PD.

The Tool for Collecting It: The Superintendent's Dashboard

Individually, each of these tools is an objective, efficient, and effective way of gauging a school's strengths and areas for growth as it puts the levers into practice. Yet the true power of these measures is that they can simply be combined into a single "dashboard," a comprehensive tracker that allows superintendents to quickly gauge exactly where each school is—and where, accordingly, to focus their attention. What might this look like? Table 9.3 presents a sample dashboard from the North Star schools.

You'll see that the seven levers are the only things measured on this dashboard, and that they all fit on one page. Then you'll notice that the categories correspond to the highest-leverage action steps mentioned, each with a target. No shading indicates that a leader is hitting or above the target; light shading means he or she is close, and dark shading means he or she is falling below the target. It becomes immediately apparent where a superintendent should focus his or her efforts with each school leader. This also allows the superintendent to see districtwide patterns and to differentiate leadership PD based on what each leader needs.

TURNAROUND: SUPPORT STRUGGLING SCHOOLS

Nowhere is the imperative of school turnaround more pressing than at the districtwide level. Frequently, superintendents will face the daunting challenge of turning multiple schools from failure to success and must do so in the face of steep pressure. What are the first steps to turnaround? The super-levers: data-driven instruction and student culture. At the district level, as at the school level, these foundations will turn chaotic, failed schools into steadily improving ones; and if time and resources are limited, it is these levers of change that will generate the most improvement. When dealing with a struggling school, you'll make an impact most quickly by limiting the parts of the dashboard you fill in to these two super-levers.

As time passes, and as change slowly takes root, superintendents can begin to implement the next important lever—feedback and observation—before starting on the others. Without the super-levers in place, further change will be impossible.

CONCLUSION: SUCCEED AT SCALE

By training her principals to focus on the right goals—and by monitoring their progress in pursuing them—superintendents like Dana Lehman create change on a districtwide scale. Although the solutions offered in this chapter cannot encompass all that a multiple-school leader does, they form the basis of a system that profoundly improves learning in even the most challenging environments. Simply put, the tools this chapter offers empower superintendents to succeed at scale, the level of success our students need and deserve.

Table 9.3   Leader Dashboard: 2nd Quarter

| Measure | Category | Target (through Dec) | School Leaders | | | | | | Principals in Training | | |
| | | | ES #1 | ES #2 | ES #3 | MS #1 | MS #2 | HS | #1 | #2 | #3 |
			Year 1	Year 2	Year 14	Year 2	Year 4	Year 1	Year 0	Year 0	Year 0
Data-driven instruction	Literacy IAs +/− last year	0	−4	−9	−2	15	8	−2	6	−1	7
	Math IAs +/− last year	0	3	5	−2	7	1	−1	9	0	−8
	Science IAs +/− last year	0	5	3	8	15			9	2	
	History IAs +/− last year	0	−7	−5	−8	−4			12	−5	
	Implementation rubric	90%	94%	89%	86%	81%	88%	88%			
Observation and feedback	Average number observations per teacher	11	21	5	10	3	13	19	8	8	11
	% of feedback measurable, actionable	90%	30%	97%	50%	55%	100%	70%	30%	—	65%
PD	PD delivery proficient	3	3.3	3.7	2.5	3.1	3.8	—	2.8		3.7
Planning	Curriculum plans proficient	90%	83%	90%	33%	67%	100%	100%			100%
Student culture	School culture rubric % categories proficient	90%	100%	71%	82%	86%	100%	95%			
Staff culture	Staff culture rubric	3	4	2	4	3	3	3			
	Teacher sense of positive staff culture	4.0	4.0	3.9	4.0	3.4	3.5	4.0			
Leadership development	Rising leaders proficient 90% of IL rubric	90%	100%	70%	70%	57%	75%	—			

Pulling the Lever
Action Planning Worksheet for Superintendent's Guide

Self-Assessment
- Which of the seven levers do you want to focus on and measure this year as you develop your principals?

_____

_____

_____

Planning for Action
- What tools from this book will you use to lead your schools? Check all that you will use (you can find all on the DVD):

☐ Superintendent's Sample Schedule

☐ Superintendent's Dashboard

☐ Monthly Map Template

☐ Sample Monthly Maps

☐ Rubrics and/or tools from specific chapters

☐ Videos of Leadership (all videos could apply)

☐ PD on the seven levers (all could apply)

- What would be the best ways to support your principals in building weekly schedules? Check all that apply.

☐ Leading principals in a professional development session

☐ Building schedules one on one with principals

☐ Sending principals instructions for scheduling, having them write their own schedules, and then monitoring their results

☐ Other:

- How will you need to change principal manager's schedules in order to support your principals face to face?

_____

_____

_____

- How will you change the sample superintendent dashboard in this book in order to make it work for you and your district?

_____

_____

_____

What are your next steps for launching the seven levers districtwide?

Action	Date

Conclusion

A Brighter Future

Throughout this book, our focus has been on the use of time and on the strategies to drive learning. In each chapter, we've offered a system to drive school growth and the ways to put it into place. Taken together, we've offered a comprehensive blueprint for building an exceptional school.

Yet this book's ultimate purpose is not time management; it's not even great school leadership. This book is about students like David Smith. In fourth grade, David was slated to be tracked into a self-contained special-needs classroom. Six years later, David is one of North Star High School's top students, a tenth grader whose Scholastic Aptitude Test scores are already above the national average. A few years ago, David and a select group of North Star students had the chance to meet Secretary of Education Arne Duncan. When Duncan prompted David to explain what North Star meant to him, David's message was unequivocal: "North Star set a vision for me and kept at it until I finally got it. I don't know who I'd be if not for this school."

This book is also about students like Wilson Rodriguez. Wilson left his family and moved to the United States from the Dominican Republic a few days before beginning sixth grade at Roxbury Prep. When asked, "Where did you go to school?" he replied, "Yes." He knew no English and had attended school for a few hours each day in his rural Dominican Republic community. With support from teachers and family and his own sheer determination, Wilson never left Roxbury Prep before 6:00 p.m., and when he went home he would complete more work there. He graduated in three years with a B average and is a thriving tenth-grade high school student.

Perhaps most of all, this book is about students like Chantaya King. Chantaya's mother never had the opportunity to go to college, but she stayed close to it, providing custodial services at a local university. When Chantaya first arrived at school, she was a quiet student who struggled academically. Few people had told her that college was in her future.

Fast forward 15 years. Chantaya not only graduated from high school, college, and earned her master's degree, she was determined to give other students the same opportunities that she had. She is currently the social worker at North Star High School.

The reason David, Wilson, Chantaya, and thousands like them are on a path toward college and success is not just an unwavering belief in them and hard work. There were complemented by doing the most *effective* work in school. These success stories were made possible in larger doses than what is considered normal because of the choices their school leaders made. Every day, leaders like Dana Lehman, Mike Mann, Julie Kennedy, Stacey Shells, and Julie Jackson are changing destinies and changing lives. In building great schools, they are building great futures.

Ultimately, the goal of what we've outlined is to give these students the education they need and deserve. The schools we studied succeeded because of their systems, yet they also succeeded because they held this as their core commitment. From this conviction, combined with the right systems, greatness is possible. It is our hope to carry that greatness to every child across the country.

Part 4

Professional Development Workshops: Overview and Highlights

HOW TO USE THESE WORKSHOPS

Use these professional development workshops to train other leaders to implement the seven key levers of leadership featured in this book.

Workshops Included in This Book

- Observation and Feedback (Chapter 2)

- Leading Planning (Chapter 3)

- Leading Professional Development (Chapter 4)

- Student Culture (Chapter 5)

- Finding the Time (Chapter 8)

Workshop Materials in the Text

- A cover page that highlights the workshop's goals and intended audience

- A workshop preparation sheet that shows what materials you need for the workshop, how long the workshop runs, and how to assess the workshop's success

- A workshop overview that outlines the subtopics covered in the workshop

- A small segment of the full-length presenter's notes to be used while presenting the workshop

Workshop Materials on the DVD

- The full-length presenter's notes to be used while presenting the workshop

- The PowerPoint presentation that accompanies each workshop

- The handouts you'll need to provide for each workshop

Other Workshops

- For the workshop on data-driven instruction (Chapter 1), see my previous book, *Driven by Data*.[1]

- Workshop materials for staff culture (Chapter 6) are still in development as of this book's publication.

Chapter 10

Observation and Feedback Workshop

Observation and Feedback

Paul Bambrick-Santoyo

Uncommon
Schools | NORTH ★ STAR

WHAT'S THE GOAL?

Make instructional leaders excellent at observing teachers and giving feedback. By the end of the workshop, leaders will know how to:

- Maintain regular observation for all teachers.

- Identify the right action steps to drive student learning.

- Implement the six steps of effective feedback.

- Hold teachers accountable for implementing feedback.

- Design specific initiatives to guide struggling teachers.

For more information about the value of building strong observation and feedback systems, see Chapter 2.

WHO'S THE AUDIENCE?

Anyone who leads teachers, either formally or informally. This may include principals, assistant principals, coaches, mentors, or department chairs.

WHEN TO USE IT

Best Time

Right before the school year begins. This gives participants the most direct opportunity to put what they learn into action.

Other Times That Work

Schools can introduce observation and feedback systems at any time, so this workshop may be fruitful at any point during the school year.

WORKSHOP PREPARATION

Workshop Objectives

1. Maintain regular observation for all teachers.

2. Identify the right action steps to drive student learning.

3. Implement the five principles of effective feedback.

4. Hold teachers accountable for implementing feedback.

5. Design specific initiatives to guide struggling teachers.

Running Time

- 7 hours

- *Short on time?* If you can only present part of the workshop, the *most important sections* to include are 1.1, 1.2, 1.3, 1.4, 1.5, and 1.6.

Making the Workshop Stick: Follow-Up Steps

- Review participants' observation trackers as a part of your regular check-ins.

- Watch video of the participants giving feedback and critique using the six steps of feedback.

- Observe teachers jointly and identify the highest-leverage action steps.

Materials

The full-length Presenter's Notes located on the DVD specify when to use each of these materials.

Materials on DVD

- Observation and Feedback PowerPoint Presentation

- Video: Clips on Observation and Feedback

- Handouts
    - 1A: Observation and Feedback Reflection
    - 2A: Case Study #1: Choosing the Right Levers
    - 3A: Six Steps for Effective Feedback
    - 5B: Action Plan Template
    - 7B: Observation Tracker Template
    - 3C: Weekly Meeting Notes Page
    - 4A: Failure Case Study: Observation and Feedback
    - 5A: Reflection on First-Year Teaching Experience
    - 5B: Managing Struggling Teachers: A Sample Six-Week Plan
    - 5C: Tightening the Feedback Loop and Increasing Change

- 7A: Serena's Observation Tracker
- 8B: Principal's Weekly-Monthly Schedule

Other Materials

- 1 binder per participant. To organize each binder, print out the handouts and place handouts that share the same number together in the same tab of the binder. *For example:* Handouts labeled 5A, 5B, and 5C would all go in Tab 5 of the binder, with 5A coming first and 5C coming last.
- 1 name tent per participant
- Green and yellow Post-it notes
- Markers
- Table tents
- 2 numbered chart paper posters per four workshop participants
- 1 basketball
- 1 basketball "hoop" (such as a trash can)
- 13 prewritten sentence strips:
  - "Co-observe another teacher with the same students."
  - "Create written, specific action plans with a timetable."
  - "Make a checklist or rubric for the struggling teacher to use while observing other teachers."
  - "Prioritize one specific action step at a time; model it."
  - "Hold regular meetings with the struggling teacher."
  - "Suggest helpful readings and tools to improve her teaching."
  - "Regularly observe the struggling teacher."
  - "Have the struggling teacher observe a 'Level 1' teacher."
  - "Assign a faculty mentor to the struggling teacher."
  - "Provide the struggling teacher with written and verbal feedback."
  - "Engage the teacher in frequent, informal conversations about her progress."

- "Videotape the struggling teacher and have her review herself on videotape."
- "Have the struggling teacher watch a videotape of a stronger teacher to see what it should look like."

COMPLETE WORKSHOP OVERVIEW

Living the Learning Components Legend

AA = *Airtight activity* that leads participants to the right conclusion mostly on their own

R = *Reflection* during which participants quietly generate and record conclusions or takeaways

S = Small- or large-group *sharing*

F = *Framing* that gives participants a common vocabulary to use to describe what they learn

A = *Application* of learned principles

For more on PD components, see Chapter 4.

Part 1: The Four Keys to Observation and Feedback

	Section	Timing	Activity	PD Step
1.1	Introduction		Quick Write: Easy and Challenging Teachers	AA, S, F
			Written Case Study: Challenges of Teacher Development	AA, S, F
			Workshop Objectives and the Four Keys to Observation and Feedback	F
1.2	The Four Keys to Observation and Feedback		Regular Observation	F
1.3	The Right Action Steps		Activity: Writing Great Action Steps	A, S, A, S, R
			Activity: Choosing the Right Action Steps	AA, S, R

(continued)

Part 1: The Four Keys to Observation and Feedback (*Continued*)

	Section	Timing	Activity	PD Step
BREAK				
1.4	Flawed Feedback		Basketball Activity	AA, S, F, R
1.5	Effective Feedback		Video: The Six Steps of Effective Feedback	AA, S, F
			Video: Precise Praise	AA, S, F
			Video: Probing	AA, S, F
			Video: Identifying the Problem and Writing the Action Step	AA, S, F
			Application: Planning Effective Feedback Meetings	A, S
			Role Play: Probe to Action Step	A, S, R, S
			Video: Practicing	AA, S, F
			Video: Planning Ahead	AA, S, F
			Video: Setting a Timeline	AA, S, F
LUNCH				
1.6	Observation and Feedback Accountability		Tools for Staying on Top of Observation and Feedback	A, F
			Role Play: Practicing, Planning Ahead, and Setting a Timeline	A, S, R, S

Part 2: Guiding Struggling Teachers

	Section	Timing	Activity	Type
2.1	Reflections of a Struggling Teacher		Activity: Challenges of Guiding Struggling Teachers	AA, S, F
			Written Case Study: Reflections of a Struggling Teacher	AA, S, F
2.2	Strategies for Guiding Struggling Teachers		Video: Classroom Intervention	AA, S, F
			Strategies for Tightening the Feedback Loop	AA, S, F
			The Six-Week Plan	AA, S
			Role Play: Guiding Struggling Teachers	A, S
2.3	Conclusion		Workshop Reflection	R, S
			Empowering Leaders	F

SPOTLIGHT ON EFFECTIVE FEEDBACK: AN EXCERPT FROM THE FULL-LENGTH PRESENTER'S NOTES

To give you a taste of what it's like to lead this workshop, here's a short excerpt from the full-length presenter's notes you'll find on the DVD.

Context

At this point in the Observation and Feedback Workshop, participants have already identified the four keys to observation and feedback: regular observation, choosing the right action steps, effective feedback, and accountability. Now, at the beginning of section 1.5 of the workshop, they are diving into the six steps of effective feedback. This segment includes an overview of the six steps and an in-depth look at each of the first three steps.

Effective Feedback

Materials	Observation and Feedback PowerPoint Presentation Slides	Video Clips	Handouts	Other Materials
	40–60	3, 4, 7, 5, 11, 12, 13	1A	

Video: The Six Steps of Effective Feedback

AA: Effective Feedback Video, Part 1 (8 minutes)

Do	Show Slide 40.

(*continued*)

Say	"We're going to watch a video clip of a leader's feedback meeting with a teacher."
Do	Show Slide 41.
Say	"In this clip, Julie is giving feedback after observing Carly's third-grade science class. Julie observed that the questions Carly asked were decreasing her class's rigor. Julie decided that Carly's best action step would be to ask less scaffolded questions. We'll watch the video of Julie and Carly's feedback meeting in two parts, and you'll take notes. Focus on this question: What steps does Julie follow to lead her meeting with Carly? Let's take a look."
Do	Have participants take notes on the steps Julie follows wherever they have space. Show Part 1 of Video Clip 3. Stop the clip when Julie finishes identifying the action step Carly has to work on.
Say	"Before we move on, take 30 seconds to finish writing down your observations."
Do	Give participants 30 seconds to finish taking notes.

S: Pair Sharing (2 minutes)

Say	"Now, turn to a partner and share your observations. What steps did Julie follow to lead her meeting with Carly? Begin sharing . . . now."
Do	Have participants pair share what steps Julie followed.

AA: Effective Feedback Video, Part 2 (5 minutes)

Say	"We'll move on to the next part of the video now. What does Julie do next? Let's find out."
Do	Have participants continue taking notes on the steps Julie follows. Show Part 2 of Video Clip 3 (from where you left off up until the end).

S: Large-Group Sharing (10 minutes)

Say	"All right. Look at all your notes, and try to piece together the steps Julie used to run the feedback meeting effectively. What process was Julie following?"
Do	Lead large-group sharing. Listen for the following key points: "Julie started by telling Carly what she'd done well that week." "Julie and Carly identified the right action step together, with Julie asking questions that got Carly to see the action step herself." "Julie and Carly practiced the action step so that Carly would know exactly *how* to do it—not just *what* it was." "Julie and Carly finished by planning how Carly would work the action step into her upcoming lessons."
Say	*If participants do not generate all the key points right away, consider asking this scaffolded follow-up question:* "Okay, and then what did Julie do right after that?"

F: Effective Feedback (5 minutes)

Do

Show Slide 42.

The Six Steps to Effective Feedback

1. PRECISE PRAISE: Narrate the positive.
2. PROBE: State targeted, open-ended question about the core issue.
3. ID PROBLEM AND ACTION STEP: Identify problem; state concrete action step that will address issue.
4. PRACTICE: Role play/simulate how teacher could have improved current class.
5. PLAN AHEAD: Design/revise upcoming lesson plan components to implement action.
6. SET TIMELINE: Establish time by which to accomplish action step.

Uncommon Schools | ▶NORTH ★ STAR◀

Say

"We call the process you just described the Six Steps of Effective Feedback. The six steps are precise praise; probing; identifying the problem and action step; practicing; planning ahead; and setting a timeline.

"As you saw, Julie opened the meeting with a precise piece of praise. Then, she began probing: asking open-ended questions that targeted the core problem she wanted Carly to address. She got Carly to identify that problem and a concrete action step that would solve it. They practiced the action. Then, Julie helped Carly plan ahead, determining where this would all fit into her upcoming lessons. Before concluding the meeting, they would also have written a timeline to set a date by which Carly would accomplish the action step.

"Julie completed all six steps in just 10 minutes—some of the highest-leverage 10 minutes in a school day. You can replicate what Julie just accomplished by learning how to carry out each of the steps effectively."

Video: Precise Praise

AA: Precise Praise Video (2 minutes)

Do	Show Slide 43.
Say	"Now that we've seen how the principles of effective feedback work together, we'll study each individually."
Do	Show Slide 44.
Say	"The first thing that happens in an effective feedback meeting is precise praise. We'll illustrate the value of precise praise with another video clip. The leader, Serena, will give precise praise. As you watch, answer the following question: What makes her praise effective? Let's take a look."
Do	Show Video Clip 4.

S: Pair Sharing (1 minute)

Say	"Okay. What made Serena's praise effective? Turn to a partner and share. Begin."
Do	Have participants pair share their observations about Serena's praise. Raise your hand to call the group back together.

S: Large-Group Sharing (2 minutes)

Say	"Time for large-group sharing! What made Serena's praise effective?"
Do	Lead large-group sharing. Listen for the following key points: "Serena's praise didn't sound hollow—it was genuine and specific." "In her praise, Serena addressed the action step she knew the teacher had been working on."
Say	*If participants do not generate all the key points right away, consider asking these scaffolded follow-up questions:* "What did you notice about the type of praise Serena gave? Was it false praise? Was it vague?" "How was Serena's praise connected to what the teacher had been working on?"

F: Precise Praise (2 minutes)

Do	Show Slide 45.

The Six Steps to Effective Feedback

Precise Praise

- **Genuine**—heart-felt, authentic
- **Precise**—target a specific action the teacher took
- **Reinforce Positive Actions**—particularly those that are connected to the teacher's development goal

Uncommon Schools | NORTH ★ STAR

Say	"What we've just noticed is that praise needs to be authentic and precise, making it clear that you observed the teacher attentively. It should reinforce the teacher's specific positive actions. Praise's purpose isn't just to start feedback meetings on a positive note: it's to tell teachers what to keep doing."

Video: Probing and Identifying the Action Step, Part 1

AA: Probing and Identifying the Action Step Video, Part 2 (3 minutes)

Do	Show Slide 46.
Say	"Next, let's look at what we call probing: asking questions that guide teachers to identify the highest-lever challenges they face. In our next video, Aja will demonstrate probing with Kristi. Aja has observed that while Kristi's students can determine the first sounds in words, they have trouble breaking down larger words and determining the sounds in the middle. Kristi, however, thinks she needs to keep working on first-letter sounds. As you watch this video clip, I'd like you to answer the question: How does Aja show Kristi the correct problem? Let's see now."
Do	Show Video Clip 7.

S: Pair Sharing (1 minute)

Say	"All right, what did Aja do to guide Kristi to the right problem? Turn and share with a partner . . . now."
Do	Have participants pair share how Aja guided Kristi to the right problem.

S: Large-Group Sharing (2 minutes)

Say

"Let's break down Aja's approach together. How did she get Kristi to the right problem?"

Do

Lead large group sharing. Listen for the following key points: "Aja asks Kristi precisely about her objective for the lesson." "Aja asks Kristi if the students are meeting the objective." "Aja presents Kristi with the data to suggest that her analysis is incomplete." "Throughout the video, Aja asks questions that help Kristi to get to the right conclusion on her own."

F: Probing and Identifying the Action Step, Part 1 (4 minutes)

Do

Show Slide 47.

The Six Steps to Effective Feedback

- **Probe—State a targeted open-ended question about the core issue.**
  - Targeted on the core area of the lesson where you want to focus
  - Scaffolded follow-up questions
  - Presenting data: allows to see how the teacher views his/her lesson
- RIGOR EXAMPLE: "What was the end goal—what should students know and be able to do at the end of your lesson?"
- MANAGEMENT EXAMPLE: "How long did you think students needed to complete the 'You Do' during the lesson?"

Uncommon Schools | ❯NORTH★STAR

Say	"As we just saw, when you start feedback with a probing question, the teacher has to think about what happened in the classroom and generate an answer. In this video, Kristi initially generated the wrong answer, but Aja continued probing with scaffolded follow-up questions she'd prepared in advance. When those follow-up questions weren't enough, Aja showed Kristi data from the lesson. Kristi remembered what her students had done and reached accurate conclusions about what was going on in her classroom. In short, when you follow the process Aja followed, you're getting the teacher to do the thinking about his or her practice."

Video: Probing and Identifying the Action Step, Part 2

AA: Probing and Identifying the Action Step Video, Part 2 (3 minutes)

Do	Show Slide 48.

Say	"Sometimes, as in this video with Kristi, teachers need a lot of guidance to identify the problem they most need to address. But even the teachers who identify the right problem easily need your guidance: after they identify the right problem, you'll need to guide them to a precise action step. Let's see how this looks. We'll watch a video now that shows what happens when a teacher, Rachel, determines the right problem quickly. How does Julie continue to guide Rachel after Rachel identifies the right problem? Pay close attention to this question as we take a look."

Do	Show Video Clip 5.

S: Pair Sharing (1 minute)

Say	"Turn to a partner. What does Julie do after Rachel identifies the right problem? Go ahead and share your observations. You may begin."
Do	Have participants pair share what Julie does.

S: Large-Group Sharing (2 minutes)

Say	"How does Julie work with a teacher who knows the right problem to address?"
Do	Lead large group sharing. Listen for the following key points: "Julie kept asking Rachel questions even after Rachel identified the main problem in her classroom." "Julie's questions led Rachel specifically to the action step Julie wanted Rachel to identify."
Say	*If participants do not provide all the key points right away, consider asking these scaffolded follow-up questions:* "Even when Rachel was quite reflective, did Julie sit back and say nothing?" "What were the types of questions Julie asked?"

F: Probing and Identifying the Action Step, Part 2 (4 minutes)

Do

Show Slide 49.

> ## The Six Steps to Effective Feedback
>
> **ID PROBLEM AND CONCRETE ACTION STEP—Get teacher to identify the problem and how to address it:**
>
> - Level 1: Teacher comes to issue by self and states clear action step to address it.
> - Level 2: Leader uses a series of scaffolded questions to lead teacher to the answer.
> - Level 3: Leader presents data from the observation; then teacher realizes the issue and states action step.
> - Level 4: Leader states the problem and action step clearly to the teacher.
>
> Uncommon Schools | **▶ NORTH ★ STAR**

Say

"When it comes to probing and identifying the teacher's action step, your approach depends on how self-reflective your teacher is. A Level 1 teacher is very self-reflective and able to identify the right action step on his or her own. Level 2 teachers require scaffolded questions. Level 3 teachers need the actual data from your observation in order to see what you saw. In rare cases, even after providing all this scaffolding, you'll just need to state the problem and action step to the teacher. Even in these cases, though, it is important to give the teacher a chance to do the thinking first. Don't assume teachers are at Level 4 before giving them chances to reflect. The value of trying each level of support is that even if nothing you try gets the teacher directly to the action step, everything you attempt makes the teacher think a little harder about teaching."

Leading Planning Workshop

Leading Planning

Paul Bambrick-Santoyo

WHAT'S THE GOAL?

Lead teachers in planning lessons and curriculum effectively. By the end of the workshop, participants will know how to:

- Drive the planning process for new teachers.
- Provide effective feedback for the lesson and curriculum plans teachers write.

  For more information about planning, see Chapter 3.

WHO'S THE AUDIENCE?

Anyone who leads teachers in the lesson planning or curriculum planning process, either formally or informally. This may include principals, assistant principals, coaches, mentors, or department chairpersons.

WHEN TO USE IT

Best Time

Right before the school year begins. This gives participants the most direct opportunity to put what they learn into action.

Other Times That Work

Either in spring, when you are training your leaders for the following school year; or in fall, as a follow-up training for leaders who have already begun coaching teachers in this way.

WORKSHOP PREPARATION

Workshop Objectives

1. Drive the planning process for new teachers.
2. Provide effective feedback for the lesson and curriculum plans teachers write.

Running Time

- 4 hours
- *Short on time?* If you can only present part of the workshop, focus this workshop *either* on lesson plan feedback *or* on leading planning meetings. If you select lesson plan feedback, the *most important sections* to include are 1.1 and 1.2. If you select leading planning meetings, the *most important sections* to include are 1.1, 1.3, 1.4, and 1.5.

Making the Workshop Stick: Follow-Up Steps

To be sure you've met this workshop's objectives:

- Use the professional development (PD) planning template to plan PD implementing Living the Learning.

- Observe PD and evaluate with the PD rubric.

Materials

The full-length Presenter's Notes located on the DVD specify when to use each of these materials.

Materials on DVD

- Leading Planning PowerPoint presentation
- Video clips on Leading Planning
- Handouts
    - 2: Leading Planning Core Handout
    - 3: Lesson Plan Feedback Samples
    - 4A: Observation-Planning Meeting One-Pager

Other Materials

- 1 binder per participant. To organize each binder, print out the handouts listed, and place handouts that share the same number together in the same tab of the binder. *For example:* Handouts labeled 2A, 2B, and 2C would all go in Tab 2 of the binder, with 2A coming first and 2C coming last.

COMPLETE WORKSHOP OVERVIEW

Living the Learning Components Legend

AA = *Airtight activity* that leads participants to the right conclusion mostly on their own

R = *Reflection* during which participants quietly generate and record conclusions or takeaways

S = Small or large-group *sharing*

F = *Framing* that gives participants a common vocabulary to use to describe what they learn

A = *Application* of learned principles

For more on PD components, see Chapter 4.

	Section	Timing	Activity	PD Step
1.1	Introduction		Quick Write: Effective Instructional Leadership	AA, S, F
1.2	Lesson Plans and Feedback		Activity: Effective Lesson Plans	AA, S, F, R
			Activity: Quality Lesson Plan Feedback	AA, S, F
			Application: Giving Lesson Plan Feedback	A, S, R, S
1.3	Setting Up Planning Meetings		Activity: Subject Area Components	AA, S, F
			Activity: Weekly Planning Grid	AA, F, R
BREAK				
1.4	Leading Planning Meetings		Activity: Effective Planning Meetings	AA, S, F
			Video: Mapping Out the Grid	AA, S, F
			Video: Setting Core Content	AA, S, F
			Video: Diving into Key Lessons	AA, S, F
1.5	Practicing Leading Planning		Role Play: Leading Planning Meetings	A, S, R
			Application: Observation, Feedback, and Planning for one Teacher	A
			Application: Observation, Feedback, and Planning for Your School	F, A
1.6	Conclusion		Workshop Takeaways	R, S, F

SPOTLIGHT ON LEADING PLANNING MEETING: AN EXCERPT FROM THE FULL-LENGTH PRESENTER'S NOTES

To give you a taste of what it's like to lead this workshop, here's a short excerpt from the full-length presenter's notes you'll find on the DVD.

Context

At this point in the Leading Planning Workshop, participants are learning how to lead weekly 20- to 50-minute planning meetings with teachers. Participants have already discovered how to guide teachers to map out weekly planning grids and set core instructional content. Now, they'll find out how to dive directly into helping teachers plan the upcoming week's most difficult lessons. After that, in Section 1.5, they'll apply what they've learned by performing role plays in which they map out a planning grid and set core content with a teacher.

VIDEO: DIVING INTO KEY LESSONS.

AA: Diving into Key Lessons Video, Part 1 (5 minutes)

Do	Show Slide 37.
Say	"Once you and the teacher have set the core content for the upcoming week's lessons, you can spend the rest of your planning meeting diving into the most difficult lessons you and the teacher have just planned. What does it look like to coach teachers on how to approach their most difficult lessons?"
Do	Show Slide 38.
Say	"To find out, we'll watch a video of a planning meeting with Kristi, an elementary teacher who is trying to determine the focus of her upcoming lesson. The instructional leader, Aja, will begin by asking Kristi about her objective for the lesson. How does Aja help Kristi to focus her lesson objective and dive into the lesson effectively?"

Do

Show clip 18 of Aja and Kristi diving into a key lesson.

S: Pair Sharing (2 minutes)

Say

"Turn and share with a partner. What did Aja do in order to dive into the key lesson with Kristi?"

Do

Have participants pair share how Aja dives into the key lesson with Kristi.

S: Large-Group Sharing (5 minutes)

Say

"What did you and your partner notice? How did Aja get Kristi to dive into this key lesson?"

Do

Lead large-group sharing.
Listen for the following key points:
"Aja starts by asking Kristi about her objective for that particular lesson."
"Aja and Kristi then plan the prompts Kristi can use when teaching that lesson."

Say

If participants do not generate all the key points right away, consider asking these scaffolded follow-up questions:
"What is Aja's opening question? Why does she start there?"
"What does she do when the teacher can't answer that question effectively?"

F: Diving into Key Lessons (2 minutes)

Do

Show Slide 40.

Diving into Key Lessons

- **Start with the Objective and Assessment**
  - Ask "What do you want students to be able to do at the end of this lesson/activity?"
  - Then ask "How will you know that students are able to do that?"
- **Link Activities to that Objective**
  - Guide teachers to make each activity aligns to the objective.
- **Set Checks for Understanding**
  - Build Checks for Understanding—including Do Nows, Questions, and Exit Tickets—into each lesson/activity.

Uncommon Schools | ▶NORTH★STAR

Say

"We've just witnessed the power of planning lessons from the end—that is, of starting by determining what you want students to leave the lesson knowing how to do, and how you'll assess whether they can do it. Just because you've mapped out the grid for the entire week doesn't mean you should start by filling in that grid with activities! Determine the activities *after* the objective and assessment, so that you can fit the activities to the objective instead of the other way around."

F: Putting It All Together (2 minutes)

Say

"We've now learned the three steps to leading a weekly planning meeting. Let's put them all together. Turn to the first page in the fourth tab of your binders, and we'll discuss what your weekly meetings with teachers will look like."

Do

Have participants turn to Handout 4A: Observation-Planning Meeting One-Pager.

(continued)

F: Putting It All Together (2 minutes) (*Continued*)

Say	"This handout shows how to combine observation and feedback with planning in your weekly meetings. Look at the time breakdown at the top of the page. You'll see that once you've spent about 10 minutes giving feedback, you have about 20 minutes to plan, depending on whether your meeting is a half-hour or a full hour long. You'll spend those planning minutes on mapping out the weekly grid, setting core content, and diving into key lessons. "One advantage of leading planning during your weekly meetings is that it gives teachers less work to do after school hours. You've helped the teachers to begin developing stronger lesson plans, so they run less risk of feeling alone or overwhelmed as they complete the process. Moreover, those lesson plans are much more likely to be high-quality, because your expertise has been there to guide the teacher from the beginning."

PRACTICING LEADING PLANNING

Materials				
	Leading Planning PowerPoint Presentation Slides	Video Clips	Handouts	Other Materials
	42–56		Leading Planning Core Handout	

Role Play: Leading Planning Meetings

A: Planning Meeting Role Play, Round 1 (10 minutes)

Do	Show Slide 42.
Say	"Now that you've learned the details of how to lead a planning meeting, it's time to practice. You're going to role play a teacher and instructional leader's first meeting of the school year. Pair up with someone else who coaches similar subjects and grade levels to the ones you coach. Prepare for your role play by determining what content your teachers are likely to be covering during the second week of school. Be sure to pick content that's familiar to both of you!"
Do	Have participants form pairs with participants who coach similar subjects and grade levels to theirs. Have pairs determine what core content they're likely to be planning with teachers during the second week of school.
Say	"You and your partner need three more things before you can begin your role play. First, you need the blank weekly grid on page 25 of the handout in the second tab in your binders, so that you can fill it in during your meeting. Second, you need the one-pager we just looked over, so you can make sure you follow it during your meeting. Lastly, if you're the first participant who will be playing the teacher, I'm going to give you a handout with a teacher personality profile that will tell you how to act during this role play. If you're playing the teacher, come and get your personality profile now. Don't let your leader see it!"
Do	Have participants playing teachers come to the front of the room for a teacher personality profile handout.

(continued)

A: Planning Meeting Role Play, Round 1 (10 minutes) (*Continued*)

Say	"In a few moments, you'll begin your role play. Map out the weekly grid and pick a difficult lesson to dive into. If you're playing the teacher, use the personality profile I just gave you. If you're the leader, pay special attention to the teacher's behavior. We'll ask you after the role play if you figured out what the teacher's greatest challenges in planning were. You will have 7 minutes for your role play. Ready? Go."
Do	Have pairs keep Handout 4A: Observation-Planning Meeting One-Pager in front of them as they role-play. Have participants playing leaders act according to the teacher personality profiles they've received. Have pairs role-play mapping out the weekly grid on page 25 of Handout 2: Leading Planning Core Handout and diving into a key lesson.

S: Pair Sharing (4 minutes)

Do	Show Slide 43.
Say	"Time! [*Wait for participants to quiet down.*] Give your partners feedback on their performances as leaders or teachers. Begin by having leaders describe what challenges they thought the teacher faced. Then, have teachers describe their profiles, and identify both strengths and areas for improvement on the part of the leader."
Do	Have pairs debrief the role play.

S: Large-Group Sharing (4 minutes)

Say	"Let's share our role play experiences as a group. What were your big takeaways from this application?"
Do	Lead large-group sharing.

A: Planning Meeting Role Play, Round 2 (10 minutes)

Do	Show Slide 44.
Say	"We'll move on to the second round of our role play now. Change roles. New teachers, come get your teacher personality profiles from me."
Do	Have participants playing teachers come to the front of the room for a teacher personality profile handout.
Say	"You will have 6 minutes. Begin your second round of role playing . . . now."
Do	Have pairs keep Handout 4A: Observation-Planning Meeting One-Pager in front of them as they role-play. Have participants playing leaders act according to the teacher personality profiles they've received. Have pairs role-play mapping out the weekly grid on Page 25 of Handout 2: Leading Planning Core Handout and diving into a key lesson.

Chapter 12

Leading Professional Development Workshop

Leading Effective Professional Development

Paul Bambrick-Santoyo

WHAT'S THE GOAL?

Train school leaders to lead professional development (PD) sessions that meet objectives. By the end of the workshop, participants will know how to:

- Design effective professional development agendas.

- Lead effective professional development sessions.

- Guarantee professional development's success through informative follow-up.

    For more information about professional development, see Chapter 4.

WHO'S THE AUDIENCE?

Anyone who leads professional development sessions.

WHEN TO USE IT

Best Time

A few months before you have a major PD that you want to deliver: summer teacher orientation, a districtwide PD session, and so on.

Other Times That Work

Pretty much any other time!

WORKSHOP PREPARATION

Workshop Objectives

1. Design effective professional development agendas.

2. Lead effective professional development sessions.

3. Guarantee professional development's success through informative follow-up.

Running Time

- 4 hours and 40 minutes

- *Short on time?* If you can only present part of the workshop, the *most important sections* are 1.1, 1.2, and 1.5.

Making the Workshop Stick: Follow-Up Steps

- By a certain deadline, have participants use the template presented in this workshop to develop an effective professional development agenda.

- By a certain deadline, have participants deliver an effective professional development session.

Materials

The full-length Presenter's Notes located on the DVD specify when to use each of these materials.

Materials on DVD

- Leading Professional Development PowerPoint Presentation
- Video clips on Leading Professional Development
  - Aja leading professional development
  - Nikki introducing a video clip
  - Julie doing video clip follow-up
  - Julie leading large-group sharing
  - Shradha leading small-group sharing
  - Serena managing small-group sharing
  - Julie getting participants to apply their learning
  - Paul leading role play
  - Jesse leading oral drill
- Handouts
  - 1A: Leading PD Reflection Template

- 2A: Leading Professional Development
- 3A: PD Template Living the Learning
- 3B: PD Template Living the Learning—Sample
- 4A: PD Rubric

Other Materials

- 1 binder per participant. To organize each binder, print out the handouts listed above, and place handouts that share the same number together in the same tab of the binder. *For example*: Handouts labeled 2A, 2B, and 2C would all go in Tab 2 of the binder, with 2A coming first and 2C coming last.

- Blank chart paper posters

- Post-it notes

- Markers

COMPLETE WORKSHOP OVERVIEW

Living the Learning Components Legend

AA = *Airtight activity* that leads participants to the right conclusion mostly on their own

R = *Reflection* during which participants quietly generate and record conclusions or takeaways

S = Small- or large-group *sharing*

F = *Framing* that gives participants a common vocabulary to use to describe what they learn

A = *Application* of learned principles

For more on PD components, see Chapter 4.

	Section	Timing	Activity	PD Step
1.1	Introduction		Workshop Objectives	F
			Video: Effective Professional Development	AA, S, F
1.2	Components of Living the Learning		Video: Airtight Activities, Part 1	AA, S, F
			Video: Airtight Activities, Part 2	AA, S, F
			Reflection	F
			Video: Large-Group Sharing	AA, S, F
			Framing	AA, S, F
			Video: Small-Group Sharing Set-Up	F, R
			Video: Managing Small-Group Sharing	AA, S, F
			Time Management	AA, A, S
			Video: Application	AA, S, F
1.3	Creating Objectives		Keys to Quality Objectives	AA, A, S
1.4	Designing Airtight Activities		Video: Effective Airtight Activities	AA, S, F
			Activity: Ineffective Airtight Activities	AA, S, R
BREAK				
			Application: Designing Airtight Activities	A, S, R
1.5	Designing an Effective Professional Development Session		Application: Designing Professional Development Agendas	A, S
1.6	Conclusion		Application: Evaluating Professional Development Sessions	A
			Workshop takeaways	R, F

SPOTLIGHT ON AIRTIGHT ACTIVITIES

An Excerpt from the Full-Length Presenter's Notes

To give you a taste of what it's like to lead this workshop, here's a short excerpt from the full-length presenter's notes you'll find on the DVD.

Context

At this point in the Leading Professional Development Workshop, participants have just watched a video that prompted them to identify the Living the Learning framework as a means by which successful school leaders make their professional development sessions effective. Now, in Section 1.2 of the workshop, the participants will examine each component of the Living the Learning framework in detail, beginning with airtight activities and reflection.

COMPONENTS OF LIVING THE LEARNING

Materials	Leading Professional Development PowerPoint Presentation Slides	Video Clips	Handouts	Other Materials
	11–17	19,20	1A	

Video: Airtight Activities, Part 1

AA: Airtight Activities Video, Part 1 (5 minutes)

Do

Show Slide 9.

> ## Four Common Airtight Activities
>
> - Video clips of teaching/learning
> - Movie clips
> - Case studies (written)
> - Role plays/simulations (acted)
>
> **Uncommon Schools** | **NORTH ★ STAR**

Say

"We'll start at the beginning of the cycle, with airtight activities. Four common types of airtight activities are videos, movie clips, written case studies, and acted-out role plays. We'll learn how to design effective airtight activities in each of these categories, beginning with videos."

Do

Show Slide 10.

Say

"How can you maximize the value of a video? The first step is introducing it well. When you watch this video, I want you to answer the following question: how does Nikki introduce her video effectively?"

Do

Show Video Clip 20.

S: Pair Sharing (2 minutes)

Say	"Turn to your partner and share what you saw. What did Nikki do to introduce the video effectively?"
Do	Have participants pair share how Nikki set up the video effectively.

S: Large-Group Sharing (4 minutes)

Say	"Time! How did Nikki introduce the video effectively? Who would like to share what you and your partner observed with the rest of the group?"
Do	Lead large-group sharing. Listen for the following key points: "Nikki gave the participants questions to answer about the video before she showed it. Then, she kept the questions up while the video played." "The questions were specific and focused on the positive: people naturally tend to look for what's wrong in video. The questions get people to look for the best practice."
Say	*If participants do not generate all the key points right away, consider asking these scaffolded follow-up questions:* "What did you notice about the type of question that Nikki asked? Were her questions being asked to critique the video?" "What was displayed while Nikki introduced the video?"

F: Airtight Activities, Part 1 (2 minutes)

Do

Show Slide 11.

> # Video Clips—How to Use Them Effectively
>
> - **Precise Question(s)**
>   - Focus the questions on observing the positive aspects of the video clip.
>   - Provide questions before showing video.
>   - Keep questions visible before, during and after clip.
> - **Keep Video Clips Short**
>   - Most should be no more than 5 minutes; on rare occasions you can show a 10-minute clip.
>
> Uncommon Schools | ▶ NORTH ★ STAR ◀

Say

"What we've just seen is that to set up a video clip effectively, a leader must ask precise questions that focus on positive observations about the video. Ask the questions before you show the clip, and keep them visible during and after the clip. Finally, keep the clip short. The most effective clips are 3 to 5 minutes long."

Video: Airtight Activities, Part 2
AA: Airtight Activities, Part 2 (5 minutes)

Do

Show Slide 13.

Say

"So if that's how leaders introduce videos, how do they then get participants to remember what they learn from those videos? Let's rewatch how Aja does it in this video. What does she do after showing her video clip?"

Do

Show Video Clip 19 again.
NOTE: Ideally you could use a different video from the one you used in the introduction. When you have leaders using the Living the Learning framework, you can videotape one of them to capture the best practices after watching a video. Until then, reuse the video clip from Aja, and focus in solely on the sharing and reflection post-video.

S: Pair Sharing (2 minutes)

Say

"Turn to a partner. What does Aja do after she shows the video? Start sharing ... now."

Do

Have participants pair share what Aja does after showing the video.

S: Large-Group Sharing (3 minutes)

Say

"What does Aja do after the video?"

Do

Lead large-group sharing.
Listen for the following key points:
"The participants had time to reflect on their own before sharing."
"The participants shared what they saw in the video in pairs before sharing in a large group."

Say

If participants do not generate all the key points right away, consider asking this scaffolded follow-up question:
"What is the value of letting people think before they share?"

F: Video Follow-Up (2 minutes)

Do

Show Slide 13.

Video Clips—How to Use Them Effectively

- **Precise Question(s)**
  - Focus the questions on observing the positive aspects of the video clip.
  - Provide questions before showing video.
  - Keep questions visible before, during and after clip.
- **Keep Video Clips Short**
  - Most should be no more than 5 minutes; on rare occasions you can show a 10-minute clip.
- **Follow Video Clips with a Think-Pair-Share (R-S)**
  - Time to reflect individually.
  - Share reflections with partner.
  - Share out to the large group.
- **Time Management**
  - Set up next video during Reflect/Sharing.

Uncommon Schools | NORTH ★ STAR

Say

"What we've discovered is that after a video, participants should do some combination of reflecting on the video, small-group sharing, and large-group sharing. Moving gradually from small- to large-group sharing is a good way to engage introverted participants."

Reflection

F: Reflection (3 minutes)

Do

Show Slide 14.

Reflection—Core Principles

- Keep It Brief
  - Most participants only need 1–3 minutes to reflect on a given topic.
- Have a Place to Write
  - Provide participants with a colorful handout where they can record all reflections.

Uncommon Schools | NORTH ★ STAR

Say

"We just saw a reflection follow an airtight activity, but reflection can occur at any time during the Living the Learning cycle. Reflection periods are brief, because participants only need a minute to collect their thoughts on a topic. When you want participants to remember their reflections after the workshop, provide handouts where they can write down their reflections."

(continued)

F: Reflection (3 minutes) (*Continued*)

Do	Show Slide 15.
Say	"We've now seen several steps of the Living the Learning cycle in action."
Do	Show Slide 16.
Say	"Aja led an airtight activity—the video—followed immediately by reflection. Then, participants shared their conclusions. Aja's next step would be to frame their conclusions, after which participants would apply what they had learned. Then, the Living the Learning cycle would repeat itself, beginning with a new airtight activity."

R: Airtight Activities and Reflection (2 minutes)

Do	Show Slide 17.
Say	"Let's put reflection into practice. Turn to the first handout in the first tab in your binders. This is where you'll write down your most important takeaways from today's workshop. Right now, record what you most want to remember about airtight activities and reflection when you plan your own professional development session. Are you ready? Go."
Do	Have participants write their takeaways on Handout 1A: Living the Learning Reflection.

Chapter 13

Student Culture Workshop

Student Culture

Paul Bambrick-Santoyo and Julie Jackson

WHAT'S THE GOAL?

Make school leaders effective student culture leaders. By the end of the workshop, participants will know how to:

- Implement keys to effective student culture.
- Identify key systems for building student culture.
- Create minute-by-minute plans that will turn their student culture visions into realities.

  For more information about student culture, see Chapter 5.

WHO'S THE AUDIENCE?

Leaders who are also responsible for schoolwide student culture
  Note: This does not have to be only people with formal responsibility.
  Strong teachers who play a critical role in student culture may also participate.

WHEN TO USE IT

Best Time

Right before the school year begins. This gives participants the best opportunity to set up a strong culture before the students arrive.

Other Times That Work

Right before resetting a broken student culture. This gives you a framework to rebuild a broken student culture.

WORKSHOP PREPARATION

Workshop Objectives

1. Implement the five keys to effective student culture.
2. Identify key systems for building student culture.
3. Create minute-by-minute plans that will turn their student culture visions into realities.

Running Time

- 4 hours

Making the Workshop Stick: Follow-Up Steps

- Evaluate the student culture action plans: Did they get implemented? What worked and what was challenging?
- Do a building walkthrough using the student culture rubric (DVD). What are the areas of proficiency and where are the areas of growth?

Materials

The full-length Presenter's Notes located on the DVD specify when to use each of these materials.

Materials on DVD

- Student Culture PowerPoint Presentation
- Video clips on Student Culture
- Handouts. Most important:
  - 3A: Steps to Strengthen School Culture: Two-Pager
  - 2A: Student Culture Breakfast Case Study.pdf
  - 4B: Sample System: Minute-by-Minute Plan for First Day of School
  - 3B: Student Culture Planning Template
  - Student Culture Planning: Sample System
  - Other handouts on DVD

Other Materials

- 1 binder per participant
  - 6B: Student Culture Breakfast Case Study: Leader Version
- 1 name tent per participant

ABBREVIATED WORKSHOP AGENDA

Living the Learning Components Legend

AA = *Airtight activity* that leads participants to the right conclusion mostly on their own

R = *Reflection* during which participants quietly generate and record conclusions or takeaways

S = Small- or large-group *sharing*

	Section	Timing	Activity	Type
1.1	Introduction to Student Culture		Quick Write: Defining Student Culture	AA, S, F
			Workshop Objectives	F
			Written Case Study: Breakfast at Blue Hill	AA, S, R
1.2	Five Steps to Effective Student Culture		Video: Morning Meeting	AA, S, F
			Overview of the Five Steps to Effective Student Culture	F
1.3	Steps 1 and 2: Establish a Vision and Identify Key Systems		Quick Write: Establish a Vision	AA, S, F
			Activity: Identify Key Systems	AA, S, F
1.4	Step 3: Create Minute-by-Minute Plans		Quick Write: Minute-by-Minute Plans	AA, S, F
			Video: Arrival	AA, S, F, R
1.5	Step 4: Practice		Quick Write: Practice	AA, F
			Video: Practice	AA, S, F, R
1.6	Step 5: Monitor and Maintain		Quick Write: Monitor and Maintain	AA, F
			Video	AA
			Tools for Monitoring and Maintaining Student Culture	F, A
1.7	Building Student Culture		Activity: Planning Systems	A
			Role Play: Practice	A
1.8	Conclusion			

F = *Framing* that gives participants a common vocabulary to use to describe what they learn

A = *Application* of learned principles

For more on PD components, see Chapter 4.

WORKSHOP PRESENTER'S NOTES: AN EXCERPT

What follows is a short segment of the full-length presenter's notes you'll use to lead this workshop. For the full-length presenter's notes, see the DVD.

Context

At this point in the Student Culture Workshop, participants have defined student culture and identified the workshop's objectives. Now, they are about to examine a written case study that will reveal to them some characteristics of strong school culture—and some pain points that can weaken it. Then, they'll begin Section 1.2 of the workshop with a video airtight activity. From this video, they'll derive five specific steps to effective student culture.

Written Case Study: Breakfast at Blue Hill

AA: Breakfast at Blue Hill Case Study (15 minutes)

Do	Show Slide 6.
Say	"The biggest challenge with student culture is translating your vision to a reality. Let's take a closer look at this challenge. You'll read a case study that narrates a morning at Blue Hill Elementary School. May I have a volunteer to read the Blue Hill Case Study background information aloud?"
Do	Have a participant read the Blue Hill Elementary School Case Study background information on the Student Culture Breakfast Case Study Handout to the rest of the group. Show Slide 7.

(continued)

AA: Breakfast at Blue Hill Case Study (15 minutes) (*Continued*)

Say	"Thanks. The questions you should consider as you read the case study are: What is going well in Blue Hill's morning routine? What are the 'pain points' where the routine breaks down? Finally, what do Blue Hill teachers and leaders need to do differently to make their student culture more effective? What expectations for student behavior need to be more firmly established?"
Do	Have participants read Student Culture Breakfast Case Study Handout. Have participants take notes on the case study.
Say	"Now that you've had a chance to read the case study yourself, get into groups of four. Move with your group to one of the blank chart paper posters attached to the wall. On the chart paper poster, write two lists: one of the pain points your group identified in the case study, and the other of your ideas for fixing those pain points."
Do	Have participants form groups. Have groups use markers to write the pain points and fixes they've identified for Blue Hill on chart paper posters.

S: Large-Group Sharing (5 minutes)

Say	"Return to your seats now, and we'll share out together. What were the major pain points in this case study?"
Do	Lead large group sharing. Listen for these correct answers: "Individual teachers have distinct methods of transitioning from breakfast." "No clear expectations for what kids should be doing once they finish eating." "The kindergarten and first-grade classes are separated, so younger students don't have older models." "Teachers still doing own prep work even while in a supervisory role." "Student backpacks and coats are left scattered on the floor."

"Students continue talking even after Dr. Anderson makes the quiet signal."
"No clear procedure for post-breakfast clean-up."

Say	*If participants do not provide the correct answers right away, consider asking these scaffolded follow-up questions:* "Did the transition at the end seem consistent or inconsistent? Were there differences in how teachers managed transition?" "What are some of the things that kids were doing after they finished eating?" "Did you notice particular parts of the room in which there was a concentration of problem areas?" "During the breakfast period, how were different teachers managing their classes?" "What happened when Dr. Anderson raised her hand? What response do you think she expected from students?" "Why were there students fighting over a backpack during transition?" "What were students doing with garbage once they finished their meals?"

F: (2 minutes)

Say	"Look around you and see all of the recommendations that you made. Each of them responds to a basic issue: there were moments when the leader was no longer defining the culture he wanted—the students were. What we're going to talk about for the rest of the day is, How do you change that? How can you as the leader drive culture in all moments of the day?"

R: Breakfast at Blue Hill Case Study Reflection (1 minute)

Do	Show Slide 8.

Say	"Before we move forward, turn to your reflection template. What are your biggest takeaways from this case study? Write them down so that you remember them after the workshop."

(continued)

R: Breakfast at Blue Hill Case Study Reflection (1 minute) (*Continued*)

Do	Have participants write takeaways on Student Culture Reflection Handout.

1.2 ESTABLISHING A VISION

Materials

Student Culture PowerPoint Presentation Slides	Video Clips	Handouts	Other Materials
8–13	25		

AA: Establishing a Vision Activity (4 minutes)

Do	Show Slide 8.
Say	"So what does a great student culture in action look like? To begin finding out, we'll watch a video of how Stacey Shells, a principal known for her exceptional skill at building student culture, kicks off each weekday morning with her students. As you watch, consider this core question: What sort of a vision does Stacey appear to have defined for her school's student culture? Let's take a look."
Do	Show Video Clip 25.

S: Pair Sharing (2 minutes)

Say	"Okay. Now turn to a partner. Based on what you just saw, what is Stacey's vision of student culture for her school? Share what you observed with your partner. Ready? Go."
Do	Give participants two minutes to pair share what vision Stacey has defined for her school's student culture.

S: Large-Group Sharing (4 minutes)

Say	"What did you and your partner notice? What vision for student culture has Stacey established?"
Do	Lead large-group sharing. Listen for the following key points: "Stacey's vision for student culture doesn't let students opt out—either in terms of learning or in terms of behavior. But she also shows them that she won't give up on them even with a wrong answer." "Stacey believes in having 100 percent engage in a learning task even in the morning." "In a student culture like this, it would be very difficult for a student to fail." "Stacey's student culture ensures that learning happens at every moment!"
Say	*If participants do not generate all the key points right away, consider asking these scaffolded follow-up questions:* "Does Stacey's school look different from the Blue Hill case study? In what ways?" "What happens when the student has the incorrect answer? How does she keep the rest of the students engaged while supporting the student to get to the right answer?" "Based on what you saw, what is Stacey's vision for morning routines at her school?"

F: Our Vision (3 minutes)

Do

Show Slide 12.

Say

"So, to sum up what you've all noticed, Stacey's vision of student culture involves joy, rigor, and order, ensuring that students constantly learn and ultimately succeed. Establishing a vision like this is a vital first step to making such an exceptional student culture a reality."

Do

Show Slide 9.

> # Five Keys to Effective Student Culture
>
> 1. Establish a vision.
> 2. Identify key systems needed.
> 3. Turn vision into minute-by-minute systems.
> 4. Practice.
> 5. Monitor and maintain.
>
> Uncommon Schools | NORTH ★ STAR

Say

"These are the five key steps to creating an effective student culture: establishing a vision, identifying the key systems that would make the vision into a reality, converting the vision into minute-by-minute systems, practicing those systems, and monitoring and maintaining your student culture on a continuous basis."

Chapter 14

Finding the Time Workshop

Finding the Time

Paul Bambrick-Santoyo

WHAT'S THE GOAL?

Give school leaders the tools to use their time effectively. By the end of the workshop, participants will know how to:

- Develop a weekly schedule that includes observation and feedback as well as all other components of the seven levers of leadership.

- Develop goals and monthly guides to managing all seven levers.

  For more information about finding the time, see Chapter 8.

WHO'S THE AUDIENCE?

All instructional leaders!

WHEN TO USE IT

Best Time

Right before the school year begins. This is the easiest time for participants to change the way they schedule and plan.

Other Times That Work

In spring, as you set up strategic planning for the year.

WORKSHOP PREPARATION

Workshop Objectives

1. Develop a weekly schedule that includes observation and feedback as well as all other components of the seven levers of leadership.

2. Develop goals and monthly guides to managing all seven levers.

Running Time

- 7 hours

- *Short on time?* If you can only present part of the workshop, focus this workshop *either* on setting measurable goals and monthly maps *or* on building weekly schedules. If you select goals and monthly maps, the most important sections to include are 1.1, 1.2, 1.3, and 1.4. If you select weekly schedules, the most important sections to include are 1.1 and 1.5.

Making the Workshop Stick: Follow-Up Steps

To be sure you've met this workshop's objectives:

- Spot check the leader's weekly schedule via the observation tracker: Are they keeping up with their planned observations?

- Evaluate implementation of each lever with the rubrics for that lever (DVD).

Materials

The full-length Presenter's Notes located on the DVD specify when to use each of these materials.

Materials on DVD

- Making Every Minute Matter PowerPoint presentation
- Video clips:
  - Final race scene from *Man on Fire*
- Handouts:
  - 1B: Finding the Time
  - 3B: How to Create Monthly Map—One-pager
  - 3E: Monthly Map MS
  - 4A: Principal Weekly Schedule Template
  - 4B: How to Create Weekly Schedule—One-pager
  - 7A: Goals for Chart Paper Exercise
  - 7B: Goals and Drivers Template

Other Materials

- 1 binder per participant. To organize each binder, print out the handouts listed above, and place handouts that share the same number together in the same tab of the binder. *For example:* Handouts labeled 2A, 2B, and 2C would all go in Tab 2 of the binder, with 2A coming first and 2C coming last.
- Table tents
- Green, yellow, pink, and blue Post-it notes
- Markers
- 1 name tent per participant

- 1 set of **7** school pillar posters per 18 participants
- 1 set of 7 goal posters per 18 participants
- 1 goal group banner per 18 participants
- 1 core questions poster per 18 participants
- 1 weekly schedule grid per participant

COMPLETE WORKSHOP OVERVIEW

Living the Learning Components Legend

AA= *Airtight activity* that leads participants to the right conclusion mostly on their own

R = *Reflection* during which participants quietly generate and record conclusions or takeaways

S = Small- or large-group *sharing*

F = *Framing* that gives participants a common vocabulary to use to describe what they learn

A = *Application* of learned principles

For more on PD components, see Chapter 4.

	Section	Timing	Activity	Type
1.1	Introduction		Making teacher development succeed	AA, S, F
1.2	Generating Measurable Goals		Generating Measurable Goals, Part 1	AA, S, F, R
			Generating Measurable Goals, Part 2	AA
			Comparing goals	AA, S, F
			Completing your goals	A, R, S
1.3	Establishing Drivers		Identifying drivers	AA, F, AA, F
			Create your own drivers	AA, R, F
1.4	Building Monthly Maps		Introduction to the monthly map	AA, F, R
			Tightening the monthly map	AA, R, S, F
1.5	Building Weekly Schedules		Building your own schedule	AA, S, R, F
			Schedule accountability	AA, S, R, S
1.6	Conclusion		Write more success stories	F, AA, F

SPOTLIGHT ON BUILDING WEEKLY SCHEDULES: AN EXCERPT FROM THE FULL-LENGTH PRESENTER'S NOTES

To give you a taste of what it's like to lead this workshop, here's a short excerpt from the full-length presenter's notes you'll find on the DVD.

Context

At this point in the Finding the Time Workshop, participants have learned how to develop and manage goals for their schools on an annual and monthly basis. Now, each participant will determine how he or she will implement those big-picture goals on a weekly basis. During the activity that begins in Section 1.5, participants will use colored Post-it notes to fill in their own weekly agendas with all the tasks that drive student learning most effectively.

BUILDING WEEKLY SCHEDULES

Materials				
	Finding the Time PowerPoint Presentation Slides	Video Clips	Handouts	Other Materials
	44–51	n/a	1B, 4B	Weekly schedule grid, Post-it notes, markers, table tents

Application: Building Weekly Schedules

A: Building Weekly Schedules Application (30 minutes)

Do	Show Slide 44.
Say	"If your Monthly Map shows what you need to do every month to make this year's big picture an image of success, now we'll look at the smaller parts of that picture: you'll build weekly schedules that show you how to manage both major goals and routine tasks from day to day. "Let's start with the basics. On a piece of paper in front of you, write down the total number of teachers you manage in your school. [*Pause*] Now write down the total number of people who have instructional leadership responsibilities in the school: yourself, any coach, assistant principal, mentor teacher, etc. You need to count everyone! [*Pause*] "Now divide the number of teachers by the number of leaders. [*Pause*] In working with major urban districts across the country, we have seen that in 95% of all schools, that ratio is 15:1 or less. "Look at the number you've just calculated. This is the number you'll use to build your weekly schedule."

Quick Tip: For The Exception—When Ratio Is More Than 15:1

In advance of your workshop, ask the workshop organizer whether or not there will be any leaders present who have higher than a 15:1 ratio of teachers to leaders in their schools. In our experience, few will. But for those rare exceptions, push those leaders to make sure they identify *all* coaches (including external coaches they've hired). Then tell them they will work on the premise of bi-weekly observations rather than weekly. In other words, if they have a 20:1 ratio, then they'll observe half of those teachers each week. They'll just write two teacher names in each observation slot on their weekly schedule—knowing they'll observe each one every other week.

Say

"Now you'll build your weekly schedule. Move to one of the sets of laminated schedules posted on the wall. Bring pens with you. "We're going to use these Post-It notes to divide up the time on these schedules. Each Post-It will represent one hour.
"We'll start by working with green Post-It notes. Green Post-Its will represent time you spend with students and parents.
"Take your green Post-Its and place them in the blocks of your schedule where you are often busy with students or parents. I'll give you a hint: these moments most often occur at breakfast, lunch, and dismissal.
"Place your green Post-Its in those moments when you need to be ready for whatever might happen. Begin... now."

Do

Have participants use green Post-It notes to schedule blocks on their Weekly Schedule Grids when they are busy with students or parents.

Show Slide 45.

Building Your Schedule

- Task 2—Yellow Post-It Notes
    - Write on Post-Its each non-teacher meeting you will have this year (individual, team, PD).
        - Each Post-It represents one hour.
- Yellow Post-It Notes, Part 2
    - Write each teacher you will meet with weekly (2 per Post-It).
    - For bi-weekly teachers, write the names of four teachers on the same Post-It.

Uncommon Schools | ▶NORTH★STAR◀

(continued)

(*Continued*)

Say	"Next, we'll use yellow Post-Its. They'll represent meetings. "Start by scheduling all non-teacher meetings. This might include professional development sessions, team meetings, or one-on-one meetings with other leaders. "Schedule non-teacher meetings on your calendar. Ready? Go."
Do	Have participants use yellow Post-It notes to schedule non-teacher meetings on their Weekly Schedule Grids. Have participants use markers to label each yellow Post-It note with the type of meeting it represents.
Say	"Keep your yellow Post-Its out. You're next going to use them to schedule teacher meetings. "On each yellow Post-It—representing one hour of teacher meetings—write the names of two different teachers. Each of those teachers will get half of this hour-long meeting block. "Use yellow Post-Its to schedule your weekly meetings with teachers . . . now."
Do	Have participants use yellow Post-It notes to schedule teacher feedback meetings on their Weekly Schedule Grids. Have participants use markers to label each yellow Post-It note with the names of the teachers they'll meet during the hour the Post-It represents. Since each Post-It represents one hour, and each feedback meeting lasts half an hour, have participants label each Post-It with two teachers' names. Show Slide 46.

Say	"Now that you have determined the best times to hold feedback meetings with each of your teachers, you need to make sure you schedule classroom observation before your feedback meeting with each teacher. "Take out your pink Post-Its. These stand for classroom observation. Label each pink Post-It with the names of three or four teachers you'd observe during the hour it represents. "Ready to schedule classroom observation? Begin."
Do	Have participants use pink Post-It notes to schedule classroom observation on their Weekly Schedule Grids. Have participants use markers to label each pink Post-It note with the names of teachers whose classrooms they will observe during the hour the Post-It represents. Since each Post-It represents one hour, and each classroom observation lasts 15 to 20 minutes, have participants label each Post-It with three to four teachers' names.
Say	"Pull out your blue Post-Its. These will signify personal work time. "Use blue Post-Its to set aside time in your weekly schedule for the big picture tasks on your Monthly Map. That time may be early in the morning, on evenings, or on weekends, but it must be completely uninterrupted. "If you schedule time for monthly tasks during the school day, plan to spend it off campus. "Schedule time to work on your big picture tasks . . . now."
Do	Have participants use blue Post-It notes to schedule big picture tasks on their Weekly Schedule Grids.
Say	"Finally, with more blue Post-It notes, schedule personal work time for responding to emails and phone calls. Complete your weekly schedules . . . now."
Do	Have participants use blue Post-It notes to schedule time to respond to messages on their Weekly Schedule Grids.

S—Small Group Sharing (2 minutes)

Say	"Step back and look at the weekly schedules displayed around the room."
Do	Have participants look at each other's Weekly Schedule Grids. Show Slide 47.
Say	"Look closely at the calendar that the person standing next to you has created. Do you see enough empty space for when things get really busy? Are there any times when this schedule wouldn't work? How would other leaders' calendars need to look in order to support these schedules? Share your feedback with your accountability trios."
Do	Have participants work in their Accountability Trios. Have trios give feedback for each other's Weekly Schedule Grids.

Quick Reference Sheet

Highlights of the Key Concepts
in *Leverage Leadership*

THE SEVEN LEVERS

Instructional Levers

1. *Data-driven instruction.* Define the roadmap for rigor and adapt teaching to meet the students' needs.

2. *Observation and feedback.* Coach teachers to improve the learning.

3. *Instructional planning.* Prevent problems and guarantee strong lessons.

4. *Professional development.* Strengthen culture and instruction with hands-on training that sticks.

Cultural Levers

5. *Student culture.* Create a strong culture where learning can thrive.

6. *Staff culture.* Build and support the right team.

7. *Leading the leaders.* Train instructional leaders to expand your impact across the school.

1. FOUR KEYS TO DATA-DRIVEN INSTRUCTION

1. *Assessment.* Define the roadmap for rigor.

2. *Analysis.* Determine where students are struggling and why.

3. *Action.* Implement new teaching plans to respond to this analysis

4. *Systems.* Create systems and procedures to ensure constant data-driven improvement.

2. SIX STEPS TO EFFECTIVE FEEDBACK

1. *Provide precise praise.* Start off the meeting with one or two pieces of precise praise from your observation.

2. *Probe.* State a targeted open-ended question about the core issue.

3. *Identify problem and concrete action step.* Identify the problem and state a clear, measurable, observable action step that will address this issue.

4. *Practice.* Role-play or simulate how the teacher could have improved current class.

5. *Plan ahead.* Design or revise upcoming lesson plan to implement this action.

6. *Set timeline.* Establish time by which the action will be accomplished.

3. EFFECTIVE PLANNING MEETINGS

- *Map out the week.* Determine how school events, classroom routines, and carryover work from last week will influence the week

- *Set the core content.* Establish the key objective for each day.

- *Dive into key lessons.* Develop tight activities for key lessons.

4. LIVING THE LEARNING FOR PROFESSIONAL DEVELOPMENT

- *Airtight activities.* Activities ensure participants will independently reach the key ideas.

- *Sharing.* Participants discuss and formulate the conclusions reached in airtight activities.

- *Framing.* The leader puts formal language to the audience's conclusions.

- *Application.* Time is allowed for participants to begin directly putting activities into practice.

- *Reflection.* Time is set aside for participants to take notes and gather their thoughts.

5. FOUR KEYS TO STUDENT CULTURE

1. *Establish a vision.* What do you want students and adults doing in school?

2. *Turn vision into minute-by-minute systems.* Build the minute-by-minute routines that will make the vision a reality.

3. *Practice.* Give multiple opportunities to practice and rehearse before stepping into the classroom.

4. *Monitor and maintain.* Evaluate your progress with a measurable tool.

6. STRATEGIES FOR SUCCESSFUL STAFF CULTURE

- *Play to your strengths.* Before you can create a powerful staff culture, you need to (1) know yourself, and (2) know your vision for staff culture at your school.

- *Get the right people on the bus.* Without great people, little else matters. Invest whatever time is necessary in hiring effectively to thoughtfully put together your team and add to it each year.

- *Put a stake in the ground.* Reflect your commitment to developing a strong staff culture by prioritizing it from the first interactions of the year.

- *Keep your ear to the rail.* Look and listen for negative culture warning signs that are coming down the tracks.

- *Lather, rinse, repeat.* Staff culture is fragile. If you're not intentional about building, maintaining, or communicating your staff culture, someone else will define it for you.

7. LEADING THE LEADERS

1. *Identify* instructional leaders.

2. *Train* initially and follow up throughout the year.

3. *Give feedback and practice.* Leverage face-to-face meetings to develop leadership.

4. *Evaluate* leaders on what matters most: the quality of their instructional leadership.

8. FINDING THE TIME

- *Build your schedule.* In creating a schedule, you can begin from regularly occurring culture events, then add group meetings, then add one-on-one meetings and check-ins, before finally adding in one-off events, such as field trips.

- *Defend your time.* Without constant vigilance, it can become easy for principals to spend their careers as "firefighters," addressing crises as they arrive without meaningfully improving instruction. To avoid this, school leaders should create systems to either contain such events or create larger, unbroken blocks of time.

ISLLC Standards

You can use the seven levers of leadership that we present in this book to help your school meet the Interstate School Leaders Licensure Consortium (ISLLC) standards for educational leadership. This table shows which chapters in the book will most support school leaders in reaching each ISLLC standard.

ISLLC Standard	"A school administrator is an educational leader who promotes the success of all students by . . ."	Chapters That Address This Standard
1	". . . facilitating the development, articulation, implementation, and stewardship of a vision of learning that is shared and supported by the school community."	1. Data-Driven Instruction 2. Observation and Feedback 3. Planning 5. Student Culture 6. Staff Culture 8. Finding the Time
2	". . . advocating, nurturing, and sustaining a school culture and instructional program conducive to student learning and staff professional growth."	1. Data-Driven Instruction 2. Observation and Feedback 3. Planning 4. Professional Development 5. Student Culture 6. Staff Culture 8. Finding the Time
3	". . . ensuring management of the organization, operations, and resources for a safe, efficient, and effective learning environment."	7. Managing Leadership Teams 8. Finding the Time
4	". . . collaborating with families and community members, responding to diverse community interests and needs, and mobilizing community resources."	6. Staff Culture 7. Managing Leadership Teams 8. Finding the Time
5	". . . acting with integrity, fairness, and in an ethical manner."	5. Student Culture 6. Staff Culture
6	". . . understanding, responding to, and influencing the larger political, social, economic, legal, and cultural context."	5. Student Culture 7. Managing Leadership Teams 8. Finding the Time

Notes

Introduction

1. TerraNova results from May 2011 for K–3 students, across all students in the school. See North Star Annual Report 2011 for TerraNova results. For reference, *percentile* refers to the median national percentile officially reported by TerraNova. This signifies that the median student at North Star—if you put all students' scores in order from lowest to highest result and take the middle student—scored as high as or higher than 99 percent of students nationally.

2. New Jersey Assessment of Skills and Knowledge (NJASK) results for North Star, May 2011. For more information on North Star's test results, see New Jersey Department of Education website's School Report Cards for results, available at http://education.state.nj.us/rc/.

3. Spring 2011 TerraNova Results for Vailsburg and West Side Park elementary schools: median national percentile on the kindergarten TerraNova. Pretest scores based on an estimate of the incoming performance of the kindergarten students.

4. Kim Marshall, *Rethinking Teacher Supervision and Evaluation: How to Work Smart, Build Collaboration, and Close the Achievement Gap* (San Francisco: Jossey-Bass, 2009).

5. Robert J. Marzano, Tony Frontier, and David Livingston, *Effective Supervision: Supporting the Art and Science of Teaching* (Alexandria, VA: Association for Supervision and Curriculum Development, 2011).

6. Ibid.

7. See, for example, Robert J. Marzano, Timothy Waters, and Brian A. McNulty, *School Leadership That Works: From Research to Results* (Alexandria, VA: Association for Supervision and Curriculum Development, 2005); Charlotte Danielson, *Enhancing Student Achievement: A Framework for School Improvement* (Alexandria, VA: Association for Supervision and Curriculum Development, 2002); Terrence E. Deal and Kent D. Peterson, *Shaping School Culture: Pitfalls, Paradoxes, and Promises* (San Francisco: Jossey-Bass, 2009); Alexander D. Platt, *The Skillful Leader: Confronting Mediocre Teaching* (Acton, MA: Ready About, 2000).

8. Paul Bambrick-Santoyo, *Driven by Data: A Practical Guide to Improve Instruction* (San Francisco: Jossey-Bass, 2010).

9. Testing results for the leaders highlighted in this book are reported throughout this text.

10. For more on the impact that effective time management can have on student achievement, see Eileen Lai Horng, Daniel Klasik, and Susanna Loeb, "Principal's Time Use and School Effectiveness," *American Journal of Education* 116 (2010): 502–521. For a description of how some school leaders put this insight into practice, see Jan Walker, "Letting Go: How Principals Can Be Better Instructional Leaders," *Middle Ground* 14 (2010): 16–17.

11. See, for example, Marzano and others, *Effective Supervision*, 107.

Chapter 1

1. See Paul Bambrick-Santoyo, *Driven by Data: A Practical Guide to Improve Instruction* (San Francisco: Jossey-Bass, 2010).

2. Ibid.

3. For some of the many definitions of rigor that have been offered, see Nel Noddings, "The New Anti-Intellectualism in America," *Education Week* 26 (2007): 29, 32; Elliot Washor and Charles Mojkowski, "What Do You Mean by Rigor?" *Educational Leadership* 64 (2007): 84–85. Daniel Baron, "Using Text-Based Protocols: The Five Rs," *Principal Leadership* 7 (2007): 50; W. Norton Grubb and Jeannie Oakes, *"Restoring Value" to the High School Diploma: The Rhetoric and Practice of Higher Standards*, Issue Brief, available at http://inpathways.net/EPSL-0710-242-EPRU.pdf;

Richard DuFour, Robert E. Eaker, and Rebecca Burnette, *On Common Ground: The Power of Professional Learning Communities* (Bloomington, IN: National Educational Service, 2005); William Daggett, "Achieving Academic Excellence Through Rigor and Relevance," Working Paper (Rexford, NY: International Center for Leadership in Education, 2012).

4. Tim Westerberg, *Becoming a Great High School: Six Strategies and One Attitude That Make a Difference* (Alexandria, VA: Association for Supervision and Curriculum Development, 2009).

5. Common Core State Standards for English Language Arts and Literacy in History/Social Studies, Rep. 2010, Common Core State Standards Initiative. Available at http://www.corestandards.org/assets/CCSSI_ELA%20Standards.pdf.

6. For more on the "backward planning" approach, see Jay McTighe and Grant P. Wiggins, *Understanding by Design: Professional Development Workbook* (Alexandria, VA: Association for Supervision and Curriculum Development, 2004).

7. Many districts, in the rush to become data driven, are overassessing their students. Assessments are critical, but once every six to eight weeks in each subject is more than sufficient. See Michael J. Schmoker, *The Results Fieldbook: Practical Strategies from Dramatically Improved Schools* (Alexandria, VA: Association for Supervision and Curriculum Development, 2001). For approaches to cut down on testing and reduce overassessment, see Bambrick-Santoyo, *Driven by Data*, 3–35.

8. Though he is reluctant to take credit for it, the idea for this sort of time distribution graph came from my friend and colleague Kim Marshall, author of *Rethinking Supervision and Evaluation: How to Work Smart, Build Collaboration, and Close the Achievement Gap* (San Francisco: Jossey-Bass, 2009).

9. Bambrick-Santoyo, *Driven by Data*, Part Two.

10. Bambrick-Santoyo, *Driven by Data*.

11. For the definitive introduction to the concept of "Good to Great," see James Collins, *Good to Great: Why Some Companies Make the Leap . . . and Others Don't* (New York: HarperBusiness, 2001).

12. Bambrick-Santoyo, *Driven by Data*.

Chapter 2

1. Mihály Csíkszentmihályi, *Flow* (New York: HarperPerennial, 2008); Jane Piirto, *Understanding Creativity* (Scottsdale, AZ: Great Potential, 2004).

2. Robert J. Marzano, Tony Frontier, and David Livingston, *Effective Supervision: Supporting the Art and Science of Teaching* (Alexandria, VA: Association for Supervision and Curriculum Development, 2011), 97.

3. Ibid., 23. For Danielson's original framework, see Charlotte Danielson, *Enhancing Professional Practice: A Framework for Teaching* (Alexandria, VA: Association for Supervision and Curriculum Development, 2007), 23.

4. Marzano and others, *Effective Supervision*, 57.

5. In schools where this sort of 15:1 ratio is an impossibility, leaders can pursue a number of approaches. One possibility is to think outside the box about other staff members who could accept a role as an instructional leader, such as a veteran teacher (this possibility is discussed at length in Chapter 8). Alternatively, though it is not ideal, leaders could switch to a biweekly cycle, observing once every two weeks. Working creatively, a solution is almost always possible.

6. Marzano and others, *Effective Supervision*, 29.

7. Doug Lemov, *Teach Like a Champion: Forty-Nine Techniques That Put Students on the Path to College* (San Francisco: Jossey-Bass, 2010).

8. See Ibid.; Jon Saphier and Robert R. Gower, *The Skillful Teacher: Building Your Teaching Skills* (Acton, MA: Research for Better Teaching, 1997).

9. Many of these techniques have been drawn from the teaching taxonomy outlined by Doug Lemov. See Lemov, *Teach Like a Champion*.

10. Daniel Coyle, *The Talent Code: Greatness Isn't Born, It's Grown. Here's How.* (London: RH Books, 2009), 168–171. For more on John Wooden's approach to success and leadership, see John Wooden and Steve Jamison, *The Wisdom of Wooden: My Century On and Off the Court* (New York: McGraw-Hill, 2010).

11. The importance of focusing on a relatively small number of concrete changes holds across almost all fields of learning and training. As an example, Washington University advises professors to limit comments on student papers to just one or two areas of improvement. See "Tips for Commenting on Student Writing" (St. Louis: Washington University, The

Teaching Center, 2009). Available at http://teachingcenter.wustl.edu/tips-commenting-student-writing.

12. Swen Nater and Ronald Gallimore, *You Haven't Taught Until They Have Learned: John Wooden's Teaching Principles and Practices* (Morgantown, WV: Fitness Information Technology, 2006), 97.

13. Saphier and Gower, *The Skillful Teacher*.

14. Kim Marshall, *Rethinking Supervision and Evaluation: How to Work Smart, Build Collaboration, and Close the Achievement Gap* (San Francisco: Jossey-Bass, 2009).

Chapter 3

1. See McTighe and Wiggins, *Understanding by Design: Professional Development Workbook* (Alexandria, VA: Association for Supervision and Curriculum Development, 2004).

2. Massachusetts Department of Elementary and Secondary Education. *Massachusetts History and Social Science Curriculum Framework*, 2003. Available at http://www.doe.mass.edu/frameworks/hss/final.pdf.

Chapter 4

1. Doug Lemov, *Teach Like a Champion: Forty-Nine Techniques That Put Students on the Path to College* (San Francisco: Jossey-Bass, 2010).

2. Ibid.

3. The importance of building in such time for reflection cannot be understated. When leadership expert Eric Jensen asked renowned neuroscientist Terry Sejnowski about effective learning strategies, he got a simple answer: "Learn, discuss, then take a walk." Though simple, Sejnowski's advice is deeply rooted in the way our brains function. "The brain is not built for continuous focused input." Instead, leaders need to make sure that "stimuli are shut down and the brain can pause to link new information." See Eric Jensen, *Teaching with the Brain in Mind,* 2nd ed. (Alexandria, VA: Association for Supervision and Curriculum Development, 2005), 56.

4. Kenneth D. Moore, *Effective Instructional Strategies: From Theory to Practice* (London: Sage, 2011), 298.f.

Chapter 5

1. Doug Lemov, *Teach Like a Champion: Forty-Nine Techniques That Put Students on the Path to College* (San Francisco: Jossey-Bass, 2010).
2. Ibid.
3. James Collins, *Good to Great: Why Some Companies Make the Leap ... and Others Don't* (New York: HarperBusiness, 2001).

Chapter 6

1. Gretchen Spreitzer and Christine Porath, "Creating Sustainable Performance," *Harvard Business Review* (January/February 2012).
2. Shawn Achor, "Positive Intelligence," *Harvard Business Review* (January/February 2012).
3. James Collins, *Good to Great: Why Some Companies Make the Leap ... and Others Don't* (New York: HarperBusiness, 2001).
4. See generally Jack and Suzy Welch, *Winning* (New York: HarperCollins, 2005), 81.

Chapter 7

1. Paul Bambrick-Santoyo, *Driven by Data: A Practical Guide to Improve Instruction* (San Francisco: Jossey-Bass, 2010).

Chapter 8

1. Kim Marshall, "How I Confronted HSPS (Hyperactive Superficial Principal Syndrome) and Began to Deal with the Heart of the Matter," *Phi Delta Kappan* 77 (1996): 336–345.
2. Maia Heyck-Merlin, *The Together Teacher: Plan Ahead, Get Organized, and Save Time!* (San Francisco: Jossey-Bass, 2012).
3. Ibid.

Chapter 9

1. See Paul Bambrick-Santoyo, *Driven by Data: A Practical Guide to Improve Instruction* (San Francisco: Jossey-Bass, 2010).

2. Malcolm Gladwell, *Blink: The Power of Thinking Without Thinking* (New York: Back Bay Books, 2007).

3. Adam Bryant, "Talk to Me. I'll Turn Off My Phone," *New York Times,* February 27, 2011, sec. B, p. 2, New York edition.

Part 4 Introduction

1. Paul Bambrick-Santoyo, *Driven by Data: A Practical Guide to Improve Instruction* (San Francisco: Jossey-Bass, 2010).

Bibliography

Amabile, Teresa, and Steven Kramer. "Do Happier People Work Harder?" *New York Times*. September 4, 2011: SR7.

Bambrick-Santoyo, Paul. *Driven by Data: A Practical Guide to Improve Instruction*. San Francisco: Jossey-Bass, 2010.

Baron, D. "Using Text-based Protocols: The Five Rs." *Principal Leadership* 7 (2007): 50–51.

Beyer, Steven. "Our School." *Principal Leadership* 12 (October 2011).

Bryant, Adam. "Talk to Me. I'll Turn Off My Phone." *New York Times*, February 27, 2011, New York edition, sec. B, p. 2.

Bryk, Anthony S., and others. *Organizing Schools for Improvement: Lessons from Chicago*. Chicago: University of Chicago Press, 2010.

Collins, James C. *Good to Great: Why Some Companies Make the Leap—and Others Don't*. New York: HarperBusiness, 2001.

Common Core State Standards for English Language Arts and Literacy in History/Social Studies. Rep. 2010. Common Core State Standards Initiative. Available at http://www.corestandards.org/assets/CCSSI_ELA%20Standards.pdf.

Coyle, Daniel. *The Talent Code: Greatness Isn't Born, It's Grown. Here's How*. New York: Bantam, 2009.

Csikszentmihalyi, Mihaly. *Creativity: Flow and the Psychology of Discovery and Invention*. New York: HarperCollins, 1996.

Danielson, Charlotte. *Enhancing Student Achievement: A Framework for School Improvement*. Alexandria, VA: Association for Supervision and Curriculum Development, 2002.

Danielson, Charlotte. *Enhancing Professional Practice: A Framework for Teaching*. Alexandria, VA: Association for Supervision and Curriculum Development, 2007.

Davenport, Patricia, and Gerald Anderson. *Closing the Achievement Gap: No Excuses*. Houston, TX: American Productivity Quality Center, 2002.

Deal, Terrence E., and Kent D. Peterson. *Shaping School Culture: Pitfalls, Paradoxes, and Promises*. San Francisco: Jossey-Bass, 2009.

DuFour, Richard, and Robert Eaker. *On Common Ground*. Bloomington, IN: National Education Service, 2005.

DuFour, Richard, and Robert Marzano. "High-Leverage Strategies for Principal Leadership." *Educational Leadership* 66 (2009): 62–68.

Eaker, Robert, and Janel Keating. "A Shift in School Culture." *Journal of Staff Development* 29 (2008): 14–17.

Firestone, William. "Accountability Nudges Districts into Changes in Culture." *Phi Delta Kappan* 29 (2010): 8.

Gladwell, Malcolm. *Blink: The Power of Thinking Without Thinking*. New York: Back Bay Books, 2007.

Grissom, Jason, and James Harrington. "Investing in Administrator Efficacy: An Examination of Professional Development as a Tool for Enhancing Principal Effectiveness." *American Journal of Education* 116 (2010): 583–612.

Grubb, W. Norton, and Jeannie Oakes. "'Restoring Value' to the High School Diploma: The Rhetoric and Practice of Higher Standards." 2007. Available online at http://epsl.asu.edu/epru/documents/EPSL-0710–242-EPRU.pdf.

Heyck-Merlin, Maia. *The Together Teacher: Plan Ahead, Get Organized, and Save Time!* San Francisco: Jossey-Bass, 2012.

Hoerr, Thomas. "Negative Feedback: Making Yourself Heard." *Principal* 82 (2004): 63–64.

Horng, Eileen Lai, Daniel Klasik, and Susanna Loeb. "Principal's Time Use and School Effectiveness." *American Journal of Education* 116 (2010): 491–523.

Jensen, Eric. *Teaching with the Brain in Mind*. Alexandria, VA: Association for Supervision and Curriculum Development, 2005.

Lemov, Doug. *Teach Like a Champion: Forty-Nine Techniques That Put Students on the Path to College*. San Francisco: Jossey-Bass, 2010.

Lovely, Suzette. "Making the Leap to Shared Leadership." *Journal of Staff Development* 26 (2005): 16–21.

Marshall, Kim. "How I Confronted HSPS (Hyperactive Superficial Principal Syndrome) and Began to Deal with the Heart of the Matter." *Phi Delta Kappan* 77 (1996): 336–345.

Marshall, Kim. "It's Time to Rethink Teacher Supervision and Evaluation." *Phi Delta Kappan* 86 (2005): 727–735.

Marshall, Kim. *Rethinking Teacher Supervision and Evaluation: How to Work Smart, Build Collaboration, and Close the Achievement Gap*. San Francisco: Jossey-Bass, 2009.

Marzano, Robert J., Timothy Waters, and Brian A. McNulty. *School Leadership That Works: From Research to Results*. Alexandria, VA: Association for Supervision and Curriculum Development, 2005.

Marzano, Robert J., Tony Frontier, and David Livingston. *Effective Supervision: Supporting the Art and Science of Teaching*. Alexandria, VA: Association for Supervision and Curriculum Development, 2011.

Massachusetts History and Social Science Curriculum Framework, 2003. Massachusetts Department of Elementary and Secondary Education. Available at http://www.doe.mass.edu/frameworks/hss/final.pdf.

Maxwell, Lesli. "Review Finds Principal-Evaluation Tools a Bit Outdated." *Education Week* (January 6, 2010): 8.

McTighe, Jay, and Grant P. Wiggins. *Understanding by Design: Professional Development Workbook*. Alexandria, VA: Association for Supervision and Curriculum Development, 2004.

Moore, Kenneth D. *Effective Instructional Strategies: From Theory to Practice*. London: Sage, 2011.

Morrish, Ronald G. *With All Due Respect: Keys for Building Effective School Discipline*. Fonthill, ONT: Woodstream, 2000.

Nater, Swen, Ronald Gallimore, Bill Walton, and Jim Sinegal. *You Haven't Taught Until They Have Learned: John Wooden's Teaching Principles and Practices*. Morgantown, WV: Fitness Information Technology, 2010.

New Jersey Department of Education Report Card. Available at http://education.state.nj.us/rc/.

Noddings, Nel. "The New Anti-intellectualism in America." *Education Week* 26 (2007): 29–32.

Piirto, Jane. *Understanding Creativity*. Scottsdale, AZ: Great Potential, 2004.

Pitler, Howard, and Bryan Goodwin. "Classroom Walkthroughs: Learning to See the Trees and the Forest." *Changing Schools* (2008). Available at http://www.mcrel.org/pdf/teacherprepretention/0125NL_ChangingSchools_58_4.pdf.

Platt, Alexander D. *The Skillful Leader: Confronting Mediocre Teaching*. Acton, MA: Ready About, 2000.

Platt, Alexander D. *The Skillful Leader II: Confronting Conditions That Undermine Learning*. Acton, MA: Ready About, 2008.

Saphier, Jon, Mary Ann Haley-Speca, and Robert Gower. *The Skillful Teacher: Building Your Teaching Skills*. 6th ed. Acton, MA: Research for Better Teaching, 2008.

Scales, Jim, and Connie Atkins. "Hamilton County Department of Education: Rethinking Teacher Evaluation Through Project COACH." *District Management* 7 (2011); 12–21.

Schmoker, Michael J. *Results: The Key to Continuous School Improvement*. Alexandria, VA: Association for Supervision and Curriculum Development, 1999.

Schmoker, Michael J. *The Results Fieldbook: Practical Strategies from Dramatically Improved Schools*. Alexandria, VA: Association for Supervision and Curriculum Development, 2001.

"Tips for Commenting on Student Writing." Available at http://teachingcenter.wustl.edu/tips-commenting-student-writing.

Toll, Cathy. "Six Steps to Learning Leadership." *Journal of Staff Development* 31 (2010: 50–56.

Vitcov, Barry, and Gary Bloom. "Managing Principals." *American School Board Journal* 198 (2011): 26–28.

Walker, Jan. "Letting Go: How Principals Can Be Better Instructional Leaders." *Middle Ground* 14 (2010): 16–17.

Washor, Elliot, and Mojkowski, Charles. "What Do You Mean by Rigor?" *Educational Leadership* 64 (2006): 84–87.

Welch, Jack, and Suzy Welch. *Winning.* New York: HarperCollins, 2005.

Westerberg, Tim. *Becoming a Great High School: Six Strategies and One Attitude That Make a Difference.* Alexandria, VA: Association for Supervision and Curriculum Development, 2009.

Whitaker, Todd. *What Great Principals Do Differently: Fifteen Things That Matter Most.* Larchmont, NY: Eye on Education, 2003.

Wiggins, Grant P., and Jay McTighe. *Understanding by Design.* Alexandria, VA: Association for Supervision and Curriculum Development, 1998.

Wooden, John, and Steve Jamison. *The Wisdom of Wooden: My Century On and Off the Court.* New York: McGraw-Hill, 2010.

Index

G

Gallimore, R., 85
Gladwell, M., 277
Golden ratio (15:1), 224, 242–243
Good to Great (Collins), 183, 194–196
Gower, R. R., 90
Great teaching, 4–6; and great learning, 4
Group meetings, locking in, 244–245
Guided practice, 149
Gulley, R., 181
Gumpper, J., 110, 124

H

Heyck-Merlin, M., 258–259
"High-rigor" questions, defined, 70
Highest-leverage action steps, 72

I

Implementation calendar, 54
In-class routines, 171
Independent practice, encouraging, 74–75
Instructional capacity, 16
Instructional leaders, 112; leading, 353; principals as, 7
Instructional leadership: rubric, 233–234; teams, 223–224
Instructional levers, 10, 168, 341; impact of, 150–154
Instructional planning, 341; as instructional lever, 10
Insufficient guidance, 112–113
Interim assessments, 29–34; and accountability, 151–153; aligned, 31–33; common, 31; observation and feedback, 70–71, 75; planning, 112, 123; professional development, 112, 123, 132, 133; working around, 34
Interruptions, choosing with care, 91
ISLLC standards, 355

J

Jackson, J., 1–2, 5, 99–100, 102, 130–131, 286, 331; action steps used by top-tier

instructional leaders, 73–75; and application, 146–147; building a schedule, 241–242; critical areas for feedback, 72; feedback, focusing on one key piece of feedback, 70–71; highest-leverage action steps, 59, 72; key action steps, reviewing, 133; key supplies for observation, 69; observation and feedback, 59–61, 63–67; observation tracker, 93–98, 132–135; opening question with evidence, 83; picking an action step, 71–72; practice, 85–86; precise praise, 78–80; probing questions, 80–81; professional development leaders, 137; and sharing, 145; struggling teachers, strategies for, 89–91; and three-hour rule, 225; timelines, 88; on training, 146–147

K

Kashner, R., 88
Kennedy, J., 6, 130, 209, 286; bias toward "yes", 206–207; boosting achievement, 216; on building better objectives, 137; and candidate interviews, 195–196; colleague's testimonial on staff culture, 214; on day-to-day excellence, 204–205; on email, 206–208; on emails, waiting before sending, 206; on feedback, openness to, 195; on first weeks of the year, 197–198; on fitting on the team, 195–196; leaders, choosing, 224–225; on listening first, 205–206; on mission alignment, 195, 207–208; on month-to-month excellence, 210–213; on openness to feedback, 195; schedule, 239; seating charts for faculty meetings, 198; on staff culture, 190–194, 214; on strategic messaging, 209; using "we" instead of "I" or "you," 206; on valuing teachers, 208–210; vision, setting, 192–193; on warning signs, 200–203; weekly schedule, 251; weekly surveys, 200–201
Key action steps: bite-sized, 61, 72, 75; converting poor action steps into effective

How to Use the DVD

SYSTEM REQUIREMENTS

PC with Microsoft Windows 2003 or later
Mac with Apple OS version 10.1 or later

USING THE DVD WITH WINDOWS

To view the items located on the DVD, follow these steps:

1. Insert the DVD into your computer's DVD drive.

2. A window appears with the following options:

    Contents: Allows you to view the files included on the DVD.

    Software: Allows you to install useful software from the DVD.

    Links: Displays a hyperlinked page of websites.

    Author: Displays a page with information about the author(s).

    Contact Us: Displays a page with information on contacting the publisher
    or author.

    Help: Displays a page with information on using the DVD.

    Exit: Closes the interface window.

If you do not have autorun enabled, or if the autorun window does not appear,
follow these steps to access the DVD:

1. Click Start → Run.

2. In the dialog box that appears, type d:\start.exe, where d is the letter of your DVD drive. This brings up the autorun window described in the preceding set of steps.

3. Choose the desired option from the menu. (See Step 2 in the preceding list for a description of these options.)

IN CASE OF TROUBLE

If you experience difficulty using the DVD, please follow these steps:

1. Make sure your hardware and systems configurations conform to the systems requirements noted under "System Requirements" above.

2. Review the installation procedure for your type of hardware and operating system. It is possible to reinstall the software if necessary.

To speak with someone in Product Technical Support, call 800-762-2974 or 317-572-3994 Monday through Friday from 8:30 a.m. to 5:00 p.m. EST. You can also contact Product Technical Support and get support information through our website at www.wiley.com/techsupport.

Before calling or writing, please have the following information available:

- Type of computer and operating system.

- Any error messages displayed.

- Complete description of the problem.

It is best if you are sitting at your computer when making the call.